PROMOTING
HIGH-TECHNOLOGY INDUSTRY

About the Book and Editors

In the wake of declining federal involvement in state affairs, state governments have taken the initiative in creating science and technology policies and programs for economic development. The contributors to this study look at the attempts of eight states—California, Florida, Massachusetts, Minnesota, New York, North Carolina, Pennsylvania, and Texas—to foster economic development through science and advanced technology industries. The contributors discuss factors common to the emergence of science and technology policies in all of these states, review the policy goals and strategies being pursued, and compare the mechanisms used to implement policies. Although it is difficult to come to conclusions about the long-term effects of the new policies and programs, the authors suggest that increased cooperation between government, educators, and the private sector; state emphasis on education and research; plus institutional innovations and heavy private-sector involvement can have beneficial effects on a state's economic health.

Jurgen Schmandt is director of The Woodlands Center for Growth Studies, Houston Area Research Center, and a professor of public affairs at the University of Texas at Austin. **Robert Wilson** is associate professor at the L.B.J. School of Public Affairs, University of Texas at Austin.

**Published in cooperation with
the Houston Area Research Center**

PROMOTING HIGH-TECHNOLOGY INDUSTRY

INITIATIVES AND POLICIES FOR STATE GOVERNMENTS

EDITED BY
JURGEN SCHMANDT
AND ROBERT WILSON

Routledge
Taylor & Francis Group

LONDON AND NEW YORK

First published 1987 by Westview Press

Published 2019 by Routledge
52 Vanderbilt Avenue, New York, NY 10017
2 Park Square, Milton Park, Abingdon, Oxon OX14 4RN

Routledge is an imprint of the Taylor & Francis Group, an informa business

Library of Congress Catalog Card Number: 87-61327

ISBN 13: 978-0-367-28446-6 (hbk)

CONTENTS

PREFACE

In recent years state governments throughout the United States have looked to advanced technology as a resource to revive old industries, create new businesses, and provide jobs. This is a difficult task. First, the link between technological innovation and economic growth is real but difficult to predict. In addition, states have long grown accustomed to the lead role of the federal government in science and technology policy. Their initiatives are mostly of recent origin and available resources are small. At the present time, the results of new state policies and programs cannot yet be measured. Nor is it possible to determine the right mix between long-term strategies, such as support of higher education, and short-term programmatic interventions. The immediate task, therefore, is to provide detailed information on the approaches taken by different states. For this purpose the Lyndon B. Johnson School of Public Affairs, The University of Texas at Austin, conducted a year-long study of initiatives in eight states: California, Florida, Massachusetts, Minnesota, New York, North Carolina, Pennsylvania, and Texas. We asked two questions:

- What role do state governments see for themselves in science and technology policy?
- What kind of institutional mechanisms have state governments created to articulate and implement their science and technology policies?

The project team consisted of sixteen graduate students and two faculty members. Members of the team visited each of the eight states. We received invaluable help from the many people we interviewed. Several of them later read drafts of the state chapters. In Texas we worked closely with the Governor's Science and Technology Council, to which we submitted a summary report in September 1986. Meg Wilson, staff coordinator of the council, was an inspiring taskmaster. Mr. Josh Farley, Department of Planning and Growth Management, City of Austin, collaborated with us throughout the year, and we wish to acknowledge our appreciation for his contribution. We also acknowledge the help of our editor, Christine Devall, and of our administrative assistant, Susan Roush.

The study was supported by The Woodlands Center for Growth Studies, Houston Area Research Center. It is part of a larger project at the Woodlands Center on state governments and technological change.

—Jurgen Schmandt and Robert Wilson

PROJECT PARTICIPANTS

STUDENTS	
Andre J. Brunel	Georgetown University
Michael P. Burke	University of Virginia
Michael Dowling	Harvard University
Harald Fischer	University of Konstanz
Michael Freudenberg	University of Konstanz
William Guillory	Stanford University
Sidney Bailey Hacker	University of Texas at Austin
Tracy L. Henderson	University of Arkansas
Mark Howard	Northwestern University
Mary Kragie	University of Virginia
Kathleen A. Merrigan	Williams College
Brian Muller	Yale University
Amy Miriam Peck	University of Michigan
Lance Silbert	University of California-Santa Cruz
Suzanne E. Smith	Vassar College
Robert D. Sommerfeld	St. Anselm College

PARTICIPATING FACULTY
Jurgen Schmandt, Ph.D.
Professor, LBJ School of Public Affairs
University of Texas at Austin

Robert Wilson, Ph.D.
Associate Professor, LBJ School of Public Affairs
University of Texas at Austin

CONSULTANT
Josh Farley
Economist
City of Austin, Texas

INTRODUCTION

The decline of traditional manufacturing sectors in many parts of the country is causing some states to seek new foundations for economic growth. The high-technology manufacturing sector is considered by many to be the most promising catalyst for future development. The traditional methods of state assistance for businesses, however, are considered inadequate for meeting the needs of this sector. States, therefore, are beginning to adopt policies specifically designed to promote the growth of high-technology industries. The problems encountered and the policy environment differ in each state; as a result, over 200 state programs with a focus on high-technology development are in operation, representing the major effort of state science and technology policies.

This book examines the science and technology policies and programs of eight states. In each case, the actors in the policy development process, their motivations, the policy directions chosen, and the science and technology programs adopted, are identified and assessed. Lessons drawn from the comparison of the eight states are presented and future policy developments are considered. The analysis is based on information from published material, internal documents and reports, and interviews with program officials, government representatives, and other participants in the policymaking process.

Historical Precedents for State Science and Technology Policy

State governments have played a role in economic development since the inception of the nation. One of the earliest and most successful examples is New York State's construction in 1826 of the Erie Canal, a major step in New York's becoming "the Empire State." The Erie Canal exemplifies the traditional emphasis at the state level on providing the basic infrastructure necessary for economic growth. A different and longstanding state role is the support of agricultural research. In this case the states joined the federal government in programs that brought the results of agricultural research to the nation's farms. Since the Civil War, the two levels of government have jointly financed agricultural research.

— This chapter was written by Michael P. Burke and Michael Dowling.

2

In addition, they developed the concepts of extension and technology transfer. These activities were critically important at a time when the majority of the work force was still employed in farming and ranching. The land-grant universities and the research and education programs initiated by them contributed greatly to increasing agricultural productivity and improving the quality of life on the farm.[1]

In recent times, the concept of agricultural extension, with its emphasis on technology transfer and education, has been used to help small businesses gain access to scientific and engineering information. There are fundamental differences, however. Farms were not expected to engage in research; high-technology businesses are. Whether and how the extension concept can be adjusted to modern conditions is a central question for states in their current efforts to develop science and technology policies.

There were other early examples of state support of science and technology, but of more modest size. States, for example, supported research aimed at finding and extracting mineral resources. Early in this century bureaus of geological research were created in several universities or as independent state agencies.[2] This tradition continues today, with states funding a variety of special research programs and institutes, many of them related to health, energy, and natural resources.

Indirectly states have long supported scientific research by funding public universities in which research is conducted. Faculty salaries, office buildings, and laboratories are paid for by the state and make it possible for research to be conducted. The federal government, since mid-century, has become the principal provider of funds for individual research projects. As a result, we now have a shared support system for research: states (or private funds in the case of private universities) pay for the "research infrastructure," and the federal government provides the additional support needed for research projects. This federal-state partnership differs in one important respect from the older model of agricultural research. In the latter case, most funds are allocated using a formula system. By contrast, funding for the physical, biological, and social sciences provided by the National Science Foundation, the National Institutes of Health, and the large federal mission agencies, requires direct applications by researchers to the federal agencies, whose decisions are based on the advice of peer review.

Until recently the state contribution to research in public universities, though important, was rarely recognized. States emphasized the educational role of universities and argued that university faculty should teach rather than lose time with research. Gradually, however, state officials came to accept the argument that higher education and research cannot be separated from each other, and that the long-term results of research will be beneficial to the state.

Some states have a longer tradition of viewing research as an investment. California is perhaps the best example. The state made a deliberate decision some sixty years ago to upgrade the research capabilities of its leading universities. This was done with the hope of improving the state's economy as well as its higher education system. The strategy paid off over time, first by improving California's agriculture, later by attracting defense, space, and other advanced technology industries.

Despite these various state efforts, the predominance of the federal government in science and technology policy has been overwhelming in recent decades. Because much of the national effort is earmarked for defense, space, and basic research, this condition will continue. Yet states are part of the modern age in which science and technology are dominant forces. Therefore, they have no choice but to define more precisely what use they plan to make of these powerful forces, and how they want to supplement the federal effort.

During the late sixties and early seventies the states made a first attempt to develop formal science and technology policies that went beyond the agricultural sector. The initiative took two forms. The first one was part of the much talked about "Moon to the Ghetto" strategy: if technology in the form of systems analysis and hardware capability could send a man to the moon, then it could be used to resolve critical economic and social issues.[3]

California, with its large defense and aerospace industries, took the lead and contracted with aerospace companies to analyze four areas: waste management, crime prevention and control, the creation of a statewide information system, and the development of an integrated transportation system.[4] Each was funded at a level of $100,000. To rely on state funds was highly unusual at a time when the federal government was perceived as an easy source of funding. A contemporary observer was impressed by the results and the process: "The four studies . . . have been notably successful. They have introduced new ways of thinking and concepts. . . . They have generated . . . an excitement about these and other new things that government can do."[5] In retrospect, little of lasting value resulted from the application of systems analysis to urban and social problems, mostly because the power of analysis was overrated and the importance of constraining political factors underestimated.

The same, by and large, was the outcome of the second effort. Congress passed the State Technical Services Act of 1965 which was designed to promote the transfer of new technology throughout the economy. The Agricultural Extension Service was the model. Visions of research spinoffs from federally financed research, such as Route 128 near Boston and the Silicon Valley near Palo Alto, California, encouraged governors to seek similar developments in their states. The most common state response, used in forty-seven states by the

4

late sixties, was the creation of science advisory boards to the governor or legislature on topics of broad concern to a state. A study of nine of these bodies, selected as a representative sample, concluded: "No state has found a useful and recognized role for science advisers in the formation of public policy."[6] Most boards suffered from lack of funds, impact, and continuity. They focused their efforts on economic development, but their initiatives were neither novel nor particularly productive. With the exception of New York and North Carolina, none of the mechanisms created at the time have survived to play a role in the current attempt to link science, technology, and regional economic growth.

Writing at the time when the failure of these earlier efforts became apparent, Long and Feller searched for an explanation from theory.[7] They concluded that regional growth was influenced by many forces and that measurement tools were not available to say whether state research and development (R&D) policy could make a significant difference. But they did not entirely dismiss the potential of state science and technology strategies. As a first step in better understanding their promise and limitation, the authors identified four state strategies, each of which made particular, but difficult to quantify, assumptions about the relationship between research and development and economic growth: (a) R&D in support of new products and processes derived from natural resources, in particular agriculture and mineral industries, (b) competition for federal R&D dollars and installations, (c) support of research in higher education with the expectation of economic spinoffs, and (d) research to support the provision of such "public goods" as housing, transportation, and environmental controls.

In recent years, the state goal of creating a diversified economic base has led to a renewed interest in science and technology. Once again the prosperity and growth of Route 128 and the Silicon Valley are cited as successful models. Though few states have developed a comprehensive state science and technology policy, many have engaged in efforts to reinvigorate existing industries, to foster the conditions for industrial growth and the creation of new companies, and to provide direct support to high-technology businesses. The ultimate goal of the states' policies and programs is to create jobs, which is expected to result from state assistance to new firms as well as existing industries that foster the development of new products and production processes. In pursuing these objectives the states are relying less on federal dollars to create new technology; rather, they are attempting to establish with their own means the R&D linkages between the private sector and the universities that the federal government tried to forge in the 1960s.

It also needs to be noted that state efforts in science and technology policy are but one example of a wave of renewed activism in state government. In the early 1970s, under President Nixon, views on federalism and the appropriate roles of federal and state governments began to change. Gradually, the political base for strengthening the state role has broadened, attracting support from the entire range of the political spectrum. At the same time, the political climate in the states has changed from passive reliance on Washington to a more active desire to shape their own future and a new confidence in their capacity to bring about desired change. The revitalized capacity of state governments is documented in a recent study by the Advisory Commission on Intergovernmental Relations, which took an in-depth look at state government capabilities today.[8] The commission report documents that states have heeded earlier criticism and had done much to reform their leadership, institutions, and processes. These reforms have occurred in many areas, including modernized constitutions, legislatures, legislative processes, increased capacity of governors to manage and lead, improved agency capabilities, and reformed judiciary systems. State governments have become more open in their operations through such mechanisms as open meeting laws, televised coverage of legislatures, broadened participation in primary elections, and increased opportunities for citizen participation in regulatory proceedings.[9] Additional studies have reached similar conclusions.[10] None of these studies have addressed science and technology policy; this report on eight states illustrates the new state activism in this area.

Definitions and Method of Study

One difficulty encountered in studying state science and technology policies is the lack of a single, commonly accepted definition of the high-technology sector. For purposes of this study, high-technology industries are identified by a high percentage of R&D funds invested in the companies and an above-average number of scientists, engineers, professionals, and technical personnel employed as a percentage of total employees.[11] Using this same definition, the Congressional Budget Office (CBO) arrived at the following list of high-technology industries: drugs, industrial organic chemicals, office and computing machines, communication equipment, electronic components, aircraft and parts, missiles and space vehicles, and instruments.[12]

Many states also use the term "advanced technology" in describing their policies and programs. They do so to demonstrate that their efforts are not focused exclusively on particular industries, but extend to the application of new technologies to all existing industries. The states realize that their efforts will not revive all declining or moribund industries, but believe that new technological processes can lead to better efficiency and competitiveness.

In selecting states for inclusion in this study, the authors examined the economic characteristics, institutional and legal structure, and policy posture of all states. A wide range of policy initiatives within a state was preferred. Using these criteria, California, Florida, Massachusetts, Minnesota, New York, North Carolina, Pennsylvania, and Texas were selected for study.

Each state chapter includes several case studies of important state programs that best illustrate the state's overall policy posture. Several selection criteria were used for inclusion of particular programs: (a) the programs should illustrate the diversity of the state's science and technology policy; (b) the programs should focus on high technology; (c) they should be innovative; (d) a policymaking body should be included for each state if possible; and (e) the programs should have a long enough history to make meaningful assessment possible.

The programs and policies of the eight states examined are relatively new and the impacts are therefore difficult to measure. In addition, full-fledged evaluations were beyond our means. There are, however, surrogate measures of research and high-technology intensity that can be used to compare the relative strengths of the states in the development of high-technology industries. These include employment shares of certain high-technology industries, a state's ability to secure federal R&D funds, R&D expenditures at universities, and numbers of employed scientists and engineers in each state.

In the states studied, employment in certain high-technology industries has increased, in some cases dramatically, over the last decade (Table 1-1).[13] This was true even in Minnesota, New York, and Pennsylvania, which experienced overall declines in total manufacturing employment. As impressive as this growth may seem, high-technology employment still remains a very small percentage of total nonagricultural employment, ranging from as low as 2.4 percent in Florida to only 7.0 percent in California. While high technology may be a source of rapidly increasing manufacturing jobs, employment growth in other sectors, such as the service industries, will be much greater in absolute terms. For example, recent forecasts predict that the high-technology sector in the United States will only account for between 3 and 17 percent of all new jobs created by 1995. The vast majority of jobs will be created in other industries.[14]

TABLE 1-1
Comparison of Employment in High-Technology
Manufacturing in the Eight States and the United States,
1972 and 1982, and Percentage of Change
(in 1,000s and %)

State	1972	1982	% Change
California	271.5	692.0	255
Florida	53.8	100.4	87
Massachusetts	103.1	157.2	52
Minnesota	35.2	67.6	92
New York	243.8	302.8	24
North Carolina	—	—	—
Pennsylvania	107.5	117.6	9
Texas	—	204.7	—
United States	2316.2	3164.0	37

Sources: See subsequent chapters.

TABLE 1-2
A Comparison of Federal Obligations
for R&D for the Eight States, 1983
(in $ million and %)

State	Funds	Percentage of United States	Percentage of U.S. Population	F/P*	Absolute Rank**	Per Capita Rank**
California	8,439.9	22.43	10.76	2.08	1	7
Florida	1,276.0	3.39	4.59	.74	8	18
Massachusetts	2,314.3	6.15	2.46	2.50	4	6
Minnesota	448.2	1.19	1.77	.67	19	21
New York	2,523.2	6.71	7.55	.89	3	16
North Carolina	312.5	.83	2.60	.32	24	30
Pennsylvania	1,173.3	3.12	5.08	.61	11	22
Texas	1,412.6	3.75	6.83	.55	6	24
Total	17,900.0	47.57	41.64			

* F/P is the ratio between the percentage of total federal R&D funds obtained by the state and the state's percentage of the total U.S. population. This ratio is a per capita measure of the federal R&D funding in the state.
** These ranks are for all of the states in the United States.
Source: National Science Foundation, *Federal Funds for Research and Development*, vol. 33, 1984, p. 150.

Federal obligations for R&D is another indicator of science and technology activity (Table 1-2). These data give a relative indication of the ability of each state to secure federal research funding that is conducted in federal laboratories, state or private universities, nonprofit institutions, and industries.[15] California is the undisputed leader in securing federal R&D funds, receiving almost one-fourth of the national total. On a per capita basis, however, Massachusetts does even better. And while some states, like Texas and New York, do relatively well in absolute terms, they do relatively poorly on a per capita basis.

TABLE 1-3
A Comparison of Academic Expenditures
for R&D from all Sources for the Eight States, 1983
(in $ million and %)

State	Funds	Percentage of United States	Percentage of U.S. Population	F/P*	Absolute Rank**	Per Capita Rank**
California	1,022.6	13.20	10.76	1.23	1	14
Florida	171.7	2.22	4.59	.48	13	45
Massachusetts	497.6	6.42	2.46	2.61	3	3
Minnesota	156.8	2.02	1.77	1.14	16	17
New York	786.3	10.15	7.55	1.34	2	11
North Carolina	180.9	2.34	2.60	.90	12	22
Pennsylvania	369.5	4.74	5.08	.93	6	25
Texas	486.0	6.28	6.83	.92	4	26
Total	3,671.4	47.37	41.64			

Source: National Science Foundation, *Academic Science/Engineering R&D Funds—Fiscal Year 1983*, 1985, p. 28.

R&D expenditures at universities give a relative measure of the research intensity of the higher-education systems in these states. These expenditures include federal, state, and private sources of funds. California is again the clear leader in absolute terms, but trails both Massachusetts and New York on a per capita basis. Most other states, which do relatively well on an absolute basis, do relatively poorly in per capita terms. This is especially the case in Florida.

TABLE 1-4
A Comparison of Number of Employed Scientists
and Engineers for the Eight States, 1982

State	Number	Percentage	Absolute Rank	Per Capita Rank
California	456,500	14.0	1	9
Florida	83,600	2.6	11	46
Massachusetts	131,800	4.1	8	3
Minnesota	61,200	1.9	17	12
New York	265,900	8.2	2	11
North Carolina	57,600	1.8	20	40
Pennsylvania	165,600	5.1	4	18
Texas	213,500	6.6	3	20
Total	1,435,700	44.3		

Source: National Science Foundation, *U.S. Scientists and Engineers 1982*, 1984, pp. 81-82.

Finally, in Table 1-4, the number of employed scientists and engineers in 1982 in each state are compared. Again, California is the clear leader on an absolute basis, and Massachusetts betters California on a per capita basis. Except for Minnesota, the other six states all do much worse ranked on a per capita basis than they do in absolute terms.

It is often argued that a certain "critical mass" of research activity is necessary for the successful development of high-technology industries. These data suggest that some of the states in this study are far behind the leading states—California, Massachusetts, and New York. Successful strategies to increase R&D intensity and create critical mass will require large investments over long periods of time.

The following chapters examine the science and technology policy and programs of the individual states. Each chapter begins with an examination of the state's demographic and economic circumstances and the policy environment that led to the adoption of a particular strategy. Next, a description and assessment of selected programs are presented. The state chapters also offer conclusions regarding the policies and programs' efficacy and prospects for the future. Two of the chapters, those of California and Texas, vary from this format. California's high-technology sector emerged without the help of specific state programs, but may have benefited from state support of higher education. Therefore, the chapter on California focuses on the higher education policy of the state, and only one high-technology program is assessed. The Texas chapter

10

provides more detail on policy development, reflecting the fact that the state is in the early stages of developing its science and technology policy and so far has few significant programs with a long enough history for assessment. The concluding chapter compares the patterns of activity found among the states and offers recommendations to assist policymakers interested in adopting or assessing their own state's policies and programs.

NOTES

1. H. C. Knoblauch, *State Agricultural Experiment Stations: A History of Research Policy and Procedures*, U.S. Department of Agriculture Miscellaneous Publications 904 (Washington, D.C.: Government Printing Office, 1962).
2. A. Hunter Dupree, *Science and the Federal Government* (Cambridge: Harvard University Press, 1957).
3. Richard R. Nelson, *The Moon and the Ghetto: An Essay on Public Policy Analysis* (New York: W. W. Norton, 1977).
4. Harold R. Walt, "The Four Aerospace Contracts: A Review of the California Experience," in National Commission on Technology, Automation, and Economic Progress, *Applying Technology to Unmet Needs, Appendix Volume 5* (February 1966): 47-73.
5. Ibid., 51.
6. Harvey M. Sapolsky, "Science Policy in American Government," *Minerva* 9 3 (July 1971): 322-348.
7. Wesley H. Long and Irwin Feller, "State Support of Research and Development," *Land Economics 48* (1972): 220-227.
8. Advisory Commission on Intergovernmental Relations, *The Question of State Government Capability*, Washington, D.C., January 1985.
9. Ibid., 363.
10. Thad F. Beyle and Lynn Muchmore, *Being Governor: Views from the Office* (Durham, NC: Duke University Press, 1983); Larry Sabato, *Goodbye to Good-Time Charlie: The American Governorship Transformed*, 2nd edition (Washington, D.C.: Congressional Quarterly, 1983).
11. U.S. Congressional Budget Office, *Federal Financial Support for High-Technology Industries* Washington, D.C., 1985, 7.
12. Ibid., 8. We use this list to examine the high-technology economic sector of the states studied.
13. Employment was measured for a set of high-technology industries as defined in ibid., 8.
14. Richard W. Riche, Daniel E. Hecker, and John U. Burgan, "High-Technology Today and Tomorrow: A Small Piece of the Employment Pie," *Monthly Labor Review* (November 1983): 52-58.
15. See tables in subsequent chapters for more detailed data on each state.

Since the early 1800s, California has been the locus for dreams of prosperity. Historically, the state's economic growth has been fueled by a series of industrial surges in mining, agriculture, oil, and aerospace. Research, development, and the commercialization of advanced technologies are the driving forces of the latest transformation, the "microelectronics rush." As a result, the basis of California's economy has changed from natural resources to technology.[1] Other states look at California as a model to emulate. What stands behind California's success?

California possesses important comparative advantages.[2] The quality of its public education system is often linked to its success in economic development. The state has exceptionally strong research facilities. Twenty-two percent of the nation's scientists and engineers work in California, conducting 50 percent of federally sponsored research and development.[3] The state is home to an exceptionally strong concentration of advanced-technology industries. Almost one-third of the national aerospace companies, one-fifth of the aircraft manufacturing companies, and three-fifths of the missile and space equipment companies are located in California.[4] Finally, the state's far western location is becoming increasingly advantageous. The Pacific rim has become a $3-trillion market and is growing at a rate of $3 billion a week.[5] Yet there are also weaknesses. The balance of trade is deteriorating; there is concern about losing the competitive edge in manufacturing. The state is often criticized for not moving more aggressively to meet international competition, and declining productivity at home is contrasted with rapidly rising productivity in the Pacific rim countries.[6]

The first part of this chapter presents an analysis of the demographic and economic structure of California. The second part discusses the state's approach to building a science and technology policy. The third part examines state policy for higher education and the Microelectronics Innovation and Computer Opportunities (MICRO) program.

— This chapter was written by Lance Silbert in collaboration with Michael P. Burke. William Guillory assisted on an earlier draft.

Demographic and Economic Profile

POPULATION CHARACTERISTICS

California has led the nation in population growth for the past six decades. Between 1970 and 1980, when the national rate of growth was 11.4 percent, California's was 18.5 percent (Table 2-1). The number of people moving to California has diminished in recent years, but still accounted for a large part of the state's growth between 1980 and 1984.[7] During this time California ranked third in growth from migration behind Florida and Texas.

TABLE 2-1

Population of California and Percentage Change
Compared to the United States, 1970, 1980, and 1984
(in 1,000s and %)

	California	Change	U.S. Change
1970	19,953,134	—	—
1980	23,667,902	18.5	11.4
1984	25,622,000	12.6	4.1

Source: U.S. Department of Commerce, Bureau of the Census, *1980 Census of Population, General Population Characteristics, California*, vol. 1, part 6, table 24, p. 20; idem, *State Population Estimates by Age and Components of Change: 1980 to 1984* , Current Population Reports, Population Estimates and Projections, series P-25, number 970, p. 9.

The racial and ethnic composition of the state is changing dramatically. The proportion of Anglo-Americans dropped from 89 percent in 1970 to 76.2 percent in 1980. The percentage of black Americans increased only slightly, from 7 percent to 7.7 percent. But the growth rate of other ethnic groups, primarily Hispanics and Asians, was an incredible 300 percent. From 1970 to 1980 this group grew from 4 percent to 16 percent of the population.[8] California's Asian-American population is expected to reach 2.8 million by the year 2000, constituting nearly one-tenth of the state's estimated total population. California will then be home to over one-third of all U.S. Asian Americans.[9] The Hispanic population will double over the next decade and a half. By the twenty-first century, the state's population will be made up of a "majority of minorities."[10] This will place a tremendous burden on California's education and training facilities, which even today have not prevented 20 percent of the adult population from being functionally illiterate.

The state's population is concentrated in metropolitan areas. In both 1970 and 1980, over 90 percent of the population resided in urban and suburban areas, as compared to the national average of 74 percent. California remains the most highly urbanized state in the country, followed by Rhode Island and New Jersey.[11]

The most distinctive feature of California's age distribution is the strong increase in the 18-44 age group between 1970 and 1980 (Table 2-2). This group represents a significantly larger share of California's population than it does in the nation as a whole. At the same time, the 0-17 age group in California is smaller than in the nation. Similar changes may occur in other states later, but California will be first in experiencing their impact. For some time to come California will benefit from the fact that a larger than average proportion of its population is in its productive years. But fifteen to twenty years from now the advantage will turn into a liability. This would not happen if the working population were increased substantially by people migrating to the state.

For both high school and college graduates, the educational level of Californians in 1980 was only slightly above the national average (Table 2-3).

TABLE 2-2
Age Distribution in California
Compared to the United States, 1970 and 1980
(%)

Age Group	1970		1980	
	California	United States	California	United States
0-17	33.4	37.8	27.0	32.0
18-44	37.4	31.7	43.5	37.2
45-64	20.2	20.6	19.2	19.7
65 & over	9.1	9.8	10.2	11.3

Source: U.S. Department of Commerce, Bureau of the Census, *State and Metropolitan Area Data Book: 1982*, table C, columns 62-81, p. 451.

TABLE 2-3
Educational Levels in California
Compared to the United States, 1980
(%)

	California	U.S.
Elementary school (less than 5 years)	4.0	3.6
High school	73.6	66.5
College (4 or more years)	9.6	16.2
Median years of school completed	12.7	12.5

Source: U.S. Department of Commerce, Bureau of the Census, *1980 Census of Population, Characteristics of Population*, vol. 1, ch. A, part 1, table 66, p. 6-109.

The median years of school completed differed only by one fifth of a percentage point. California's comparative advantage in education, therefore, is not due to the number of educated residents or the length of time they attend school. The difference is more likely to be related to the quality of education and training.

ECONOMIC PROFILE

Before World War II, California's was still a resource-based economy driven largely by agriculture, oil, and mining.[12] During the war, massive federal investments in California's universities and industry, which were just reaching world-class quality, transformed the state into a center of science and technology. In the 1950s the state facilitated the continued growth of technology-based industries by investing heavily in the infrastructure necessary for development—highways, water systems, and higher education.[13] Strong new industries emerged in microelectronics, aerospace, and biotechnology. Old industries began to adopt a value-added strategy to produce goods and services characterized by increased sophistication and a more effective ratio of price to cost. Examples include specialty agricultural products: designer clothing; specialized printing; enhanced petroleum recovery; aerospace industries; new telecommunications and microelectronics products; and new financial, engineering, business, and research services.[14]

While California's high-technology industries attract world-wide attention, the most unique features of the state's economy are diversity and size. California grows more crops, raises more cotton, builds more airplanes, and manufactures more computers, space equipment, and military hardware than any other state in the nation. If California were a nation, its gross national product would rank sixth in the world.

California is the leading agricultural state in the United States. In 1983, direct sales of $13.8 billion led to $54.4 billion in economic output, constituting 12 percent of the state's total output.[15] Eight California counties rank among the top ten in the country in terms of total value of agricultural production, and Fresno County leads all others, as well as twenty states, in agricultural output.[16]

Yet success in agriculture can only be maintained by a continued shift in emphasis from production of commodity crops to more effective product differentiation and international marketing. The research base needed for this strategy is strong. In biotechnology, California is a world leader. The state has and will continue to benefit strongly from research and development in the agricultural sector. Much of this work has been conducted by researchers of the University of California system.

The state is less successful in marketing its agricultural products internationally. California exports over one-fifth of its agricultural products and ranks among the top three exporting states; however, the value of California agricultural exports fell by 30 percent between 1981 and 1984. Increased competition, the high value of the dollar, and insufficient marketing efforts contributed to the decline.[17]

The state's nonagricultural sector employed almost 10 million people in 1982. Wholesale and retail trade, services, and manufacturing industries had the highest employment shares. Growth rates between 1972 and 1982 were highest in the mining, services, and finance and insurance industries (Table 2-4).

California's economic growth between 1970 and 1980 resulted in a 39 percent increase in the total number of jobs; in the nation, the increase was 24 percent. In 1980 alone, a net total of 202,000 new jobs were created in the state, accounting for over one-fourth of new jobs in the United States.[18] Since 1980, job growth in the state has slowed down. Plant closures and layoffs have accounted for 61 percent of the unemployed. In 1982, for example, 283 plants were closed, resulting in the layoff of over 50,000 workers.[19] Between 1979 and 1982, California lost over 27,000 jobs in the auto industry and over 6,000 in steel as major plants closed. Fortunately, California never relied much on the traditional heavy industries, as did other states.[20] Even so, structural problems exist, and some observers see them becoming more ominous. A recent SRI International study put it this way:

Loss of global competitiveness shows up most sharply in California's growing trade deficit, but this trend is the result of deeper problems. Nearly half of the trade deficit is due to slow productivity growth, lagging civilian R&D expenditures, declining quality of education, and eroding manufacturing capacity. Each of California's major export industries shows signs of long-term erosion of competitive advantage.[21]

TABLE 2-4

Nonagricultural Employment in California by Sector,
1972, 1977 and 1982, and Percentage of Change between 1972 and 1982
(employees in 1,000s, share and change in %)

	1972 Emp.	1972 Share	1977 Emp.	1977 Share	1982 Emp.	1982 Share	1972-1982 Change
Mining	29.2	0.4	35.6	0.4	50.1	0.5	71.6
Construction	320.7	4.5	366.1	4.3	366.1	3.7	14.2
Mfg.	1536.0	21.3	1728.3	20.1	1928.4	19.6	25.5
Trans.	454.1	6.3	476.5	5.5	543.1	5.5	19.6
Wholesale & retail	1608.6	22.3	1982.4	23.1	2275.4	23.0	41.5
Finance & insurance	409.3	5.7	505.4	5.9	645.1	6.6	57.6
Government	1492.7	20.7	1740.7	20.2	1733.2	17.6	16.1
Services	1359.4	18.9	1764.7	20.5	2284.0	23.3	68.0
Total	7210.0	100.0	8599.7	100.0	9825.4	100.0	36.3

Source: U.S. Department of Labor, Bureau of Labor Statistics, *Employment, Hours, and Earnings, States and Areas, 1939-1982*, vol. 1, bulletin 1370-17, pp. 47-62.

In 1982, almost two million people were employed in manufacturing, the majority (over two-thirds) in the durable goods industries. The largest industries, in descending order, were electrical equipment, transportation equipment, nonelectrical machinery, and instruments. Three of these industries grew by more than 83 percent in the ten years preceding 1982; fabricated metals experienced modest growth, and transportation equipment decreased slightly (Table 2-5).

Since 1970 California's employment in the managerial and technical fields has been above the national average. Per capita income has also been higher, surpassing the national figure by $1,698 in 1984.[22] These data reinforce the image of the California economy as having a relatively highly skilled, well-paid, and rapidly growing labor force.

HIGH-TECHNOLOGY SECTOR

The high-technology sector in California has exhibited fast growth and serves as a standard for other states. In 1972, 17.6 percent of the state's total nonagricultural employment was in the industries that have been designated as high technology; by 1982, this share had almost doubled (Table 2-6). During this period high-technology employment grew 155 percent, or more than five times as much as the manufacturing sector as a whole.

A recent ten-year forecast by the California Commission on State Finance predicts continued growth in the high-technology industries. For the period 1986-1996 the California economy is expected to outperform the national economy; this will be due largely to superior performance in three high-technology sectors—office machines (mainly computers), electronics, and aerospace industries.[23] Throughout this period California is expected to remain competitive in attracting new businesses. In just one industry—electrical machinery—California's share of the national industry has risen from 13 percent in 1975 to 19 percent in 1985. A share of 26 percent is predicted for 1996.[24]

High-technology industry in California, while more diversified than in other states, shows a high concentration in communication equipment, electronic components, computers and office machines, and aircraft.[25] Four industry groups—microelectronics, communications, computers and office equipment, and instruments—contributed 51 percent of California's manufacturing value-added in 1982. The same groups were responsible for 71 percent of the state's total manufacturing exports in 1983. Increased foreign competition, however, has led to losses in the last few years. In 1985 California lost 5,600 jobs in microelectronics and computers. In recent years many microelectronics firms have become research and design centers for manufacturing outside the state.[26] Other firms have countered by producing customized semiconductors or automating their production facilities. Both strategies have been highly successful and have resulted in improved productivity and lowered labor costs.

TABLE 2-5
Manufacturing Employment and Share in California by Industry,
1972, 1977, and 1982 and Percentage Change between 1972 and 1982
(employees in 1,000s, shares and change in %)

	1972		1977		1982		1972-1982
	Emp.	Share	Emp.	Share	Emp.	Share	Change
Nondurable							
Food/kindred	155.0	10.5	163.4	9.6	174.0	13.4	12.3
Tobacco	—	—	—	—	—	—	—
Textile	12.2	0.8	16.4	1.0	12.4	1.0	1.6
Apparel	82.2	5.6	101.1	6.0	106.0	8 .2	29.0
Paper products	34.5	2.3	35.9	2.1	35.5	2.7	2.9
Printing/ publishing		6.0	97.1	5.8	131.0	10.1	48.9
Chemicals	45.2	3.1	52.7	3.1	52.6	4.1	16.4
Petroleum refining	16.1	1.1	18.5	1.1	18.8	1.5	16.7
Rubber & plastic	50.8	3.5	63.6	3.7	66.1	3.5	30.1
Leather	—	—	11.6	0.7	10.5	0.8	—
Total nondurable	484.0	32.9	560.3	33.1	606.9	46.9	25.4
Durable							
Lumber & wood	62.6	4.2	67.1	4.1	48.4	2.5	-22.7
Furniture & fixtures	43.2	2.9	51.9	3.1	52.6	2.8	21.8
Stone, clay, glass	50.3	3.4	53.0	3.1	49.0	2.6	-2.6
Primary metal	49.9	3.4	49.0	2.9	42.2	2.2	-15.4
Fabricated metal	120.1	8.2	136.2	8.1	139.9	7.3	16.4
Nonelectric machinery	135.0	9.2	174.3	10.3	247.9	13.0	83.6
Electrical equipment	176.9	12.0	228.8	13.5	331.8	17.4	87.6
Transportation equipment	268.3	18.2	253.5	15.0	258.3	13.6	-3.7
Instruments	48.1	3.3	69.0	4.1	91.8	4.8	90.1
Misc.	34.7	2.4	40.0	2.4	38.3	2.0	10.4
Total durable	989.1	67.1	1,127.8	111.9	1,300.2	68.2	31.5
Total mfg.	1,473.1	100.1	1,688.1	100.0	1,907.0	100.0	29.5

Source: U.S. Department of Commerce, Bureau of the Census, *1977 Census of Manufactures, General Summary, Alabama-Montana*, vol. 3, pp. 5-12 — 5-24; idem, 1982 *Census of Manufactures, Geographic Area Series, California*, pp. 12-19.

The California economy has greatly benefited from increased federal spending for defense, including the Strategic Defense Initiative (SDI) and the space station. The state has reached the highest employment level in the production of aircraft, guided missiles and space vehicles since the slowdown in defense spending in the early 1970s. In July 1985 226,000 workers were employed in

TABLE 2-6
High-Technology Employment in California
and Percentage Change, 1972, 1977, and 1982

	1972 Emp.	Change	1977 Emp.	Change	1982 Emp.	1972-1982 Change
Drugs	8.7	35.6	11.8	26.3	14.9	71.3
Industrial organic chemicals	—	—	3.9	-28.3	2.8	—
Office/computing machines	43.2	46.8	63.4	77.8	112.7	160.9
Communication equipment	75.7	18.2	89.5	53.4	137.3	81.4
Electronic components	53.8	58.4	85.2	58.6	135.1	151.1
Aircraft & parts	—	—	93.9	19.7	112.1	—
Missiles/space vehicles	42.0	—	—	—	85.0	102.4
Instruments	48.1	43.5	69.0	33.0	91.8	90.9
Total high-tech employment	271.5	53.5	416.7	66.1	692.0	154.9
All mfg.	1545.9	13.3	1751.5	14.5	2005.0	29.7
Percentage of high-tech.	17.6	—	23.8	—	34.5	—

Note: Statistics for some industry groups are withheld to avoid disclosing figures for individual companies.
Source: U.S. Department of Commerce, Bureau of the Census, *1977 Census of Manufactures, General Summary, Alabama-Montana,* vol. 3, table 4, pp. 5-11—5-24; idem, *1982 Census of Manufactures, Geographic Area Series, California,* pp. 12-19.

defense industries. The UCLA model of the California economy estimates that as much as 30 percent of the state's employment growth since 1981 is attributable to defense spending.[27]

In 1983, 19.4 percent of all federal procurements for defense as well as civilian purposes went to California. The Department of Defense (DOD) spent $26.4 billion, or 22.2 percent of its prime contracts, and the National Aeronautics and Space Administration (NASA) spent $2.1 billion, or 38 percent of its prime contracts.[28] Future spending levels will stabilize or be somewhat lower in the years ahead. The California Commission on State Finance estimates that defense spending currently accounts for 16.3 percent of total manufacturing output. If the Gramm-Rudman deficit cuts were strictly adhered to, the resulting 1987 drop in federal spending could lead to a 1.2 percent loss in employment in the state.[29]

In 1983 California ranked first among states in federal R&D obligations, receiving 22.4 percent of all federal obligations. Eighty percent of the total

TABLE 2-7

Share of Federal Obligations for R&D in California
by Agency Source Compared to the United States, 1983

(%)

Agency	California	United States
Agriculture	0.6	2.2
Commerce	0.2	0.9
Defense	71.1	61.0
Energy	10.1	12.0
Health & Human Services	5.7	11.5
Interior	0.5	1.0
Transportation	0.4	0.9
EPA	0.3	0.6
NASA	9.2	7.0
NSF	1.9	2.8
Total ($ million)	8,440.0	37,628.0

Source: National Science Foundation, *Federal Funds for Research and Development*, vol. 33, 1984, p. 150.

TABLE 2-8

Federal Obligations for R&D by Performer
in California and Share Compared to the United States, 1983

($ million and %)

Performer	Funds	Share	U.S. Share
Federal facilities	1,143.2	13.6	27.1
Industry	5,191.1	61.5	49.1
Universities	1,641.0	19.4	18.8
State & local government	444.4	5.3	4.5
Other	20.3	0.3	0.5
Total	8,439.9	100.0	100.0

Source: National Science Foundation, *Federal Funds for Research and Development*, vol. 33, 1984, p. 142.

came from DOD and NASA. On a per capita basis, California ranked seventh. Of the states in this study, only Massachusetts ranked higher (Table 2-8).

Approximately 62 percent of 1983 federal R&D obligations in California went to private industry; this accounted for almost half of all federal obligations for R&D performed by industry. This may well be the single most revealing indicator of the exceptional strength of California's high-technology industry (Table 2-8). Federal obligations provided 71 percent of R&D conducted at California universities. Both industry and university R&D depend heavily on

20

TABLE 2-9
Occupational Structure in California for Employed Persons Sixteen Years and Over Compared to the United States, 1980
(workers in 1,000s and %)

	California		United States	
	Workers	Share	Workers	Share
Managerial & professional	2,671.8	25.1	22,151.6	22.7
Technical, sales & admin.	3,469.3	32.6	29,593.5	30.3
Service	1,340.3	12.6	12,629.4	12.9
Farming, forestry & fishing	301.5	2.8	2,811.3	2.9
Production, craft & repair	1,313.3	12.3	12,594.2	12.9
Operators & laborers	544.2	14.5	17,859.3	18.3
Total	10,640.4	100.0	97,639.3	100.0

Source: U.S. Department of Commerce, Bureau of the Census, *1980 Census of Population, Characteristics of the Population*, vol. 1, ch. A, part 6, p. 6-104.

the federal government, leading to increased strength when federal R&D spending is completed, but also making the advanced-technology sector vulnerable to federal budget cuts.

The rapid growth of the high-technology sector in California has produced an occupational structure slightly different from the rest of the nation. Both the professional and technical sectors comprise a larger percentage of the work force (Table 2-9). In 1982 California universities and firms employed 456,500 of the nation's scientists and engineers, almost twice as much as New York (265,900) and Texas (213,500), which ranked second and third, respectively.[30]

California's economy is often described as post-industrial, meaning that traditional industries play a relatively small role in the economy. This description ignores the fact that many of the high-technology industries *are* manufacturing industries. The production of goods remains important. What has changed is an increasing interdependence of manufacturing and services. Advanced-technology manufacturing depends on sophisticated research, engineering, and business services. According to recent research, "upwards of 25 percent of jobs are service jobs which are tightly linked to manufacturing."[31] Using this finding, SRI estimates that manufacturing-related employment in California could be as high as 50 percent if tightly linked services were included.[32] Linked services include research, engineering, and design as well as maintenance and customer and financial services. This line of argument implies that the emergence of a high-technology economy in California has progressed much further than a simple interpretation of the statistics suggests. We now ask what role the state government has assumed in promoting the new economy.

Science and Technology Policy

The development of high-technology industries in California was the result of a rare combination of events. The major actors were the federal government, business companies, and universities. Most of the time, the state government played a secondary role.

During World War II the federal government conducted defense research and development at a scale hitherto unknown. Instead of creating federal laboratories for the task, the government contracted with civilian scientists and engineers who remained, for the most part, in their previous settings—universities and private industry. The use of the contract mechanism to buy brain power led to strong cooperative programs between the public and private sectors. The approach was further expanded during the Cold War era, and was later used for R&D in areas other than defense like space, transportation, and telecommunications. Under this policy federal funds were channeled to the states on a competitive basis: states competed for grants and contracts on the basis of the quality of their scientists, engineers and production facilities. California showed great competitive strength and consistently attracted a lion's share of federal R&D and procurement dollars.

Today the federal government continues to dominate research funding in the country. Although state governments have played important roles in agricultural research for a century, in the years following World War II, they saw little need to develop explicit science and technology policies. California was no exception to this rule. However, the state made one decision about sixty years ago which, with the advantage of hindsight, is recognized as having laid the foundation for the state's science and technology policy: to explicitly support research in higher education. Long before defense research brought the federal government into play, the state made a broad-based, long-term commitment to excellence of research in its public universities. A well-thought-out master plan for higher education, passed in 1960, reinforced the early initiative and enabled the state university system to maintain world leadership in research and attract businesses dependent on advanced technology.

One report seeking to explain California's success has identified three reasons: a large and well-trained work force, the state's location on the West Coast and Pacific Basin, and good amenities.[33] Another report adds more technology-specific factors: leadership in technological innovation and entrepreneurship, high industrial productivity, and excellence in education and training.[34] The growth of Silicon Valley shows these various factors at work and highlights the important contribution made by the private sector.

The foundation for the private-sector contribution to technology-related growth was laid at Stanford University when Vice-President Frederick Terman encouraged two graduate students, Bill Hewlett and Dave Packard, to collaborate on commercializing their work. Hewlett and Packard enjoyed minor success selling variable-frequency oscillators; with the advent of World War II, business picked up significantly. The company continued to prosper in the postwar period, but by 1950 the firm still employed only about 200 people.

Meanwhile, Stanford University was searching for ways to raise revenue to expand its academic programs. The university was prohibited from selling unused land in the Palo Alto area, but the concept of a high-technology industrial park there was suggested and approved. The Stanford Industrial Park was created in 1951. The idea of building an industrial park near a university was new, and Terman became a strong advocate of its unique advantages, for both the university and industry. The first tenant was Varian Associates, a Stanford University spin-off. Hewlett Packard signed a lease in 1954.

The development of the semiconductor technology and the rapid growth of microelectronics firms triggered a high-technology boom for the entire region, and later for the state and nation. In 1960 thirty-two firms were located in the Stanford Research Park; by 1970 the number of tenants had more than doubled. Initially the industry depended largely on military purchases. At one point sales to the military accounted for 40 percent of all sales. Later civilian purchases became more important.[35] In 1971 the name Silicon Valley was coined.[36]

Prior to the development of the Stanford Industrial Park, the existence of systematic university-industry technology transfer and sustained two-way communication had long been recognized as important. The University of California system, though highly regarded in many fields of science and engineering, was not as successful as Stanford in implementing the concept. Frederick Terman's leadership was vital, and "a very strong case can be made that Silicon Valley would not exist today if it were not for Stanford University since hundreds of high-technology corporations trace their origins and success to Stanford training and research."[37]

By the late 1970s other countries and states were successfully competing with California in a number of high-technology sectors. Governor Jerry Brown, in response to what he perceived as a dangerous weakening of the state's economy, formed the California Commission on Industrial Innovation (CCII). The commission's mandate was "to provide policy guidance . . . on the role of technological innovation in maintaining California's leadership in the national economy."[38] Commission members included representatives from business—among them Steven Jobs of Apple Computers and David Packard—labor, universities, and the government.

Like many of the other state high-technology commissions formed at this time, the CCII recognized the need to apply technological innovation to the dual tasks of restoring traditional industries and promoting the growth of the high-technology sector. But unlike other commissions, the CCII also examined national strategies for improving the economy. In its 1981 report, the commission observed that economic problems in the United States as well as California stemmed from poorly formulated national policies leading to declining productivity, R&D expenditures, and educational standards. Business leaders were also held accountable for the declines.[39] Japanese competition was cited as a third villain; the CCII's concern with Japanese competition was so great that it co-sponsored a study on Japanese and American semiconductor firms.[40]

The commission's recommendations encompassed three areas: investments, including both government and private-sector initiatives; education and job training at all levels; and measures to enhance the productivity of management and workers. In contrast to other state high-technology study groups most of the CCII recommendations were not aimed at the state level; rather, policy proposals concentrated on federal actions to aid high-technology industries. Of the fourteen recommendations related to investment, eleven called for federal action and one was addressed to the state. The rationale for the level of the proposals was that damage was being inflicted on the state's high-technology sector by foreign competition and exacerbated by the lack of a national response. Similarly, the CCII called for a "Sputnik-like" push to reverse declining educational standards. The university systems' declining capability to conduct research, cited as a contributing factor to the state's problems, required national remedies in addition to state efforts.

The commission's 1981 report accurately predicted the problems that today afflict the California economy. Foreign producers, especially within the semiconductor industry, are gaining increased market shares in the United States and the world. The CCII also rightly argued that educational reform had to play a major role in the policy response. Yet the commission did not have a significant impact. Just as the report was released, Governor Jerry Brown was defeated in his bid for reelection. Brown, an ardent proponent of high-technology and a believer in an active government role, was replaced by George Deukmajian in 1982.

The new governor advocated a less active state role in the economy. The high-technology sector, in his view, should rely on market forces the same way the more traditional parts of the economy do. High-technology was not to be de-emphasized, but other sectors were of equal interest to the new administration in strengthening the California economy.[41] The state's new attitude was perhaps best expressed in the following statement:

Rather than government targeting on technologies or industries or products or companies in trying to pick the winners and losers, government should target on the process of innovation. That is, it should create an environment in which new ideas and technological advances can flourish.[42]

In one important regard, this philosophy agrees with the CCII report, which had called for national policies to stimulate high-technology growth rather than a multitude of state programs to aid businesses. The Deukmajian administration has not attempted to initiate economic or science and technology programs.

The legislature does not wholly agree with the administration's stance and has pushed for state initiatives in support of science and technology policy. The Democratic leadership was particularly concerned when the Microelectronics and Computer Technology Corporation (MCC) decided to locate in Texas. As a result, two legislative committees were formed, the Joint Committee on Science and Technology and the Assembly Committee on Economic Development and New Technologies. Both have the mandate to assess the state of high-technology industries and to recommend action.

The Assembly Committee, formed in early 1983, has been the more visible of the two groups, holding numerous hearings, conducting on-site investigations, meeting with constituent groups, and forming task forces. The Assembly Committee has looked at a wide range of issues, including state and local economic development, international trade, small businesses, economic disaster relief, and legislation dealing with the development of new technologies. So far the Assembly Committee's work has been largely investigative in nature, although legislation has been proposed in several instances.

The Joint Committee on Science and Technology is focusing its work on all five stages of the "innovation cycle"—basic research, applied research, product development, manufacturing, and marketing. The committee has attempted to devise programs to strengthen each of these components.[43] Many of the committee's proposals emphasize the linkage of industry to universities and are designed to facilitate greater interaction between the two. Like the Assembly Committee, the Joint Committee has yet to articulate a comprehensive policy statement or proposal.

The legislature cannot yet consider bold action because the public does not perceive the seriousness of the problems facing the state's high-technology sector. This may change if the semiconductor industry encounters more setbacks. At present, the administration as well as the Democratic legislative leadership have limited their action proposals to a relatively narrow call for increased R&D cooperation between state universities and industry. California's political structure, with strong gubernatorial powers, will make it difficult for the legislature to play the lead role in implementing a comprehensive state science and technology policy.

Existing state programs are not focused specifically on high-technology industries. Several, like the Small Business Loan Guarantee Program and the Economic Development Loan Program, are standard general assistance programs. The state has also begun to provide nonfinancial assistance to small businesses through Small Business Development Centers. Currently only two are in operation, but the state hopes to expand the program.

A cluster of programs that is unique to California encourages innovation in energy conservation and small-scale technologies. The Energy Technologies Research, Development, and Demonstration Act of 1985 provides low-interest loans and contract research funds to both the public and private sectors. Administered by the California Energy Commission, the act is designed to enhance the commercialization of California's indigenous energy resources by improving market acceptance of new energy technologies. The program funds demonstrations and a limited number of research projects on specific technological problems.

A related program is the State Assistance Fund for Energy, California Business and Industrial Development Corporation (SAFE-BIDCO). The program focuses on small-scale innovative energy conservation efforts and alternative energy projects. SAFE-BIDCO depends on a federal Small Business Administration guarantee of 90 percent on its loans, which can provide up to $5,000,000 for an individual case. The loans may be used to purchase machinery, fund plant expansion, or finance the development of equipment that saves energy or develops new energy sources. The money cannot be used to invest in new firms. Once the loan is made, the federal portion is sold to investors with financial institutions acting as intermediaries. SAFE-BIDCO risks only 10 percent of its own funds, and the program shows some success.

Program Assessments

The successes of California's high-technology industries cannot be attributed to programmatic state intervention. While other states have initiated numerous science and technology programs in recent years, California has not. Rather, the state has followed a different strategy focused on long-term structural needs. While cause and effect are difficult to establish, it may be that the state's most important contribution to the growth of its high-technology economy has been in meeting infrastructure needs. Using primarily federal funds, the state has over a period of years built a sound physical and human infrastructure to benefit industry. Physical infrastructure was provided through the financing and construction of roads, water systems, and sewage systems. Human infrastructure was built through a long-term commitment to all levels of education, particularly higher education. As a result, California has a population supportive of science-based industry and is a leader in producing highly trained scientists and engineers. State policy has also been effective, under several governors, in reconciling economic growth with environmental goals. Finally, the state's work force has benefited from the services offered by the three-tiered California educational system.

Whether more specific state programs will be needed in the future, however, is an open question. Many policymakers in the state see a need for programs that create closer university-industry cooperation. There is concern that public universities have not played a greater role in the growth of the high-technology sector. An intensive debate is presently under way about refocusing the higher education system to better meet the needs of industry.

For now, the state has few of the high-technology programs that we found in other states in this study. To illustrate California's focus on structural policy we shall review state policy for higher education. An assessment of the single high-technology-specific program that does exist, Microelectronics Innovation and Computer Research Opportunities, follows.

THE HIGHER EDUCATION SYSTEM

California's public system of higher education has it origins in the Organic Act of 1868 which established the University of California and laid out in detail the first academic structure and curricula.[44] In the 1920s the state made a long-term commitment to raise the quality of its research universities to world standards. From that time on the state has accepted the proposition that education and research are closely related to economic prosperity. State education expenditures are viewed as investments that produce tangible economic results and improve the human capital of the state. An early product of this strategy was the design by Berkeley scientists of a statewide water system which made possible the irrigation-based California agriculture, with its focus on specialty crops and high added value.

Shortly before World War II, a critical mass of first-class researchers was assembled at the University of California. The group of nuclear physicists around Robert Oppenheimer and Edward Teller pioneered the close cooperation between the university and the federal government that has since sustained the excellence of higher education in California. Over time, the agricultural, industrial, and service sectors of the economy have all derived benefits from this policy. The growth of the defense, aerospace, and high-technology industries attests to the success of the strategy.

The state's educational institutions multiplied and eventually included a large number of universities, state colleges, and community colleges. In 1960 the Donahoe Higher Education Act consolidated these institutions into a three-tiered system differentiated by function. The California master plan has been a model for the organization of higher education in many other states.

The top tier is the selective, research-oriented University of California system (UC). Its nine campuses are designed to conduct world-class research. UC is the only tier authorized by the master plan to engage in research and grant doctoral degrees. The California Education Code also designates UC as the primary state-supported academic agency for research in the fields of water, energy, agriculture, health, and other engineering fields. The state has long supported specialization of individual campuses in order to create centers of excellence and avoid duplication of effort.

The second tier, consisting of nineteen institutions, is the California State University (CSU) system, whose mission is to provide a four-year college education to the majority of California students. Heavier teaching loads underscore the educational mission of the institutions. This legislative intent has been partially circumvented by an oversupply of trained PhDs during the 1970s. As these scientists accepted jobs in the CSU system, they brought with them the desire to be involved in research and to apply for federal funding for their work. Some of the new faculty members, however, used their talents to forge new links of service with surrounding industries and communities.[45]

The bottom tier, some 100 institutions, is the California Community College (CCC) system. The community colleges offer the first two years of college education to all state residents who want to enroll. The CCCs also provide vocational and technical training to adults.

The 1970s ushered in a decade of difficulties in state-university relations. Several governors resented the role played by the universities during the period of student unrest. There was also increasing criticism that the universities did not follow through in the transfer of research results and therefore failed to give a fair return to the state for the funding they received. To make things worse, the financial condition of state government deteriorated. Governors Reagan and Brown responded by reducing state funding for the education system. Equipment purchases were reduced, faculty salaries were cut, and less institutional support was provided.[46] Proposition 13, passed in 1975, worsened the financial difficulties. The CCC lost taxing authority and became dependent on state financing. All three tiers of the higher education system suffered funding cuts, and there was concern that the quality of the institutions was endangered.

The turning point came in 1983. Newly selected UC President David Garner warned Governor Deukmajian that the UC system was loosing its competitive edge and that the state's high-technology industries would suffer irreparable damage unless the state renewed its commitment to support higher education.[47] The argument was presented forcefully and brought a positive response from the state. The result has been three years of increased funding for the university systems. State support of higher education represented 15.4 percent of the state budget in 1986. It is expected to reach $3.7 billion in 1987-1988.[48] The legislature has reviewed in detail the funding needs of the UC system, and has renewed its commitment to research in the UC system. The CCC, while not being treated as well, received a one-time special equipment fund and $33 million from the state lottery fund. CCC officials do not feel that this will be sufficient to rectify the decline that the system has experienced.

State officials and educators agree that financial problems are not the only ones besetting the higher education system. They feel that the entire system needs to be examined and made more responsive to current social and economic needs. The Commission for the Review of the Master Plan for Higher Education was created for this purpose. The commission has completed its study of the CCC and expects to publish the results of its UC review in 1987.

Regarding the CCC, the commission calls for a reaffirmation of the goals originally assigned to the system in the master plan: to prepare young people for college so that they can find jobs in tomorrow's economy. In recent years increased emphasis on remedial and vocational education has left many students unprepared to continue on to four-year universities. According to the commission, the CCC should not divert from its primary mission. The continued influx of immigrants will increase the importance of the CCC. Higher standards are seen as essential to ensure that educated workers are available to meet industry needs. Vocational and remedial education should continue, but only as a secondary mission.[49]

The UC review is in the initial phase and the commission's findings and recommendations are not yet known. Preliminary indications are that the commission will place more emphasis on applied research and improved linkages with industry.

In recent years relations between the university and state government have improved markedly. Some of the credit goes to the California Policy Seminar, an innovative program that provides legislators and executive agencies with research support from UC faculty. The program was started in the 1970s, when the legislature considered reducing UC research appropriations by $5 million and using the funds for research on issues of interest to the state. In response to the threat, UC initiated the seminar, a group of seven faculty members from various campuses of the UC system, the governor's cabinet members, and several members of the legislature. Each year the UC faculty is invited to submit short proposals on policy issues that will become critical for the state in five to ten years. Some seventy proposals are received, and fifteen are funded modestly to develop more detailed proposals. Ultimately four or five are selected for full funding. The annual cost is about $350,000. In recent years the process has been refined, and state agencies issue formal requests for proposals on issues that are important to them. The program has attracted much faculty interest and has been well received by the legislature and the executive branch.[50]

MICROELECTRONICS INNOVATION
AND COMPUTER RESEARCH OPPORTUNITIES (MICRO)

MICRO is the only high-technology program in California comparable to the kind of state programs discussed in other chapters. This chapter has argued that support of California's higher education system is an important state contribution to economic development. This view is shared by the leaders of MICRO, who see their program as building a bridge between UC and the microelectronics industry.[51]

MICRO was established by the legislature in 1981 in response to a proposal by Governor Jerry Brown. The organization's goal is to support:

> ... innovative research in microelectronics technology, its applications in computer and information sciences, and its necessary antecedents in other physical science disciplines ... and to help the California electronics and computer industries maintain their leadership by expanding relevant research and graduate student training at the university.[52]

Legislative intent has been interpreted to mean that sponsoring industries must have relevant manufacturing and/or research facilities in California and that the sponsorship of projects must benefit California industry. It has also been assumed that one of the program's purposes is to stimulate and cooperate with small businesses in the fields covered by MICRO.

Policy decisions are made by the MICRO policy board, which is comprised of three members each from industry, state government, and the University of California. The five-member executive committee includes faculty members from five of the nine UC campuses and manages the day-to-day operations of the program. The committee is responsible for development of the program guidelines, which are then submitted to the board for approval. The committee also forms peer review committees, makes recommendations on funding levels for the accepted proposals, and attempts to equitably distribute available funds among campuses.

In early spring, the MICRO executive committee sends out requests for proposals to UC faculty members. Those interested in submitting a proposal contact one or more firms for support of their research projects. When a suitable sponsor is found, the faculty member and his industry counterpart prepare a research proposal and budget. The supporting industry issues a letter of intent to fund at least 50 percent of the budget, and the proposal and the letter of intent are submitted to the executive committee.

The faculty member is responsible for arranging private-sector support and must explain all MICRO policies concerning the binding letter of support, delivery of product, termination procedures, and patent provisions. Any patentable result of a MICRO project is subject to the university's patent policy, which limits a cooperating company's interest in resulting patents to nonexclusive royalty-bearing rights. In other words, interested parties may have to pay royalties for the use of a patent, but they may not be denied its use.

Industry support is normally in cash but can take the form of new equipment valued at 50 percent of list price. Software may be donated at 10 percent of list price. The UC president's office allocates the full amount of the university's contribution to each campus. The chancellor's office at each campus allocates 20 percent of the university's share for each approved MICRO project. The remaining 80 percent is held back until award documents have been received from the industrial sponsors.

MICRO is not meant to support product development or pure research, but to help California industries maintain their technological lead. Foremost in the program's goals is the training of graduate students, not only in technology but also in entrepreneurship. Graduate fellowships have grown from $95,000 in 1981-1982 to $500,000 in 1985-1986. The number of projects supported has also grown, from 31 in 1981-1982 to 120 in 1985-86. The number of industrial sponsors has remained at about 60. Industry cash contributions have grown from $1.34 million in 1981-1982 to over $4.5 million in 1985-1986.[53] Total industry contributions peaked at over $8 million in 1984-1985.

Funding by the state has increased significantly during the program's existence. State funding in 1981-1982 was $.83 million, increasing in 1982-1983 to $1.66 million, twice that of the previous year. In 1983-1984 funding did not increase, but in 1984-1985 it again more than doubled to $3.4 million. In 1985-1986 state funding leveled off at $4 million.

To our knowledge, no independent evaluation of MICRO exists. There is a general perception among California observers that the program is successful and well received by industry. Due to the short history of the program, the number of finished projects is not yet a good measure of success. MICRO favors research projects that will yield results in the mid- to long-term future.

Nor, according to Professor Chand Viswanathan, chairman of the executive committee, is the present amount of state funding a good measure of success. He points out that, although state funding has leveled off, industry funding continues to grown and more closely approximate a two-to-one match than the half that is required.

Conclusions

California's past and present emphasis in science and technology policy has been on support of its higher education system. While general public education, accessible to all residents, has been an important focus, it is in support of higher education that California truly distinguished itself. Instead of creating programs directly helping industrial enterprises, the state has provided business with first-class universities from which to hire scientists, engineers, and trained workers and to which it can turn for research support. Few state-initiated programs exist because few have been needed in California. MICRO is an important exception. By maintaining first-class research institutions, the state has continued to attract a disproportionately large share of federal research, development, and procurement dollars. By following this strategy over many decades, and reinforcing it after a period of neglect, the state has generated jobs and fostered economic growth.

NOTES

1. SRI International, *Meeting California's Competitiveness Challenge*, Menlo Park, 1985, 14. A report to the Senate Select Committee on Long Range Policy Planning.
2. SRI International, *Promoting Advanced Technology Appropriate to a State's Economy: Beyond "High Tech" Highways*, Menlo Park, n.d., 1.
3. SRI International, *California's Economic Future: Building New Foundations for a Competitive Society*, Menlo Park, 1986, 4. A Report to the Joint Legislative Committee on Science and Technology.
4. Charles Bell and Charles Price, *California Government Today* (Homewood, IL: Dorsey Press, 1984), 18.
5. California Legislature, Assembly Committee on Economic Development and New Technologies, *The Pacific Rim and the Competitive Future of California's Industries*, Sacramento, n.d., 1.
6. SRI International, *California's Economic Future*, 15.
7. U.S. Department of Commerce, Bureau of the Census, *State Population Estimates by Age and Components of Change: 1980-1984, Current Population Reports, Population Estimates and Projections*, Washington, D.C., 1985, 9.
8. U.S. Department of Commerce, Bureau of the Census, *1980 Census of Population, General Population Characteristics, California*, vol. 1, part 6, Washington, D.C., 1985.
9. California Legislature, *The Pacific Rim*, 2.
10. SRI International, *California's Economic Future*, 6.
11. U.S. Department of Commerce, Bureau of the Census, *1980 Census of Population, Characteristics of the Population*, vol. 1, ch. A, Washington, D.C., 1984, 1-58.
12. SRI International, *California's Economic Future*, 4.
13. Ibid.
14. Ibid., 16.
15. Ibid., 22.

32

16. Bell and Price, *California Government Today*, 16.
17. SRI International, *California's Economic Future*, 10.
18. *A New Approach For Economic Growth*, Sacramento, 1983, 10. Briefing paper for the Assembly Committee on Economic Development and New Technologies.
19. Ibid.
20. SRI International, *California's Economic Future*, 18.
21. Ibid., 15.
22. U.S. Department of Commerce, Bureau of the Census, *Statistical Abstract of the United States, 1984*, Washington, D.C., 1984, 457.
23. State of California, Commission on State Finance, *Annual Long-Term General Fund Forecast: Fiscal Years 1985-86 Through 1995-96*, Sacramento, 1986, 27.
24. Ibid.
25. John Campbell, "Comparative High-Technology Industrial Growth: Texas, California, Massachusetts, and North Carolina," Bureau of Business Research, The University of Texas at Austin, 1986, 6.
26. SRI International, *California's Economic Future*, 17-18.
27. Ibid., 19.
28. California Legislature, Assembly Committee on Economic Development and New Technologies, *The Impact of Defense and Aerospace Spending on California's Economic Development*, n.d., 12.
29. State of California, Commission on State Finance, *Impact of Federal Expenditures on California*, Sacramento, 1986, 3.
30. National Science Foundation, *U.S. Scientists and Engineers, 1982*, Washington, D.C., 1984, 81-82.
31. SRI International, *California's Economic Future*, 16.
32. Ibid.
33. The California Post-Secondary Education Commission, *The Wealth of Knowledge*, Sacramento, 1984, 15.
34. SRI International, *California's Economic Future*, 7-8.
35. Everett M. Rogers and Judith K. Larsen, *Silicon Valley Fever*, (New York: Basic Books, Inc., 1984), 39.
36. Ibid., 25-43.
37. The California Post-Secondary Education Commission, *The Wealth of Knowledge*, 11.
38. California Commission on Industrial Innovation, *Winning Technologies, A New Industrial Strategy for California and the Nation*, Sacramento, 1981, ii.
39. Ibid., 13-14.
40. Ibid., 24.
41. Christy Campbell Walters, director, California Department of Commerce, as quoted by John Cox in "The Politics of Innovation," *PSA Magazine*, November 1983.
42. Ralph Landau, "Government Policies for Innovation and Growth," in Ralph Landau and Nathan Rosenberg, editors, *The Positive Sum Strategy: Harnessing Technology for Economic Growth*, (Washington, D.C.: National Academy Press, 1986), 535.
43. Bill Bradley, "Industrial Strategy," November, 1985. Draft for the Senate Office of Research.

44. The University of California UC, *A Multi-Campus System in the 1980s: Report of the Joint Planning Committee*, Berkeley, 1979, A-1.

45. Frank A. and Edith Darknell, "State College Science and Engineering Faculty: Collaborative Links with Private Business and Industry in California and Other States," in *University-Industry Research Relationships*, (Washington, D.C.: National Science Foundation, 1983), 163-192.

46. UC, *A Multi-Campus System*, B-2.

47. David Savage, "Higher Education," *California Journal*, (September 1985), 12.

48. State of California, *Annual Long-Term General Fund Forecast*, 46 and 52.

49. Commission for the Review of the Master Plan for Higher Education, *The Challenge of Change: A Reassessment of the California Community Colleges*, Sacramento, 1986, 1-9.

50. Irwin Feller, *Universities and State Governments*, (New York: Praeger, 1986); Todd R. La Porte, "California," in *The University and the State*, (proceedings of a conference sponsored by the Bureau of Governmental Research, University of Maryland, College Park, 1980), 16-18; telephone interview with Todd R. La Porte, December 18, 1986.

51. Interview with Professor Chand Viswanathan, chairman, executive committee, MICRO, Los Angeles, January 6, 1986.

52. The Microelectronics Innovation and Computer Research Opportunities Program, *Progress Report*, January 1985.

53. Ibid.

High-technology policy in Florida is relatively new. The Florida economy has traditionally been quite dependent on a few principal sectors like tourism and agriculture. The economic slump of the late 1970s promoted the state to begin strengthening the industrial sectors, especially the high-technology industries. Recognizing the state's ability to attract industries and workers, the state government has established and implemented policies toward high-technology development in the 1980s.

Demographic and Economic Profile

POPULATION CHARACTERISTICS

Three characteristics in Florida's demographic profile are striking: its rapid population increase, its high share of residents of Hispanic origin, and its citizens' age distribution.

In 1984, more than ten million people were living in Florida, making it the sixth most populous state in the country. During the 1970s, Florida experienced a rapid population increase. While the total U.S. population grew about 11 percent between 1970 and 1980, Florida's population grew over four times this amount (Table 3-1). Only two other states, Nevada and Arizona, experienced faster growth during that period.[1]

In absolute numbers of new residents Florida was also third, this time trailing California and Texas. This boom continued through the early 1980s: between 1980 and 1984, Florida's growth rate of 12.6 percent was more than three times the national growth rate. During this period, more than one million people immigrated to Florida from other states and from abroad — over 88 percent of its population increase was due to this factor.[2] If the trend holds, Florida will be the third most populous state in the country in the year 2000, exceeded only by California and Texas.[3]

While, in 1980, Florida still had a higher proportion of blacks than the United States as a whole did, the percentage had decreased since 1970, a trend contrary to the national tendency (Table 3-2). Other races experienced a vast increase in Florida in the 1970s, although when compared to the national increase, they remained a marginal group. In 1980 Florida reported a significantly higher proportion of residents of Hispanic origin, many of whom were Cubans, than the United States did (Table 3-3).[4]

— *This chapter was written by Michael Freudenberg and Tracy L. Henderson.*

36

Florida is a highly urbanized state (Table 3-4). Most of the population increase of the 1970s occurred in urbanized areas — over 50 percent, as compared to a growth rate of about 16 percent in rural areas.

The level of education of Florida residents is similar to that of most Americans in that about 67 percent complete high school (Table 3-5). The median years of school completed are also the same as the national average. But while 16.2 percent of all Americans 25 years old and older in 1980 completed four or more years of college, only 14.9 percent did in Florida. The weaker performance on the college level is one reason for Florida's current emphasis on higher education.

TABLE 3-1

Population of Florida and Percentage
Change Compared to the United States, 1970, 1980, and 1984
(in 1,000s and %)

	Florida	Change	U.S. Change
1970	6,789	—	—
1980	9,746	43.6	11.4
1984	10,976	12.6	4.1

Source: U.S. Department of Commerce, Bureau of the Census, State Population Estimates by Age and Components of Change: 1980 and 1984, p. 7; idem, 1980 Census of Population, vol. 1, part 1, p. 1; idem,1970 Census of Population, vol. 1, part 11, p. 8.

TABLE 3-2

Racial Distribution in Florida
Compared to the United States, 1970 and 1980
(%)

	1970 Florida	1970 United States	1980 Florida	1980 United States
White	84.2	87.5	84.0	83.1
Black	15.3	11.1	13.8	11.7
Other	0.4	1.4	2.2	5.1

Source: U.S. Department of Commerce, Bureau of the Census, 1980 Census of Population, ch. B, part 11, p. 17; ibid., part 1, p. 42; idem, 1970 Census of Population, vol. 1, part 11, p. 60.

TABLE 3-3
Population of Hispanic Origin
in Florida Compared to the United States, 1980
(%)

	Florida	United States
Hispanic origin	8.8	6.4
Non-Hispanic-origin	91.2	93.6

Source: U.S. Department of Commerce, Bureau of the Census, *1980 Census of Population,* ch. B, part 11, p. 7.; ibid., vol. 1, part 1, p. 19.

TABLE 3-4
Urban and Rural Composition of Florida
Compared to the United States, 1970 and 1980
(%)

	1970		1980	
	Florida	United States	Florida	United States
Urban	80.5	73.6	84.3	73.7
Rural	19.5	26.4	15.7	26.3

Source: U.S. Department of Commerce, Bureau of the Census, *1980 Census of Population,* vol. 1, part 11, p. 17.; ibid., part 1, p. 37; idem, *1970 Census of Population,* vol. 1, part 11, p. 8.

TABLE 3-5
Educational Levels in Florida
Compared to the United States, 1980
(%)

	Florida	United States
Elementary school (less than 5 years)	3.5	3.6
High school	66.7	66.5
College (4 or more years)	14.9	16.2
Median years of school completed	12.5	12.5

Source: U.S. Department of Commerce, Bureau of the Census, *1980 Census of Population,* ch. C, part 11, p. 91.

TABLE 3-6
Age Distribution in Florida
Compared to the United States, 1970 and 1980
(%)

Age Group	1970 Florida	1970 United States	1980 Florida	1980 United States
0-19	34.3	37.8	27.6	32.0
20-44	29.6	31.7	33.5	37.2
45-64	21.6	20.6	21.7	19.7
65+	14.6	9.8	17.3	11.3

Source: U.S. Department of Commerce, Bureau of the Census, *1980 Census of Population*, ch. B, part 11, p. 37; ibid., vol. 1, ch. B, part 1, p. 42; idem, *1970 Census of Population*, vol. 1, part 11, p. 69.

The most remarkable element in Florida's age distribution is its relatively high share of older persons (Table 3-6). Florida has a higher proportion of people aged 65 or older than any other state, and its share increased during the 1970s. As in the nation, the category of persons aged 19 or younger experienced a decline in Florida, but the share of this age group remained at a lower level in Florida.

The median age in Florida in 1980 was 34.7 years.[5] However, differences among regions in Florida are great; for example, Orlando City's median age of 29.5 years in 1970 decreased to 28.5 years in 1980, while Pompano Beach's increased from 43.3 years to 50.9 years during the same period. While most Florida cities did grow older, certain cities experiencing rapid economic growth began to attract large numbers of young professionals.

The rapid increase in Florida's population has tended to improve the state's business climate. But it has also generated corresponding problems of keeping up with demand — homes, jobs, sewers, roads, schools, and hospitals are in short supply.[6]

THE ECONOMY OF THE STATE

Florida's economy has historically depended on industries subject to economic elements beyond the state's control, that is, construction, agriculture, and tourism. Construction is seasonal, and slowdowns are experienced by all industries in the state. Agriculture is very sensitive to extremes of weather —

one freeze or one hurricane can destroy most of the state's citrus crop. Tourism is directly related to the overall U.S. economy; as national inflation rates rise, the number of tourists in the state declines. During the recession of the 1970s, the Florida economy suffered revenue shortfalls.

Tourism is Florida's largest industry. In 1984 it brought over $15 billion into the state economy and almost $700 million in state and local revenues.[7] International trade is also important; in 1984, exports accounted for 46 percent of Florida's trade sector.[8] Other factors influential to the Florida economy include retirement pay and the payrolls at numerous military bases in the state; these factors act as stabilizers.

The tourist industry contributes to the two largest employment sectors, services and wholesale and retail trade (Table 3-7). The dominant employers in the service sector are the health care industries, business services, and tourist-related services such as hotels and amusements. The service sector experienced rapid growth between 1972 and 1982, while shares of all other employment sectors stayed relatively constant. This change is consistent with the growth of the service sector on a national level.

TABLE 3-7

Nonagricultural Employment and Share in Florida by Sector,
1972, 1977, 1982 and Percentage Change between 1972 and 1982
(employees in 1,000s, shares and changes in %)

	1972		1977		1982		1972-1982
	Emp.	Share	Emp.	Share	Emp.	Share	Change
Mining	8.3	.4	9.6	.3	10.2	.2	22.9
Construction	230.1	9.2	256.6	7.0	319.4	8.0	38.8
Manufacturing	351.3	14.0	456.7	12.0	502.3	12.0	43.0
Transportation	173.5	7.0	229.9	6.0	242.5	6.0	39.8
Wholesale & retail	643.5	26.0	998.0	27.0	1114.1	26.0	73.1
Finance & insurance	162.4	6.5	276.6	7.0	298.7	7.0	83.9
Government	437.9	17.4	632.5	17.0	652.6	16.0	49.0
Services	505.6	20.1	902.0	24.0	1068.4	25.0	113.1
Total	2513.1	100.0	3761.9	100.0	4208.2	100.0	67.5

Source: U.S. Department of Labor, Bureau of Labor Statistics, *Employment, Hours, and Earnings, States and Areas, 1939-1982*, vol. 1, pp. 170-177.

The state is presently trying to reduce its economic dependence on those industries affected by external factors by strengthening the manufacturing sector. Government officials are trying to achieve a balance among tourism, agriculture, and manufacturing, especially high-technology manufacturing. Although in 1982 Florida was still well behind the national average in manufacturing percentages of employment, the migration of firms has contributed to growth in this sector, especially in electronics; large federal contracts also figure importantly into increases in manufacturing. The largest areas of employment within the manufacturing sector in 1982 were the electronics, transportation, food processing, and printing industries (Table 3-8). According to an article by David Avery and B. Frank King in *Economic Review*, "Florida's industrial sector has shifted from being a construction-driven and therefore volatile sector to one driven by technology closely allied to the recession-immune defense industry."[9] This shift resulted in a decrease of the sector's overall share of Florida employment between 1972 and 1982.

Florida's overall occupational structure is similar to that of the United States as a whole (Table 3-9). The main difference lies in the number of operators and laborers, in which Florida falls behind the United States. Florida's growth in per capita income since 1970 almost equals national growth rates (Table 3-10). The absolute difference between the dollar figures is diminishing as Florida's growth rate accelerates. When compared to the national average, Florida has a higher percentage of individuals living below the poverty level (Table 3-11). The unemployment rate, however, is normally lower than the national rate. The exception to the trend occurred during 1974-1979, when Florida's rate of unemployment exceeded the U.S. rate. Economists predict that renewed vigor in economic growth will cause the unemployment rate to level off in the next few years.

HIGH-TECHNOLOGY SECTOR

The high-technology division within the manufacturing industry underwent a marked growth spurt between 1977 and 1982 (Table 3-12). In 1972-1977 the high-technology growth rate was 5.4 percent, well below the national figure. In 1977 and 1982, however, the 77 percent growth rate of the high-technology industries in Florida substantially exceeded the national average of 26 percent.

During the 1980s, Florida has consistently ranked among the top ten states receiving federal R&D obligations, although between 1982 and 1983 Florida's position fell from fourth to eighth. Florida's ranking on a per capita basis is not as impressive: the state ranked eighteenth in 1983 (Table 1-2).

TABLE 3-8

Manufacturing Employment and Share in Florida by Industry,
1972, 1977, 1982, and Percentage Change between 1972 and 1982
(employees in 1,000s, share in %, and change in %)

	1972		1977		1982		1972-82
	Emp.	Share	Emp.	Share	Emp.	Share	Change
Nondurable							
Food/kindred	44.3	13.4	45.1	12.9	45.3	10.3	2.3
Tobacco	4.4	1.3	2.7	.9	1.7	.4	-61.4
Textile	3.7	1.1	4.7	1.3	3.0	.7	-18.9
Apparel	28.4	8.6	32.0	9.3	33.5	7.6	18.0
Paper products	15.8	4.8	15.3	4.3	15.3	3.5	-3.2
Printing & publishing	26.6	8.0	29.8	8.5	44.6	10.1	67.7
Chemicals	19.2	5.8	14.7	6.1	22.7	5.2	18.2
Petroleum refining	.8	.2	.8	.2	1.4	.3	75.0
Rubber & plastic	8.9	2.7	10.8	3.1	16.0	3.6	79.8
Leather	3.5	1.1	3.9	1.1	4.7	1.1	34.3
Total nondurable	155.6	47.0	166.6	47.6	188.2	42.8	21.0
Durable							
Leather	3.5	1.1	3.9	1.1	4.7	1.1	34.3
Lumber & wood	20.2	6.1	16.5	4.7	19.0	4.3	-5.9
Furniture & fixtures	10.2	.1	9.3	2.7	11.7	2.7	14.7
Stone, clay, glass	18.5	5.6	13.9	4.0	18.4	4.2	-.5
Primary metal	4.0	1.2	4.8	1.3	4.3	1.0	7.5
Fabricated metal	25.7	7.7	24.3	6.9	29.6	6.7	15.2
Nonelectric machinery	17.0	5.1	20.9	6.0	33.5	7.6	97.1
Electrical equipment	33.5	10.1	41.9	12.0	67.3	15.3	100.9
Transportation equipment	40.7	12.3	36.7	10.3	47.2	10.7	16.0
Instruments	5.4	1.6	8.3	2.9	12.4	2.8	129.6
Miscellaneous	5.9	1.7	7.0	2.0	8.5	1.9	44.1
Total durable	175.2	53.0	183.6	52.4	251.9	57.2	5.1
Total manufacturing	330.8	100.0	350.2	100.0	440.1	100.0	32.5

Note: Auxiliary and administrative employees have been omitted from this table.
Source: U.S. Department of Commerce, Bureau of the Census, *1982 Census of Manufactures, General Summary, Florida,* pp. 10-17; idem, *1977 Census of Manufactures, General Summary, Florida,* pp. 10-17.

42

TABLE 3-9
Occupational Structure in Florida for Employed Persons
Sixteen Years and Over Compared to the United States, 1980
(workers in 1,000s, shares in %)

| | Florida | | United States | |
	Workers	Share	Workers	Share
Managerial & professional	912,741	22.8	22,151.6	22.7
Technical, sales, & admin.	1,294,815	32.3	29,593.5	30.3
Service	583,920	14.6	12,629.4	12.9
Farming, forestry, & fishing	125,827	3.1	2,811.3	2.9
Production, craft, & repair	530,330	13.3	12,594.2	12.9
Operators & laborers	554,697	13.9	17,859.3	18.3
Total	4,002,330	100.0	97,639.3	100.0

Source: U.S. Department of Commerce, Bureau of the Census, *1980 Census of Population,* ch. C, sec. 2, pp. 93-94.

TABLE 3-10
Per Capita Income and Percentage Change
in Florida Compared to the United States, 1970, 1980, and 1984
(dollars and change in %)

	Florida	Change	United States	Change
1970	3,779	—	3,945	—
1980	9,245	144.0	9,494	140.7
1984	12,763	38.0	12,789	34.7

Source: U.S. Department of Commerce, Bureau of Economic Analysis, *1984 Survey of Current Business*, p. 18; U.S. Department of Commerce, *1980 Statistical Abstract of the United States 1984*, p.457.

TABLE 3-11

Individuals below the Poverty Level in Florida
Compared to the United States, 1970 and 1980
(%)

	Florida	United States
1970	—	13.0
1980	13.5	12.1

Source: U.S. Department of the Commerce, Bureau of
the Census, *1980 Census of Population*, ch C, sec. 2,
p. 86.

TABLE 3-12

High-Technology Manufacturing Employment
in Florida and Rate of Change, 1972, 1977, and 1982
(employees in 1,000s, change in %)

	1972	Change	1977	Change	1982
Drugs	1.1	36.4	1.5	140.0	3.6
Industrial organic chemicals	2.1	- 4.8	2.0	5.0	2.1
Office/computing machines	4.9	38.8	6.8	86.7	12.7
Communication equipment	16.6	22.9	20.4	87.7	38.3
Electronic components	9.2	7.6	9.9	61.6	16.0
Aircraft & parts	—	—	—	—	15.3
Missiles & space vehicles	14.5	- 46.2	7.8	—	—
Instruments	5.4	53.7	8.3	49.4	12.4
Total high-tech employment	53.8	5.4	56.7	77.1	100.4
All manufacturing	330.8	5.9	350.2	25.7	440.1
Percentage of high-tech	16.3		16.3		22.8

Note: Statistics for some industry groups are withheld to avoid disclosing figures for
individual companies. Auxiliary and administrative employees have been omitted
from this table.
Source: U.S. Department of Commerce, Bureau of the Census, *1982 Census of
Manufactures, Geographic Area Series*, Florida, pp. 9-15; idem, *1977 Census of
Manufactures, Geographic Area Statistics*, pp. 10.10 - 10.17.

Florida universities receive a strikingly small share of federal obligations: only about 7 percent of the total, compared to a national average of almost 19 percent (Table 3-13). Florida industries, on the other hand, receive almost two-thirds of the R&D obligations, compared to a national average of about 50 percent. The Department of Defense and the National Aeronautics and Space Administration (NASA) are the two dominant federal sources for R&D funds (Table 3-14). NASA's share is about four times the U.S. average, reflecting its major installations in the state.

Federal funds, though slim, constitute half of the R&D monies awarded to Florida's universities and colleges. The second most important source is institutions, with about 30 percent, or twice the national average. The life sciences are the main recipients in the universities, followed by engineering and the environmental sciences. Florida's weakness in education is demonstrated in Table 1-3: although the state ranked thirteenth in the nation for total academic R&D expenditures of $171 million in 1983, its per capita ranking was forty-fifth. Likewise, although the state held eleventh place in the number of employed scientists and engineers in 1983, its per capita ranking dropped to forty-sixth place (Table 1-4).

TABLE 3-13

Federal Obligations for R&D by Performer
in Florida and Share Compared to the United States, 1983
($ million and %)

Performer	Funds	Share	U.S. Share
Federal facilities	339.61	26.62	27.1
Industry	827.71	64.87	49.1
Universities	91.73	7.19	18.8
State & local government	12.33	0.97	4.5
Other	4.63	0.36	0.5
Total	1,276.02	100.00	100.0

Source: National Science Foundation, *Federal Funds for Research and Development*, vol. 33, 1984, p. 142.

TABLE 3-14
Share of Federal Obligations for R&D in Florida
by Agency Source Compared to the United States, 1983
(%)

Agency	Florida	United States
Agriculture	1.7	2.2
Commerce	1.9	0.9
Defense	63.3	61.0
Energy	0.7	12.0
Health & Human Services	3.5	11.5
Interior	0.4	1.0
Transportation	0.3	0.9
EPA	0.5	0.6
NASA	26.4	7.0
NSF	1.4	2.8

Source: National Science Foundation, *Federal Funds for Research and Development,* vol. 33, 1984, p. 150.

Science and Technology Policy

HISTORICAL ACCOUNT

Florida's high-technology industry emerged in the 1950s with the establishment of Cape Canaveral. The cape has generated growth by attracting new industries to the state, many of which are space and defense contractors. Reduced space funding depressed the Space Coast area in the 1970s; however, renewed space interests (such as the Space Shuttle) in conjunction with greater defense expenditures have placed Florida in a more prosperous economic position. Economists credit the state's large defense contractors, such as Martin Marietta and Honeywell, with sparking much of Florida's high-technology growth because they both recruited skilled engineers from out of state and trained local workers.[10]

The improvement of infrastructure, especially transportation, in the state has contributed to the development of high-technology industries. According to a Department of Commerce brochure, "a firm located in Florida is guaranteed an integrated transportation system with multiple capabilities for reaching both national and world markets."[11] In 1985 Florida ranked sixth in the nation in the number of public airports.[12] The extensive rail and highway network provides complete access throughout the state. The twenty seven ports, including fourteen deepwater ports, allow Florida to serve as a point for importing and exporting goods. Canals and rivers traverse the state to provide an alternative method of shipping. Having access to alternative modes of transportation is an incentive for firms to locate in a state.

Businesses looking for new locations find in Florida an attractive business climate. There is no personal income tax in Florida and corporate income tax is 5.5 percent. In 1983 Floridians retained 91.65 percent of their personal income after state and local taxes. [13] Florida has right-to-work laws, and only a small percentage of the manufacturing employees are unionized. In addition, businesses located in enterprise zones have corporate tax credits. The legislature has even provided incentives expressly for high-technology industries. Manufacturers are exempt from the sales and use tax of tangible property used in R&D. Trade secrets and patentable ideas are exempt from Florida's Public Records Law if in the hands of university staff. The cost of establishing R&D facilities has been reduced through industrial revenue bonds.

The development of major spin-off industries in Florida will depend on significant improvements to Florida's risk capital, which ranked forty-seventh nationwide in 1981-1982. Florida has expanded business incentives for venture capital formation. By offering equity investments as venture capital, the state can bypass a Florida constitutional amendment prohibiting state-funded loans and loan guarantee programs. [14] To overcome the lack of risk capital devoted to technology transfer, the 1985 legislature appropriated $1.5 million to fund technology startups. [15] A $5 million venture capital program for minority entrepreneurs is to be initiated in 1985-1987. Venture capital, when linked to the state's research programs, provides a valuable basis for entrepreneurial creativity.

CURRENT STRATEGIES

The Florida state government has become increasingly involved in the pursuit of high-technology development. Since Governor Bob Graham came into office in 1978, many new agencies, commissions, and committees focusing on economic development have been created. There seem to be three main strategies.

First, science and technology policy is being made more explicit, especially since the creation of the Florida High Technology and Industry Council (FHTIC) in 1983. This policymaking body tries to promote state economic development by coordinating the actions of state agencies, universities, and industry.

Second, there is an emphasis on education on all levels. Since Florida's educational system has been perceived as inferior, and a major location consideration of high-technology companies is the availability of a skilled work force, Florida leaders are seeking to improve education on all levels, including vocational education. [16] In 1981, the State Board of Education declared that the state education system would "equal that of the upper-quartile states within five years, as indicated by commonly accepted criteria of attainment."[17] To compare state university systems, Florida is participating in a study on establishing common educational criteria. These indicators of excellence include faculty services at university and community college levels and appropriations per student. In addition, Florida has created its own indicators to compare the individual school districts and universities within the state. State indicators include state licensing examination results of graduates, SAT and ACT test scores, and student-teacher ratios.

The board's expressed goal was not only the achievement of a better educational system, but also one more responsive to industry's needs — one, according to Governor Graham, "pro-active in meeting the demands of the economy. . . . The university system, therefore, will move conditions from being place-bound to being responsive and dynamic to the demands of tomorrow's industrial, business, and cultural conditions."[18] The state legislature appropriated more than one-third of its budget to educational expenses in 1984-1985. Funds to expand public school computer facilities have been provided. Gifted-student programs have been implemented. Universities have received special funds for engineering science programs. Community colleges and vocational-technical centers have received strong financial backing. Florida is considering toughening its high school curriculum and graduation requirements, extending the school day, and providing merit pay for faculty.

The third strategy is diversifying the state's involvements. Although the emphasis has been on education, programs covering the range of possible state involvements have been created. Overall, when compared to other states in terms of science and technology policy, Florida is a newcomer.

MAJOR POLICY COMPONENTS

Policymaking Bodies
The High Technology and Industry Council was created to promote Florida's economy by coordinating the efforts of different state agencies and representatives of high-technology business, industry, and academia. Its task is planning, coordinating, assisting in, and making recommendations about high-technology programs and policies.[19]

Education and Training
The Industry Services Training Program was created to provide customized training of employees for new and diversifying industries in Florida. The program is implemented through public schools, community colleges, and vocational-technical centers located near plant sites. It is concerned primarily with training skilled and semiskilled workers.

The Florida Center for Industrial Excellence is a facility created to provide ongoing industrial training and continuing education for vocational and technical instructors, thus assuring a skilled work force. The center, which is still in the planning stages, will try to meet industry's needs by providing laboratories, classrooms, and limited office space in which to update technicians in state-of-the-art skills and to showcase equipment and new technologies. The companies themselves will have to equip the classrooms and laboratories and agree to conduct workshops and training sessions.

The Postsecondary Education Programs of Excellence in Mathematics, Science, and Computer Education award funds to institutions of higher education to develop high-technology programs for all levels of education. Some programs link schools and industries. All public universities and community colleges are eligible to apply for funds.

The Regional Centers of Excellence in Mathematics, Science, Computers, and Technology were established by the legislature in 1983 at the University of South Florida in Tampa and in 1984 at Florida Atlantic University in Boca Raton. Created to bring together resources — both human and fiscal — from both the public and private sectors, the centers foster cooperative arrangements among business and industry, community colleges, state universities, private colleges and universities, and public school districts.[20] Activities include summer camps for students in math, science, computers, and technology, mentor programs for advanced high school students, and extensive in-service programs for teachers.

The Special University Funding is used to enhance engineering education within the state university system. A total of $54 million for five years is used to increase the production of engineers, improve engineering programs and facilities, and upgrade scientific and technical equipment.

The Florida Engineering Education Delivery System conducts statewide off-campus instruction at the master's level by using tutored videotapes and closed-circuit live video and electronic blackboard instruction. The program was created to meet the needs of Florida's high-technology community for the continuing education of technical professionals.

Basic and Applied Research

The former Research and Development Commission was created in 1978 with the authority to create research and development parks in association with state universities. As of 1985, three such parks were under development in Tampa, Orlando, and Tallahassee, and others are in the planning stages for Boca Raton, Jacksonville, and Miami. The purpose of the parks is to provide linkages between industry and business for research and development.

Technology and Management Assistance

The Florida Entrepreneurship Program, created in 1983, promotes the formation and expansion of organizations that provide opportunities for entrepreneurs to make more frequent contact with each other and to be more accessible to potential investors. Its goal is to achieve a critical mass supportive of successful entrepreneurs statewide. Local councils facilitate the exchange of information through activities such as venture fairs, workshops, forums, and seminars. The councils also promote awareness of opportunities to invest in new, innovative local companies.

Financial Assistance

The Commercialization Technology Fund is administered by the High Technology and Industry Council. It is a venture capital fund to finance entrepreneurs who are bringing their projects to the marketplace.

Program Assessments

This section contains assessments of selected high-technology programs in Florida. Programs were chosen on the basis of (a) funding — programs with larger budgets were preferred because they are more likely to have greater impacts; (b) history — established programs are more usefully evaluated; (c) success — programs that are credited with visible achievements were preferred; (d) scope — programs implemented on a statewide basis were preferred to local programs; and (e) innovativeness — programs showing new approaches in policy were preferred.

We selected four education and training programs and one policy development program for assessment. Our selection does not cover the range of possible state involvements described in the previous section because many such programs in Florida are too new to evaluate. Florida's economic development strategy places an emphasis on education; therefore, several educational programs were chosen for review.

The programs selected are:

- the Florida High Technology and Industry Council, (FHTIC);
- the Special University Funding for Engineering and Science Programs;
- the Florida Engineering Education Delivery System, (FEEDS);
- the Industry Services Training Program (ISTP); and
- the Postsecondary Education Programs of Excellence in Mathematics, Science, and Computer Education.

To our knowledge, only one evaluation on FEEDS has been conducted previously. A study was in progress early in 1986 that examined the engineering programs. The following research is based on in-house literature as well as newspaper articles, magazines, and personal interviews conducted in Tallahassee in January 1986.

FLORIDA HIGH TECHNOLOGY AND INDUSTRY COUNCIL

Legislative History and Goals

The Florida High Technology and Industry Council (FHTIC) was created in 1983 by the state legislature. The FHTIC was granted more authority than any previous high-technology advisory body because the legislature wanted an agency to coordinate the efforts of academia, government, and industry. The mission of the council is "to promote the development of the State economy by coordinating the efforts of the Department of Education, public and private postsecondary educational institutions, leaders in high technology business and industry, and in cooperation with the Executive Office of the Governor and other executive agencies to meet the needs of high technology business and industry."[21]

Administration and Implementation

The FHTIC consists of the council and an administrative staff. The council is comprised of twenty-three members from government, education, and business. The government representatives include the governor, the commissioner of education, the secretary of commerce (or their designees), as well as one member of the Senate and the House of Representatives. Two members are from academia. The remainder are from business: eleven are leaders in the high-technology industry, four are from the area of investment and banking, and one is the chairman of the Council of 100, a private organization of the top 100 businessmen in Florida. The FHTIC meets about four times annually and the subcommittees with specific concerns meet regularly.

The council's executive director, Ray Iannucci, stated that the role of the FHTIC is basically that of a broker.[22] The FHTIC employs specialists, gives them a work plan, and monitors their work, reserving the right to reject or modify their proposals. To accomplish committee goals, the FHTIC provides access to additional sources of information and some planning capability. From studies and reports generated from this procedure, the FHTIC advises the governor and the legislative and educational communities on policy changes and resource allocations needed to support and attract high-technology industry.[23] The FHTIC also assists government agencies and private organizations in coordinating and establishing training programs, and in assuring that development efforts are compatible with state efforts and resource allocation is consistent with state priorities.[24]

The budget is divided into operating expenses and specific appropriations administered by the council. The operation portion for FY 1985 was $180,000, which included salaries, travel expenses, and printing costs. The legislature has appropriated funds for the implementation of specific programs. The FHTIC received $1.5 million for the Commercialization of Technology Fund (a venture capital fund) "to bring the ideas and talents of Florida's entrepreneurs into the marketplace."[25] It received $1.6 million to create the Planning, Program Development, and Operational Grants program, the purpose of which is to strengthen applied research and encourage industry-university partnerships. The council received $1.3 million to establish Centers of Electronic Emphasis at five vocational-technical centers and five community colleges to produce one of the finest electronic education systems in the nation through industry responsiveness and uniform curricula. Additionally, $3.5 million was appropriated for basic research; however, the state university system administers this program with the FHTIC's input.

Some of these programs were recommended in a series of panel reports conducted by the FHTIC. The FHTIC recruited Florida scientists and businessmen to serve on panels to determine the technological strengths of industry and the universities and to suggest a policy direction. The eight panel reports were presented to a review board created by the FHTIC; the members of the board were nationally known scientists and industry representatives from outside the state. The review board identified the need to (a) strengthen applied research and (b) foster viable relationships between the universities and industry.[26] Three clusters of technology sectors were targeted for investment of state funds: (a) materials science, microelectronics, and lightwave technology; (b) computer software and robotics; and (c) medical biotechnology and biomedical devices and technology.[27]

Assessment of Goal Attainment

The size and the role of the council are the main contributors to its success. Because the staff is small and facilitates coordination, it has a significant impact in the state when working with large numbers of people.[28] The staff has direct contact with business professionals in the state and thus creates a personal relationship. When the staff size is coupled with the "brokerage" role, the FHTIC's contact and influence within the state is somewhat maximized.

By sometimes assembling out-of-state experts to judge potential projects for the state, bias toward a particular university is reduced. Bias can also be avoided through good geographic distribution of team members and utilization of large numbers of businesses. FHTIC has thus built a reputation for fairness among the government, business, and education sectors.

Through its roles of advisor and policy implementor, the council is starting to meet the high-technology industry's needs. The policy coordination around the panel report recommendations is effective because programs are targeted to correspond to existing strengths. However, with more money from the legislature, more projects could be funded that could further Florida's goals for economic development.

Issues and Questions

The main question facing the FHTIC is whether the staff can pursue so many activities without destroying its compatible relationship with industry and education. Will conflicts of interest emerge as the state further develops its high-technology programs? The number of programs the FHTIC oversees is likely to increase as the panel report recommendations are approved and other initiatives are identified by council members; a breakdown of the brokerage role may result from increased numbers of programs, contacts, and exposure in the state. Also, how much coordination does the FHTIC have with previously existing programs? Does the presence of other governmental departments on the FHTIC alleviate a problem of conflicting agendas? The FHTIC does seem to have some influence over how other areas should be developed.

SPECIAL UNIVERSITY FUNDING

Legislative History and Goals

In 1980, a board of regents Task Force on Science, Engineering, and Technology Service to Industry identified three important industry needs as:

• Continuing education — there is a great need for expanded continuing education opportunities, especially graduate courses, for employees in high-technology industries;

• Quality improvement — high-technology industry depends on high quality engineers and scientists. Therefore, there is a need to improve the quality of engineering in related areas (especially engineering technology and computer science); and

• Increased production — there is a strong demand for additional engineers to serve high-technology industry. Therefore there is a need to increase the production of new engineers.[29]

In 1982, a study reviewed the Florida engineering programs and found that "the state engineering schools have overcrowding in the classrooms. Buildings are inadequate . . . additional faculty are difficult to recruit. . . . All of the engineering programs have great needs for additional laboratory equipment."[30] The author of the study, Dr. Joseph Hogan, estimated that $15 million was needed to update equipment, and more than $40 million was needed for new buildings at the four graduate engineering schools — the University of Florida in Gainesville, the University of Central Florida in Orlando, the University of South Florida in Tampa, and Florida Atlantic University in Boca Raton.[31] The establishment of a special university funding was recommended. The Special University Funding was created in 1982. Its goals are twofold: to produce more engineers for industry, and to enhance the quality of the engineering programs.

Administration and Implementation

There are no administrative staff members for the program. The strategy of the board of regents is not to monitor the universities closely. Dr. Henry Hector, director of Planning and Research for the Florida State University system, oversees the program.

The Special University Funding has a budget of $54 million for five years (1982-83 through 1986-87). The four universities receive the main share of the funding, although it was extended to Florida A&M University, Florida State University, and Florida International University.[32]

The funding provides the means to replace obsolete equipment, purchase new equipment, reward and acquire faculty and staff, and initiate new programs. In addition, it delivers the means to develop an off-campus statewide continuing education program for graduate engineers.[33] FEEDS, which is also included in our study, is part of the program.

The universities made requests for the allocations and, in the Hogan Report, recommendations were made for each university. According to Mr. Hector, there is "surprisingly little resentment" among the recipient universities, but other disciplines feel that money is taken away from them.[34]

Assessment of Goal Attainment

This program is highly decentralized; the use of funds by universities is not closely monitored by the state university system. The universities, however, do report to the legislature. Since there are so many education programs, it is hard to isolate the effects of the Special University Funding.

Five buildings were built early in 1986, and the enrollment in engineering programs increased about 30 percent in five years.[35] Whether this increase has reached the goal of more engineers depends on the yardsticks: 30 percent in itself seems quite high, but Florida's population also experienced a strong increase. The 18-24 age group, however, did not increase significantly over this time.[36]

According to Mr. Hector, the universities are satisfied with the improved faculty-to-student ratio, but would like a continuation of the program for equipment purchasing after the 1982-1987 period.[37]

The recipient universities were able to attract more contracts and grants, both federal and state. For example, IBM contributed equipment worth $2.3 million. However, we do not have any information about the size of industry commitments compared to the $54 million in state appropriations.

Issues and Questions

The program's last year is 1987. There are efforts being made to extend the funding, but with a shift in the goals. The emphasis will be not on enlarging the faculty, but on upgrading the equipment. The new funding will not be on the same scale as the previous five-year plan, but the legislature realizes its commitment must continue and that areas still exist that need further assistance. How long these additional funds will continue has not yet been determined. Funding the engineering departments is viewed as an investment in the universities as well as the state. With adequate facilities and equipment, Florida universities are better prepared to compete for federal R&D funds.

FLORIDA ENGINEERING EDUCATION DELIVERY SYSTEM

Legislative History and Goals

FEEDS is an off-campus engineering program modeled after a previous successful state program called GENESYS (the Graduate Engineering Education System). This was an educational TV network with two-way audio capability that permitted a student at one location to ask questions and be answered by a professor at another location during the class session. The system connected many high-technology industrial centers into a statewide network. The program became operational in 1965, and although it was a success in its service to industry, it was shut down in 1971. There were two reasons. One was that enrollment and therefore tuition income dropped drastically with the federal government's cutbacks in space activities. About the same time, Florida opened two new colleges of engineering.[38]

Changing economic and political situations caused the 1980 Task Force on Science, Engineering, and Technology Service to Industry to perceive a renewed demand for additional engineers in high-technology industries. In 1982, the Hogan Report concluded that Florida "must have a supply of engineers to meet the manpower needs now in the state as well as the future needs of those companies that are moving into the state."[39] Industrialists wanted the state to "supply continuing graduate engineering education for engineers already employed in industry, by either delivering courses in the industry's facilities or in nearby communities."[40] Dr. Joseph Hogan, who conducted the study, made recommendations for enhancing the educational system; one of the recommendations was the establishment of an off-campus delivery system.[41]

The goal of FEEDS is to produce more engineers in Florida. To overcome constraints of distance and time, FEEDS can serve engineers that are not within commuting distance of one of the four graduate engineering schools, and it can offer evening courses for engineers with full-time jobs.

Administration and Implementation

FEEDS is coordinated by the Industry Advisory Board, which consists of representatives of eighteen major corporations in Florida and the nine universities in the university system. The board is dominated by industry. It coordinates the courses that are produced by the universities, and provides feedback about how successful FEEDS is perceived to be by industry. There is no special staff for FEEDS. The director of planning and research of the board of regents, Dr. Henry Hector, oversees the program.

FEEDS is part of the Special University Funding budget. In 1984 the budget for FEEDS was $1.4 million. This is a "small price to pay compared to building an engineering school in every place in the state."[42] One reason for the relatively small budget (compared to output) is that courses are not produced specially for FEEDS; rather, they are already taught on campus for regular students. Each of the four graduate schools of engineering is expected to produce fifty courses a year for the system. Principal costs are for tapes and their delivery, for the tutors, and for studio costs. If the classes are held on a business site, the programs are less costly to the state, since the companies have to provide the classrooms and equipment and pay for the tutors.

FEEDS provides a tutored videotape program for engineering students at the master's level. A regular university lecture for a "studio class" is recorded on tape and sent to "FEEDS classes" throughout Florida. For each class of about four to eight students, there is a tutor who supervises the class and leads the discussions. In addition, FEEDS provides live instruction, instructional television fixed service, and a computer-based education.[43]

FEEDS offers degrees in civil engineering, computer and information sciences, electrical engineering, industrial and systems engineering, and mechanical engineering. Additional courses taught include aerospace, chemical and coastal engineering, environmental engineering, nuclear and ocean engineering, and materials science and engineering. Because FEEDS classes in 1985 were offered through the nine universities of the system and in thirty-three different business sites all over Florida, there is "no need yet to do so in community colleges or vocational education centers."[44]

Whether students are admitted as degree or nondegree students, they adhere to the same admission guidelines, take the same tests, and pay the same tuition (about $130 per course). A regular degree can be attained in three years; FEEDS students generally remain in the program for three-and-a-half to four years. The enrollment in 1984 was about 2,500 students, making FEEDS the largest program of its type in the United States.[45] It is expected that enrollment will stabilize at around 3,000 students.

Assessment of Goal Attainment

FEEDS' goal is to produce more engineers. Has this goal been reached? The program served about 2,500 students in 1984. Not all these students, however, are continuing students — some left the regular university programs to participate in the FEEDS program because they preferred its flexibility. Unfortunately, there are no data for how many students fall into this category.

An evaluation of the first year of FEEDS' existence was performed in 1984.[46] Questionnaires were administered to students, faculty, and institutional administrators; about 20 percent were returned. According to this study, students were satisfied with the FEEDS course. They felt that the courses were convenient and relevant to their professional careers. One finding was that most of the industrial-site FEEDS students were non-degree-seeking students, and their course of study was more for personal development.

In this evaluation, the researchers concluded that, based on the average response, FEEDS was "meeting the needs of the engineers desiring further education and meeting the objectives laid down by the State FEEDS Policy

Board."[47] However, the study did not discuss whether industry's needs — a greater number of engineers — were being met.

Quantitative data like performance records that would help determine the success of the program are not available. There is an opinion that "students in the field actually do better than the students on campus."[48] Industry seems to be quite content with the program. There is some support for FEEDS classes on business sites; for example, some employees are allowed free time to go to class. According to Dr. Hector, the program is "so successful that a lot of the industry is willing to work with the university system on a lot of other areas."[49]

Issues and Questions

There is no report on FEEDS' impact yet. According to a study, GENESYS' "impacts on Florida's industry and on the nation's space programs were considerable. A large number of engineers . . . in responsible positions in Florida's high-technology industries earned their master's degrees or took courses for professional development in the GENESYS program."[50]

FEEDS offers new dimensions in ways to deliver education: it combines conventional teaching methods with new technology, and allows greater flexibility for both students and professors. This might change academic approaches to teaching and research. Time saved by videotaping lectures can be used for research and more interactive forms of teaching, like seminars. In this regard, FEEDS is an interesting additional method of teaching.

The small budget for the program creates a minor problem for the advisory board office: the tapes have to be erased after each semester because they are needed for the next one. A larger budget would easily remedy this problem. If the tapes are used more than once, instructors will have to be compensated for additional lectures.

The advisory board is presently trying to expand FEEDS beyond the five existing engineering degrees. The board is considering the addition of business courses to the system.

INDUSTRY SERVICES TRAINING PROGRAM

Legislative History and Goals

The Industry Services Training Program (ISTP) is a supplemental program to the federal Job Training Partnership Act which provides training for Florida citizens for employment in new, expanding, and diversifying industries.[51] Located in the Division of Vocational Education, ISTP is one of Florida's oldest industry-related programs. ISTP was created in 1968 but did not provide services until 1974 due to lack of support and funding. The ISTP now has political support from both state and local leaders. The purpose of the ISTP is to assist relocating and expanding firms in startup with a minimum loss of competitive position in the marketplace.

Administration and Implementation

The ISTP staff consists of three former industry businessmen. The program is assisted by the Industry Services Advisory Board, an interdepartmental council. The board relays business concerns to the ISTP but has no authority over it. The budget has increased considerably since the ISTP's first appropriation of $200,000 in 1978. The state appropriation for FY 1985 is $1.211 million. Additionally, the program receives approximately $30,000 from federal sources.

The ISTP works directly with the Department of Commerce's Division of Economic Development. The Department of Commerce recruits firms to Florida and then directs them to the ISTP. Local agencies, chambers of commerce, and schools also refer firms to the ISTP. The firm selects potential business locations in the state and the ISTP defines the training capabilities at the various locations. The ISTP represents the firm at the local school district, community college, or vocational school to acquire facilities for necessary training. The firm may also choose to use its own facilities. School districts are autonomous and can refuse to assist in the training program. If denied school district facilities, the ISTP has the legal authority to enter into agreements for a training facility with other agencies or institutions — state, local, county, or private. The training program must not duplicate a course at a community college or vocational-technical school in the state.

Requirements for a firm's participation in the training program are few. First and foremost, the training must be for new positions, not for employees to advance within a firm. The firm must be environmentally safe. The size of the firm has no effect on the creation of a program, but the number of jobs to be created is considered. The required learning time of the skill must be less than one year.

There are many benefits provided by the program, and all are at no cost to the company. The ISTP will find and hire the most qualified instructor for the training program — no teacher certification is required. The ISTP appoints a "team of specialists to analyze manufacturing processes, develop job descriptions, and establish time frames" to create the firm's training program.[52] No two training programs are ever alike. All classroom materials and supplies — textbooks, workbooks, paper, audiovisuals, and learning devices — are furnished by the ISTP. The ISTP can recruit potential students and even advertise the training program, if necessary. Travel expenses of trainees can be covered. If required, the ISTP will install special machinery and the purchase of necessary equipment can be negotiated. In 1985, approximately 5,000 people were trained in about thirty-five programs.[53]

The ISTP relies on other sources helpful in the implementation of a program. In recruiting trainees for a program, the ISTP uses its unique placement service, the Cooperative Agency Placement System (CAPS). CAPS provides a computer printout of the "names and specialties of vocational

58

students who have completed their training programs and are willing to relocate within the state."[54] Retired military personnel are an additional source of technical expertise. Local employment service offices and the Department of Labor's Division of Employment Security are also used to supply potential trainees. The ISTP monitors the trainees' performance and adjustment during the course of training. The ISTP encourages the firms hiring trainees to allow these employees to further their training through vocational-technical courses.

Assessment of Goal Attainment

The ISTP believes its success is dependent on flexibility. The ISTP is grateful to the government officials who have allowed it to pursue its goals with little interference. The director of vocational education who oversees the ISTP, Joe Mills, spoke highly of the program.[55] He believed that the ISTP was meeting the needs of industry and that its success was based on targeting industry's needs.[56]

Success can also be attributed to a relationship of trust between the ISTP and local agencies, schools, and firms; the ISTP is not threatening to their activities. The local agencies are made to feel as if they are a part of the programs. Credit for success of a program goes to the school involved, while the ISTP takes the blame for failures. According to a Kentucky Department of Education national survey on industry training programs, Florida's ISTP had a job placement rate of 90 percent in 1981.[57]

The ISTP could probably do even more programs if it were widely known throughout the state. The staff does not contact existing industries to determine if vocational education can be of assistance. The ISTP relies almost entirely on referrals, though it does publish some literature. According to this literature, the ISTP is geared toward high-technology industries; in fact, all industries participate: "Approximately 15 percent of the programs are for high technology industries."[58] However, most programs use some form of state-of-the-art training. Final reports of completed programs are not available to the public due to disclosure rights of the firms involved in the programs. The ISTP does no evaluations, but is in the process of accumulating data from past programs.

Issues and Questions

With additional funds, the ISTP could undertake more training programs. But it is not clear that more training programs are needed. Mr. Jesse Burt, director of the ISTP, states that the number of potential workers in the state is declining due to the rising employment rate.

In the future, the ISTP may concentrate on developing training programs for a more local clientele. New firms will continue to move into the state, but according to Mr. Burt, the act of recruitment has somewhat lessened.[59] Thus, the ISTP's future clients will probably come from within the state. The ISTP is preparing for this transition by forming good business relations with firms and agencies already existing in the state.

POSTSECONDARY PROGRAMS OF EXCELLENCE
IN MATHEMATICS, SCIENCE, AND COMPUTER EDUCATION

Legislative History and Goals

The Postsecondary Programs of Excellence are designed to improve mathematics, science, and computer science curricula. The programs attempt to bridge the gap between education and high technology by preparing students for a constantly changing technological society. Also, these programs support Florida's upper-quartile goal for student learning. The legislature first appropriated funds in 1983 for postsecondary institutions, universities, and community colleges to create programs for the 1983-1984 school year. Due to the support of the participating institutions and program beneficiaries, the legislature has continued funding through 1986.

Administration and Implementation

The Postsecondary Programs of Excellence are administered by the Postsecondary Education Policy Unit — Planning, Budgeting, and Evaluation. The director, Jack Tebo, forms a committee to review applications for the current-year funds. The funding for FY 1985 was $1.92 million — the same level of legislative appropriation since the creation of the programs. The selection committee includes one legislator, representatives from the community college and university systems and the governor's office, and the director. Each of the state universities and community colleges apply for state funding to create its own program. The selection committee grades the applications by criteria derived from Florida's stated goals in education.

To be eligible for funding, proposals must be consistent with state goals to promote student achievement and excellence in education.[60] The proposals must relate to at least one of the seven program types discussed below and they must be feasible. They must have an impact in the state "by producing products or processes with a potential for use by other postsecondary education institutions."[61] State funds received must be matched by the applying institution on a one-to-one basis with available funds or in-kind services. The project should involve joint efforts of at least two departments at the institution. The proposal must require no more than $110,000 in state funds. Joint proposals may be funded between two or more cooperating institutions. Each institution is limited to one full grant plus any portion of one joint grant.[62]

The application must contain a summary of the proposal narrative, a completed application form for the project grant, a copy of the proposed budget, and a proposal narrative. The proposal narrative must describe the program type and how it meets the state's goals and commitment to academic excellence. The program types include:

- cooperative programs involving postsecondary institutions and private industry;

60

- cooperative programs involving public school districts;
- training programs for teachers;
- instructional research grants for faculty;
- updating of faculty training;
- joint appointments of personnel to industry, universities, and community colleges; and
- feasibility planning grants to establish or expand centers for academically talented students in mathematics, science and computer education.[63]

All applications received before the deadline that meet the guidelines are at least partially funded. Outstanding proposals that meet all guidelines receive full funding. If proposals do not meet all the guidelines, only the portion of the application that does is considered for funding. Merely adequate programs that meet the guidelines receive some funding. Once the outstanding proposals are funded, the balance is prorated among the remaining approved programs.

Individual programs vary because applying institutions design their own programs and are at liberty to choose the target population. A majority of the programs, however, benefit high school students and teachers. In 1985, two programs were fully funded. The first was a joint program with Florida State University and Florida A&M University entitled the Model Microcomputer Trainer Program. Selected teacher participants were trained in microcomputer education so that they might in turn train other teachers and students in the educational setting. The project has the potential to affect computer education in the entire state. The thirty participants benefit directly; over 2,000 professionals and 100,000 students benefit indirectly.

The other fully funded program was at Florida Keys Community College. The first phase of the project is the continuation of a previous grant to promote computer literacy in faculty, students, and the community at large. The second phase is the continued updating of high-technology awareness of kindergarten through secondary-level teachers. The final phase, the Neptune program, consists of research at sea, an underwater classroom habitat, and courses in marine environmental studies.

Assessment of Goal Attainment

Flexibility is a strong characteristic of the Postsecondary Programs of Excellence. The state provides the guidelines, and the universities and community colleges proceed from there. Mr. Tebo believes that the state benefits every time a person learns to cope with technology.[64] The institutions benefit by becoming visible educational resources for the community. Legislators have continued the funding through 1986, which suggests that there is support in the home districts for this program.

The main problem with the programs is a lack of communication among institutions. There is little exchange of ideas and programs. Mr. Tebo provides the names of contact personnel from all institutions, but the initiative belongs to them. The Postsecondary Education Policy Unit does not keep evaluations or accumulate statistics on the programs — each project director is required to maintain that information.

The programs fit nicely into Florida's commitment to excellence. They can benefit students of all ages as well as faculty and administrators. The fact that all qualified applications are funded precludes the exclusion of smaller institutions. Outstanding programs challenge institutions to create even more exceptional programs the following year. As always, results are difficult to quantify, but the programs do contribute to math, science, and computer education curricula.

Issues and Questions

The issue of funding the programs should be considered. Since all proposals are not fully funded, would an increase in available funds enhance the program substantially? If so, how much should the increase be? How much more will the schools, faculty and students benefit from this increase? These questions cannot be answered fully; however, benefits are likely to emerge in the future. Programs are likely to continue to be funded since they are relatively inexpensive for the benefits received.

Conclusions

The five programs assessed here demonstrate Florida's concern with education at all levels. They also reflect the developing relationships between education and industry and show a consensus that a good education system is necessary for economic development. Each level of education depends on the quality of the preceding level. Since industry, especially high-technology industry, relies on an adequate supply of qualified engineers and a trained labor force, the relationship of education to economic development is obvious. Also, a primary consideration of relocating high-technology companies is the availability of skilled workers.

The programs reviewed here complement each other in their efforts to improve education on all levels and contribute to meeting Florida's upper-quartile goal for academic excellence. However, their effects have not yet been determined. The interdependence of variables makes measurement difficult. Program outputs are better-educated and -adjusted students, computer-knowledgeable teachers, and a work force trained for designated industries. Indirect benefits include university research that contributes to improved products and the exchange of information between industry and education. Industry benefits from both indirect and direct outputs. Efforts to improve the educational system can only be felt over a long term and therefore should to a certain degree be free from economic constraints.

Flexibility allows the programs to adapt fairly easily to changes in policy as new objectives are created. The FHTIC responds to the needs of government, education, and industry, while the members of the educational program boards are receptive to the needs of students, teachers, and business. In the past, state government has not been a dominant influence on business; however, Governor Graham's administration has been more responsive to industry and has encouraged Florida's business climate. The government has observed that a steady increase in the work force due to population growth is important for this climate; however, the poorly regarded educational system in Florida has discouraged companies from locating in Florida.

The evaluated programs raise some issues that the state has begun to address. These new challenges center on the transfer of information between industry and academia — the granting of state funds for basic and applied research, the creation of research parks and incubator facilities, and the formation of regional coalitions among education, industry, and government. Another issue is whether adequate state funds are being allocated to the necessary programs.

These questions are difficult to answer because the relationship between educational programs and industrial output is hard to assess. Florida's indicators of excellence are an attempt to define this relationship.

The effectiveness of the emphasis on education has yet to be determined, but it seems that the need for this emphasis was real. Good general business incentives already existed in the state. Education was a weak link in attracting the development of new business in the state. Since the fruits of an improved educational system cannot be reaped overnight, Florida also engages in other high-technology programs, such as state venture capital funding and increased funding for basic and applied research. While educational programs have dominated this evaluation, Florida is pursuing other avenues of high-technology to provide a balanced program for economic development.

NOTES

1. U.S. Department of Commerce, Bureau of the Census, *State Population Estimates, by Age and Components of Change: 1980 and 1984,* table B, 3.
2. Ibid., 7.
3. Florida Department of Commerce, Bureau of Economic Analysis, Division of Economic Development, *Florida and the Other Forty-nine,* 6th ed., (Tallahassee, September 1985), table 3, 8.
4. U.S. Department of Commerce, Bureau of the Census, *1980 Census of Population,* ch. B, *General Population Characteristics,* part 11, *Florida,* 51.
5. Ibid., 7.
6. "Florida: Pacesetter for a Nation," *Advertising Age* (January 9, 1984): M-9.
7. David Avery and Frank B. King, "Florida: Sunny with No Clouds, " *Economic Review* 70, (February 1984): 12.

8. Florida Department of Commerce, Division of Economic Development, *Florida: Industrial Trends in 1984,* Tallahassee, January 1985, 21. This was a report on the government and legislature.
9. Avery and King, "Florida," 73.
10. "Call to Arm," *Miami Herald,* September 16, 1985.
11. Florida Department of Commerce, Division of Economic Development, *Build Your Future Where the Future Is: Florida.,* Brochure.
12. Department of Commerce, *Florida and the Other Forty-nine,* table 12, 26.
13. Ibid., table 31, 68.
14. Florida Department of Commerce, Bureau of Economic Analysis, "The Florida Entrepreneurial Network," Tallahassee, January 1984, 1. Mimeograph.
15. Florida High Technology and Industry Council, *High Technology and Economic Development: A Technology Innovation and Commercialization Policy Statement,* Tallahassee, 1985, 23.
16. U.S. Joint Economic Committee, *Location of High Technology Firms and Regional Economic Development,* Washington, D.C., 1982, 23-25.
17. Florida State University System, *Quest for Excellence: The Master Plan of the State University System of Florida,* Tallahassee, 1983, 3.
18. Ibid., as cited by Governor Graham, 10.
19. Florida *Statutes,* sec. 229.8053.
20. "Centers of Excellence Spur Educational Collaboration," *Ed Tech News* 4, 6 (January-February 1985): 2.
21. Florida *Statutes,* sec. 230.66.
22. Interview with Ray Iannucci, Florida High Technology and Industry Council, Tallahassee, January 15, 1986.
23. Florida High Technology and Industry Council, "Background," Tallahassee, 1985, 1. Mimeograph.
24. Ibid.
25. Ibid., 3.
26. Florida High Technology and Industry Council, "Results of the Planning, Program Development, and Operations Grant Program," Tallahassee, 1985. 1. Mimeograph.
27. Florida High Technology and Industry Council, "Background," 3.
28. Interview with Iannucci.
29. Joseph Hogan, *Engineering Excellence for the Decade Ahead* (May 1982), 30.
30. Ibid., 16.
31. Ibid., 50.
32. Interview with Dr. Henry Hector, Planning and Research, the Florida State University System, Tallahassee, January 16, 1986.
33. Florida State University System, *Quest for Excellence,* 12.
34. Interview with Hector.
35. Ibid.
36. Florida State University System, *Quest for Excellence,* 4.
37. Interview with Hector.
38. Hogan, *Engineering Excellence,* 3.
39. Ibid., 22.
40. Ibid., 31.
41. Ibid., 44. FEEDS was created in 1983.

64

42. Interview with Hector.
43. "Florida Engineering Education Delivery System," n.d. Pamphlet.
44. Interview with Hector.
45. Ibid.
46. Charles Hutinger, "FEEDS: Evaluation Summary for the Academic Year: 1983-84," May 1984. Mimeograph.
47. Ibid., 9.
48. Interview with Hector.
49. Ibid.
50. "The Florida Engineering Education Delivery System: Serving the Needs of Industries," September 1982, 3.
51. Florida *Statutes*, sec. 230.66.
52. Florida Department of Education, Industry Services Training Program, "The Gem of the Southeast Has Some Brilliant New Facets," Tallahassee, 1982. Pamphlet.
53. Interview with Jesse Burt, Industry Services Training Program, Tallahassee, January 13, 1986.
54. Department of Education, "The Gem of the Southeast," 7.
55. Interview with Joe Mills, Florida Department of Vocational Education, Tallahassee, January 14, 1986.
56. Ibid.
57. John F. Loyd, *New/Expanding Industry Training Program Survey* (Frankfort, Kentucky) "Memorandum to Presidents, State Universities and Community Colleges," Programs of Excellence in Mathematics, Science, and Computer Education, Tallahassee, June 26, 1985, 1.
58. Interview with Burt.
59. Ibid.
60. Ralph Turlington, "Memorandum to Presidents, State Universities and Community Colleges," Programs of Excellence in Mathematics, Science, and Computer Education, (Tallahassee, June 26, 1985), 1.
61. Ibid., 1.
62. Ibid., 2.
63. Postsecondary Education Policy Unit, 1985-86 Application Instructions, 1-2. Mimeograph.
64. Interview with Jack Tebo, Postsecondary Programs of Excellence, Tallahassee, January 15, 1986.

Massachusetts has virtually no valuable natural resources. The economy of the state has historically depended upon the cultivation of skill, imagination, and resourcefulness in its citizenry. Over the past two centuries, Massachusetts has been responsible for innovations in science, industrial organization, art, medicine, education, and the law. Throughout American industrial history, Massachusetts has been involved in the technologies of change—the American steam engine; the electrical transformer; the analog and digital computers; instant photography; and since the 1970s, research in robotics and biotechnology. Concentrated educational facilities and an educated and curious populous have created an environment for innovation, sparking such phenomena as the high concentration of technology-based industries on Route 128. Industries riding the wave of new technologies have largely defined Massachusetts' entire economic history, from the early manufacturing technologies of cotton and firearms production to the technically advanced manufacturing of CAD/CAM machinery.

Massachusetts' industrial base before the 1970s consisted largely of traditional industries such as shoes, textiles, and tool manufacturing. These industries have been hit the hardest by foreign competition and innovation. Between 1969 and 1976 the state lost 730,000 jobs, recording in 1975 the highest unemployment rate in any industrialized state.[1]

Several years later, however, the state experienced an amazing comeback. It went from having the highest unemployment rate in the 1975 recession to having the lowest unemployment rate during the 1982 recession.[2] Massachusetts' long-term investment in education had paid off; Massachusetts was able to take advantage of the transition of the nation's businesses from traditional industries to more technology-based ones. In 1984 the state reported the largest annual increase in employment since pre-World War I with the creation of 159,000 new jobs. Massachusetts now ranks first among all states in high-technology employment growth, and it is determined to keep its lead.[3]

Demographic and Economic Profile

POPULATION CHARACTERISTICS

Massachusetts has a population of over 5.7 million people who are largely concentrated on the eastern shore (Table 4-1). The proportion of urban residents to rural residents is heavily one-sided — over 83 percent of the state's population lives in urban areas. However, recent trends indicate that the western, rural part of the state is growing and there is a slow decline in the urban centers (Table 4-2). Ninety-three percent of the population is white, 4 percent is black, and 3 percent is composed of other minorities (Table 4-3).

— This chapter was written by Kathleen A. Merrigan and Suzanne E. Smith.

TABLE 4-1

Population of Massachusetts and Percentage
Change Compared to the United States, 1970, 1980, and 1984
(in 1,000s and %)

	Massachusetts	Change	U.S. Change
1970	5,689	—	—
1980	5,737	.8	11.4
1984	—	—	4.1

Source: U.S. Dept. of Commerce, Bureau of the Census, *1980 Census of Population*, vol. 1, part 23, p. 7; idem, *1979 Census of Population*, vol. 1, part 23, p. 7.

From 1970 to 1980, changes in Massachusetts' population characteristics were minimal; the state experienced only a .8 percent increase in total population (Table 4-1). Much of this growth occurred among blacks and other minorities. A .1 percent decrease in the white population totals was reported.

Compared to the national average of educational attainment, the population of Massachusetts is highly educated (Table 4-4). Over 72 percent of the people 25 years or older in the state had completed high school in 1980—six percent more than the national average. The share of persons having five years or fewer of education was also lower in the state than in the nation. From 1970 to 1980 the number of persons completing high school increased over 107 percent; of those completing college, over 63 percent. In a society where a well-educated work force creates a comparative advantage in the competition for industrial locations and developments, Massachusetts is well ahead of the nation.

As is true for most of the nation, the age distribution of the state shows a young average age (Table 4-5). In 1980, although the state has a slightly higher share of older people than the nation, over 60 percent of the total population was under the age of 44; over 37 percent of the population in 1980 was between 20 and 44 years old. This age distribution leaves Massachusetts with a large sector of working-age people.

TABLE 4-2

Urban and Rural Composition
of Massachusetts Compared to the United States, 1970 and 1980
(%)

	1970		1980	
	Massachusetts	United States	Massachusetts	United States
Urban	84.6	73.6	83.8	73.7
Rural	15.4	26.4	16.2	26.3

Source: U.S. Dept. of Commerce, Bureau of the Census, *1980 Census of Population*, vol. 1, ch. B, part 23, p. 7; *1970 Census of Population*, vol. 1, ch. B, part 23, p. 7.

TABLE 4-3
Racial Distribution in Massachusetts
Compared to the United States, 1970 and 1980
(%)

	1970 Massachusetts	1970 United States	1980 Massachusetts	1980 United States
White	96.2	87.5	93.7	83.1
Black	3.1	11.1	3.9	11.7
Other	0.6	1.4	3.4	5.1

Source: U.S. Dept. of Commerce, *1980 Census of Population*, vol. 1, ch. B, part 23, p. 39; idem, *1970 Census of Population*, vol. 1, ch. B, part 23, p. 49.

TABLE 4-4
Educational Levels in Massachusetts
Compared to the United States, 1980
(%)

	Massachusetts	United States
Elementary school (less than 5 years)	2.8	3.6
High school	72.2	66.5
College (4 or more years)	20.0	16.2
Median years of school completed	12.5	12.5

Source: U.S. Department of Commerce, Bureau of the Census, *1980 Census of Population*, vol. 1, ch. B, part 23, p. 71.

TABLE 4-5
Age Distribution in Massachusetts
Compared to the United States, 1970 and 1980
(%)

Age Group	1970 Massachusetts	1970 United States	1980 Massachusetts	1980 United States
0-19	36.6	37.8	30.2	32.0
20-44	30.9	31.7	36.9	37.2
45-64	21.3	20.6	20.4	19.7
65+	11.2	9.8	12.7	11.3

Source: U.S. Dept. of Commerce, Bureau of the Census, *1980 Census of Population*, vol. 1, ch. B, part 23, p. 7; idem, *1970 Census of Population*, vol. 1, ch. B, part 23, p. 52.

ECONOMIC PROFILE

According to the 1985 economic analysis prepared for the Massachusetts Senate Ways and Means Committee, the Massachusetts economy is currently one of the most robust in the nation.[4] Statistics collected from reports of the U.S. Department of Commerce and the Bureau of Labor support this conclusion.

In all areas of employment except the government sector, Massachusetts experienced growth between 1977 and 1984 (Table 4-6). The greatest sectoral shares of employment are claimed by wholesale and retail sales, service industries, and manufacturing categories, which together make up 73 percent of Massachusetts' total nonagricultural employment. Of these three sectors, the service industry expanded the most, increasing its employment share by 30 percent between 1977 and 1984, overtaking manufacturing as the largest employment sector. The other two major employment sectors displayed less growth. Total nonagricultural employment for the seven-year period increased by approximately 450,000 jobs.

TABLE 4-6

Nonagricultural Employment and Share in Massachusetts by Sector, 1977, 1982, and 1984 and Percentage Change between 1977 and 1984

(employees in 1,000s, share in %, change in %)

| | 1977 | | 1982 | | 1984 | | 1977-1984 |
	Emp.	Share	Emp.	Share	Emp.	Share	Change
Mining	1.0	0.04	1.1	0.04	1.1	0.04	10.0
Construction	72.7	3.0	78.4	2.9	96.0	3.3	32.0
Manufacturing	611.5	25.5	640.1	24.3	675.9	23.6	10.5
Transportation	112.8	4.7	120.0	4.5	122.9	4.3	8.9
Wholesale & retail	542.6	22.6	577.0	21.8	657.9	23.0	21.2
Finance & insurance	135.5	5.7	168.7	6.4	177.4	6.2	30.9
Government	374.3	15.6	370.7	14.1	369.7	12.9	-1.2
Services	545.1	22.8	682.0	25.8	750.7	26.3	37.7
Total	2,395.5	100.0	2,638.0	100.0	2,857.7	100.0	19.3

Source: U. S. Department of Labor, Bureau of Labor Statistics, Annual Averages, Employment and Earnings, vol. 32, 5 May 1985, pp. 124-126; idem, vol. 24, July 1977.

Within the manufacturing sector, national comparisons reveal that while Massachusetts was on the road to recovery by 1977, it was still behind the national growth rate of 7 percent. By 1984, however, almost 55,000 more jobs had been created and Massachusetts experienced a higher than national growth rate in manufacturing.

Of categories within the manufacturing sector, nonelectrical machinery remained the largest employer, increasing its number of jobs by almost 22,000 jobs between 1972 and 1982 (Table 4-7). Electrical equipment also showed substantial growth during the same time, adding approximately 17,000 new jobs to Massachusetts' employment total. Many job losses occurred, however, in the more traditional industries. The textile and leather industries showed the greatest decline, together losing nearly 19,000 jobs. In spite of these losses the job totals reflect that Massachusetts, after 1977, was creating more jobs in manufacturing than it was losing.

HIGH-TECHNOLOGY SECTOR

The 1985 Massachusetts Senate Ways and Means Committee report states that 60 percent of the new employment created over the past nine years lies in the high-technology and service industries.[5] High-technology industries, according to the U.S. Bureau of Labor Statistics, increased in their total share of employment to almost one-fourth of all manufacturing industries, and their growth rate was nearly ten times that of manufacturing as a whole. The Census of Manufactures documents that, within the high-technology industries, the greatest growth areas were in drugs, industrial organic chemicals, and electronic components (Table 4-8).

However, the data from the census describing another large growth area—the office machine industry—are incomplete. Employment growth in this category from 1977 to 1984 was almost 150 percent. This category contains the computer industry, and more specifically the minicomputer industry, which was begun in Massachusetts in the 1950s at MIT. The minicomputer makes up almost the entire computer industry in the state. Of total U.S. production, 60 percent is produced in the state.[6] Massachusetts is home to major computer companies such as Wang Laboratories, Digital Equipment, Data General, and Prime Computer.

TABLE 4-7

Manufacturing Employment and Share in Massachusetts by Industry,
1972, 1977, and 1982, and Percentage Change between 1972 and 1982
(employees in 1,000s, share in %, and change in %)

	1972 Emp.	1972 Share	1977 Emp.	1977 Share	1982 Emp.	1982 Share	1972-1982 Change
Nondurable							
Food/kindred	32.6	5.6	26.8	4.7	26.0	4.4	-20.3
Textile	29.1	5.0	26.3	4.6	20.9	3.5	-28.2
Apparel	43.3	7.9	42.4	7.5	38.3	6.5	-11.5
Paper products	28.2	4.8	29.8	5.2	26.2	4.4	- 7.1
Printing/ publishing	42.6	7.3	41.8	7.3	48.0	8.1	12.7
Chemicals	16.4	2.8	15.8	2.8	15.1	2.5	- 7.9
Petroleum refining	—	—	1.3	0.2	1.2	0.2	—
Rubber & plastic	31.6	5.4	30.4	5.4	31.4	5.3	- 0.6
Leather	28.4	4.6	22.1	3.9	17.1	2.9	-39.8
Total nondurable	255.3	43.7	263.7	41.7	224.2	37.9	-12.2
Durable							
Lumber & wood	6.0	1.0	6.0	1.1	—	—	—
Furniture & fixtures	9.2	1.6	7.6	1.3	7.0	1.2	-23.9
Stone, clay, glass	12.4	2.1	—	—	11.7	2.0	- 5.6
Primary metal	14.0	2.4	14.0	2.5	13.7	2.3	- 2.2
Fabricated metal	46.1	7.9	47.4	8.3	50.7	8.5	10.0
Nonelectric machinery	74.3	12.7	81.2	14.3	96.2	16.2	29.5
Electrical equipment	78.8	13.5	77.9	13.7	95.7	16.2	21.4
Transportation equipment	23.1	3.9	22.2	3.9	20.2	3.4	-12.5
Instruments	37.0	6.3	47.5	8.3	49.4	8.3	33.5
Miscellaneous	27.9	4.8	27.2	4.8	22.2	3.8	-20.4
Total durable	328.8	56.3	331.0	58.3	366.8	62.1	11.6
Total mfg.	548.1	100.0	567.7	100.0	591.0	100.0	1.2

Source: U.S. Department of Commerce, Bureau of the Census, *1982 Census of Manufactures, Geographic Area Series, Massachusetts*, pp. 10-16; idem, *1972 Census of Manufactures, Geographic Area Statistics*, pp. 22.11-22.19.

TABLE 4-8

High-Technology Manufacturing Employment in Massachusetts
and Percentage Change, 1972, 1977, and 1982
(employees in 1,000s, change in %)

	1972	Change	1977	Change	1982
Drugs	0.8	75.0	1.4	21.0	1.7
Industrial organic chemicals	0.6	150.0	1.5	6.6	1.6
Office/computing machines	18.2	—	—	—	36.6
Communication equipment	28.7	7.6	30.9	17.4	36.3
Electronic components	17.8	21.9	21.7	45.6	31.6
Aircraft & parts	—	—	—	—	—
Missiles/space vehicles	—	—	—	—	—
Instruments	37.0	28.3	47.5	4.0	49.4
Total high-tech employment	103.1	21.0	102.7	17.4	157.2
All manufacturing	618.9	- 0.008	613.4	3.1	640.1
Percentage of high-tech	16.7		16.7		24.5

Note: Statistics for some industry groups are withheld to avoid disclosing figures for individual companies.
Source: U.S. Department of Commerce, Bureau of the Census, *Census of Manufactures, Geographic Area Series, Massachusetts,* pp. 10-16; idem, *1977 Census of Manufactures, Geographic Area Statistics,* pp. 22.11-22.19.

RESEARCH AND DEVELOPMENT FUNDING

From World War II to the present, Massachusetts has been a steady receiver of maximum federal research funds. Military spending was critical to the emergence of the electronics sector. It subsidized research efforts that advanced electronic technologies such as transistors and integrated circuits, fostered the establishment of electronic firms, and supported a scientific community in Massachusetts.

Massachusetts began to lose some of its share of military dollars in the late 1960s.[7] However, in 1983 Massachusetts continued to rank at the top in receiving federal R&D funds (Table 4-9). Massachusetts received over $2.3 billion in FY 1983, ranking fourth in the nation. The biggest investment came from the Department of Defense (DOD) (Table 4-10), which contributed over three times the amount of any other federal agency and granted Massachusetts a larger allotment than any state in 1983.[8] With such a high percentage from DOD, Massachusetts officials worry that the federal effort to reduce the deficit will severely reduce research funding levels.

TABLE 4-9

Federal Obligations for R&D by Performer in Massachusetts
and Share Compared to the United States, 1983
($ million and %)

Performer	Funds	Massachusetts	United States
Federal facilities	147.3	6.4	27.1
Industry	1208.6	52.2	49.1
Universities	501.2	21.6	18.8
State & local government	6.8	0.3	4.5
Other	450.3	19.5	0.5
Total	2314.3	100.0	100.0

Source: National Science Foundation, *Federal Funds for Research and Development*, vol. 33, 1984, p. 142.

TABLE 4-10

Share of Federal Obligations for R&D in Massachusetts
by Agency Source Compared to the United States, 1983

Agency	Massachusetts	United States
Agriculture	0.8	2.2
Commerce	0.5	0.9
Defense	71.4	61.0
Energy	4.3	12.0
Health & Human Services	14.5	11.5
Interior	0.2	0.9
Transportation	1.5	0.5
EPA	0.6	0.3
NASA	2.4	7.0
NSF	3.8	2.8

Source: National Science Foundation, *Federal Funds for Research and Development*, vol. 33,1984, p. 150.

Most of the federal obligations were granted to Massachusetts' private industries or for research at Massachusetts' universities and colleges. In both of these categories, Massachusetts received a funding amount higher than the national average, the larger share going to industry (Table 4-9). Massachusetts ranked behind only California and New York in receiving government funds, and additionally behind Pennsylvania in receiving industry-sponsored research funds.

Industry funding was nearly three times the amount as that granted to the universities, yet over three-fourths of research occurring at the universities receives funding from the federal government. The largest share of this research is in the life sciences, in areas such as biotechnology. In comparison with the other states, however, Massachusetts leads in the field of engineering, with over $99 million committed to this science.[9]

Science and Technology Policy

HISTORICAL ACCOUNT

Massachusetts' economy was once dominated by traditional mill industries, led by textiles and then shoes. By 1975 the employment numbers for these industries had been cut in half, reflecting the decline in traditional industries between 1950 and 1975.[10] From 1950 to 1975 the traditional industries were declining. Four high-technology-related industries — nonelectrical machinery, instruments, electrical equipment, and transportation equipment — were growing enough to take up some slack but not enough to keep the employment totals from declining.[11] These industries were supported, as noted earlier, by military contracts. During the early 1970s, military spending decreased, and many of the electronics firms were forced to cut back. However, a growing nonmilitary market for electronics-based goods had emerged. The infrastructure was in place and Massachusetts was able to move quickly from communications equipment for military use to computers and electronic components for commercial markets.

The success of the science and technology sector in Massachusetts is also due in large measure to a rich history of partnerships between public and private institutions of higher learning, industry, and government. Route 128, "America's Technology Highway," is a roadway encircling the city of Boston on which most of the state's science and technology firms are located. This area was developed soon after the end of World War II. Scientists and engineers came to the state from all parts of the world to work on weapons technology and eventually chose to settle in Massachusetts. Some were offered teaching posts at the various colleges and universities, including the Massachusetts Institute of Technology (MIT). Others joined together and established businesses along Route 128 that were primarily supported by military research and development contracts. By the mid-1960s, MIT labs alone had spawned approximately 100 new technology companies, and almost 70 percent of the high-technology sales in the state were made to the government.[12] Military contracts have continued to be of great importance to the state; a combination of strong academic research, entrepreneurial skill, and the fact that the first three science advisors to the president were affiliated either with MIT or Harvard accounts for the generous portion of federal R&D dollars flowing into the state.[13]

Massachusetts is home to 120 institutions of higher education. Most technology firms cite the quality of the state's work force as their primary reason for locating in Massachusetts.[14] There are over 15,000 graduate faculty members in the greater Boston area alone, and many private university-industry research partnerships have developed, such as those between Exxon and MIT and between Dupont and Harvard. The presence of the universities is also responsible for the creation of fine teaching hospitals like Massachusetts General and a sizable medical research community.

The state government has both helped and hindered science and technology development. In the mid-1970s Massachusetts faced a budget deficit of $450 million, an inflation rate of 9.1 percent, and an unemployment rate of 11.2 percent. Governor Michael Dukakis, having won his election on a platform of "no new taxes," was forced to make severe and politically unpopular budget cuts and to impose a surtax on personal income. Occurring at a time when the state was losing ground in its industrial base, this was an extremely unpopular action. Dukakis was defeated in the next gubernatorial race by a pro-business candidate, Edward King. Growing resentment over the high tax rates also lead to a citizen's tax revolt and the passage of referendum Proposition 2 1/2, a property-tax-cutting mechanism. People were determined to lower their tax rates and shed the "Taxachusetts" label affixed to their state.

During Governor King's administration, the state began searching for ways to better its business climate. Several tax provisions specifically designed to promote science and technology were enacted in the late 1970s. While King did improve the business climate, he was defeated in his reelection bid due to some questionable political actions. Dukakis, elected to his second term of office in 1982, worked to trim state spending. By 1985 the state had a revenue surplus of over $200 million, with the total state budget totaling over $8.6 million.

Although Massachusetts pays far more than the national average for debt service and has a $11-billion unfunded pension liability, the state generally is on very sound financial footing and is seeking to invest its surplus dollars in the state's future economic growth.

POLICYMAKING BODIES

In his second term of office, Governor Dukakis has made economic development his highest priority and the Centers of Excellence program, discussed later in this chapter, his administration's centerpiece. He has developed very close ties to several science and technology industry leaders. Dukakis, an often-mentioned candidate for the presidency, is concerned about his legacy and wants to establish a reputation as an innovator. During the 1984 Democratic National Convention, he chaired a committee on national science and technology development.

The Executive Office of Economic Affairs (EOEA), authorized and funded by the state legislature, is responsible for carrying out the major economic policy objectives of the commonwealth. Its projects are wide-ranging, from partnerships with technology firms to tourist booths along the state's highways. EOEA budget totaled $24 million in FY 1985; the lion's share of this money supported programs for science and technology development. Programs under the EOEA umbrella include the Massachusetts Centers of Excellence Corporation, the Massachusetts Manpower Development Department, the Massachusetts Technology Development Corporation, the Small Business Development Centers, the Foreign Business Council, and the Bay State Skills Corporation.

In 1983, Governor Dukakis established the Governor's Office of Economic Development. Several staff members in this office are responsible for projects related to science and technology. Its agenda may be more closely tied to the governor's own political agenda than that developed at EOEA. How this office differs in function from EOEA is not clear and several territorial battles have occurred. The state legislature has threatened every year to remove the office from the state budget.

Unquestionably the most important decisionmaker in science and technology policy is private industry.[15] In Massachusetts, the numerous partnerships among government, industry, and academia have served to link strongly industry leaders and public decisionmakers. The Massachusetts High Tech Council, an organization of 160 businesses, began in 1979 when business leaders entered into a social contract with the state: the council would create 60,000 new jobs if the state brought the tax burden more in line with other industrial states. This joint venture was so successful that decisions affecting the state's economy are now made following consultation with the council. Massachusetts state officials also listen to the Massachusetts Business Round Table which, while representing a broader business community, often teams up with the High Tech Council in lobbying efforts at the State House. A new high-technology business council, the Software Council, was established in 1985. This new organization is perceived as a splinter group from the High Tech Council, one which more readily supports government-business ventures.

STRATEGIES

Massachusetts has pursued several strategies to encourage the development of the state's science and technology sector. First, the state recognizes the importance of a sound education system and has invested heavily in public education. There are 120 public and private institutions of higher education in the state. In Boston alone, there are over 15,000 graduate faculty. These institutions provide the highly skilled professional work force which many firms cite as their primary reason for locating in the state. University research staffs, faculty, and graduates are a main source of entrepreneurs who start up the new firms that have played such an important role in the state's economy. The abundance of universities in the Boston area contributes to the cultural and professional climate that helps induce the professionals and entrepreneurs that local universities turn out to remain in the region.

Second, Massachusetts is one of the leading export states in the country.

The number of foreign firms doing business in the state increased from just over 50 in 1971 to over 250 in 1985. The state has developed numerous programs to help Massachusetts businesses market their products overseas. Governor Dukakis has also met several times in Japan and Massachusetts with business leaders in efforts to locate Japanese technology enterprises in Massachusetts. For example, the Biotechnology Center of Excellence is expected to house several Japanese firms.

Third, the state has invested in training and retraining its work force. The very low unemployment in 1986 may be partly attributed to the state's efforts at retraining dislocated workers and homemakers, training workers for high-demand occupations, and training public-assistance recipients for job placement.

Fourth, Massachusetts has established a variety of development finance programs to assist new expanding industries in securing necessary capital for growth. The state also encouraged privately owned and operated financial assistance programs. From long-term, fixed-rate lending at the Massachusetts Industrial Finance Authority (MIFA) to high-risk financing at the Massachusetts Capital Resource Company, Massachusetts has covered the financing needs of its business community. Massachusetts recognizes that different clients have different needs and provides resources accordingly. High-technology firms are favored, but basic industries in economically depressed areas are also included.

These initiatives show the variety of ways in which the state functions. Some allow for complete public control; others are privately owned, managed, and funded. Cooperation between the business community and the state and local governments within Massachusetts has culminated in the development of these mutually beneficial public-private partnerships.

Fifth, the state has reduced the overall tax burden. Until 1982 the state was disparagingly referred to as "Taxachusetts" because its taxes were among the highest in the country. By 1986 the tax on businesses and the tax burden as a percentage of personal income fell below the national average. The state is aware of the impact taxation has on industry investment decisions and has sought to use its tax program to encourage science and technology development.

Sixth, the state, although assisting its declining businesses, has emphasized the development of new products and industries. The Route 128 success story has become a model for state policy. The state is investing in industry-academia research endeavors with hopes that new industries will result.

Massachusetts Programs

Massachusetts offers a variety of programs that encourage science and technology development in accordance with state strategies.

• A strong education system — The 1985 Education Reform legislation provided $210 million in assistance to elementary and secondary schools over a three-year period. Much of this money is earmarked for faculty salaries and recruitment. This bill also established a science and technology advisory committee to recommend a plan for long-term state assistance in science education.

In the last several years, the state has dramatically increased its expenditures for higher education—from 1982 to 1985, for example, the state contribution increased 54 percent with $529 million being spent in 1985 alone. A significant amount of this increase is for engineering and science studies. There has been a large increase in expenditures for engineering and laboratory equipment and for computer literature and journals. The state has also exempted 2 percent of all university faculty from collective bargaining and salary ceiling agreements. The universities now have the flexibility to recruit top-notch scientists for their graduate programs and are expending considerable effort to do so.

Several private universities also have significant science and technology programs. Northeastern, with the largest private engineering enrollment in the country and long-established work-study and evening programs, is not noted for its research, but it produces over 200 degree holders in electrical and computer engineering every year. Harvard University, which has been in the forefront of computer design since Howard Aiken's development of Mark I in the early 1940s, discourages faculty participation in business, and its engineering department is part of its College of Arts and Sciences. However, its electronics graduates, including An Wang, have significantly contributed to the state's economy. MIT has had by far the greatest impact. With one of the two leading electrical engineering departments in the nation and a host of distinguished research labs, it has provided not only outstanding degree holders for the local job market, but also hundreds of entrepreneurs who have started high-technology firms in the area.

• Developing foreign markets — The Office of International Trade and Investment (OITI), a division of EOEA, oversees international trade activities primarily through the development of a state export promotion program and reverse investment efforts.

EOEA established the Foreign Business Council, a quasi-public organization, to provide assistance to foreign investors. The council answers questions on site evaluations, investment studies, financing assistance, and helps with general liaison problems with public authorities.

The Massport Small Business Export Program (SBEP) and the Trade Development Program offer marketing services for small businesses. Specifically these organizations provide export assistance for firms involved with information technology, electronic components and electronic industrial production equipment, health care and biomedical supplies and equipment, and engineering and data processing services.

• Training a skilled work force — The Office of Training and Employment Policy (OTEP) administers the $60 million federal Job Training Partnership Act (JTPA) program. The training programs are provided through a network of Private Industry Councils, business-led organizations that plan and oversee a comprehensive program of locally developed employment and training services. OTEP performs job-matching services, provides on-the-job training, and if federal eligibility requirements are met, reimburses employers for up to 50 percent of their new employees' wages during training periods.

The Bay State Skills Corporation (BSSC) is a quasi-public agency that provides training programs for high-demand occupations in the state, especially in high technology. BSSC is one of the four programs evaluated later in this paper.

In addition, the state operates fifteen vocational high schools across the common-wealth.

• Assisting business with planning and capital information — In 1978 the state created the Massachusetts Technology Development Corporation (MTDC), which provides capital and technical assistance to Massachusetts businesses. This program will be discussed later in this paper. Other agencies with less of a high-technology focus have also been established to encourage growth in the private sector. The Massachusetts Industrial Finance Authority (MIFA) provides low-cost financing for private businesses through the issuance of tax-exempt industrial revenue bonds and loan guarantees. MIFA has helped 1,000 industrial and urban revitalization projects since its inception in 1979 and has created an estimated 50,000 new jobs.[16] Economically depressed areas can find an additional source of public venture capital funds through the Massachusetts Community Development Finance Corporation (MCDFC).

The Massachusetts Business Development Corporation (MBDC) is a state-chartered but privately owned corporation funded by Massachusetts' financial institutions. The banks pool funds to provide medium- and long-term loans to promising businesses that do not qualify for loans through conventional sources. The Massachusetts Capital Resource Company is another state-chartered, privately owned capital provider. It is a limited partnership funded by Massachusetts-based life insurance companies which provides high-risk capital for Massachusetts businesses. The Economic Stabilization Trust (EST) is a quasi-public financing agency designed to make high-risk loans to firms in mature industries. The EST received $2 million in FY 1985. This trust was established as part of the 1984 Mature Industries Legislation to aid businesses and employees in declining industries. Financing through the EST can be used to help a business find a new buyer, restructure the company, or for employee buy-outs.

• Providing tax incentives — There are several tax provisions specifically designed to encourage science and technology development. They include deductions and exemptions for R&D expenditures; exploration and development costs; purchase of materials, tools, fuels, and machinery used in R&D; qualified research contributions; and gifts of scientific equipment to the schools. A 1985 Massachusetts Taxation Commission report recommended that the state eliminate these special provisions in favor of reducing the overall tax burden on businesses. The study concluded that while these tax programs do provide some cash-flow advantages to small and new businesses, the business climate would be better served and the system more equitable if the tax expenditures were eliminated.

The state has also provided tax relief to certain industries in exchange for capital formation assistance. In 1985 the state established the Massachusetts Thrift Institution Fund for Economic Development. The Thrift Fund is a $100-million lending pool to be invested over a ten-year period for a variety of economic development and job-generating purposes. Funding for the $100 million loan pool is contributed by the state's thrift banks and savings and loan associations in return for certain tax allowances. The predecessor of the Thrift Fund is the previously mentioned MCRC, established in 1978. MCRC is a $100 million loan pool financed by the domestic life insurance companies in exchange for tax relief—MCRC is one of the four programs evaluated later in this report.

• Encouraging innovation — The Massachusetts Product Development Corporation (MPDC) is a quasi-public corporation that provides financial aid for the development of inventions and new products. The aid is awarded to businesses that are likely to experience a loss of employment due to declining industries, foreign competition, automation, or other factors. The production of the product must be instrumental in maintaining employment of all or part of the existing work force and thus reducing the social and public cost of employment dislocation. MPDC's FY 1986 budget was $2 million.

The Massachusetts Centers of Excellence (MCEC) and the Massachusetts Technology Park Corporation (MTPC) are programs that encourage partnerships between academia and business in university-based research, the establishment of incubator facilities, and the creation of new industries for the commonwealth. MCEC and MTPC are also further evaluated in the case study portion of this chapter.

Program Assessments

Four Massachusetts programs were chosen for evaluation: the Bay State Skills Corporation (BSSC), the Massachusetts Technology Development Corporation, the Massachusetts Capital Resources Company, and the Massachusetts Centers of Excellence Corporation, including the Massachusetts Technology Park Corporation.

It was difficult to choose from the wide variety of programs Massachusetts offers. These four programs have attracted national attention and are often examined by other states considering economic development programs of their own. Selections were made on the basis of the following criteria:

• Emphasis on partnerships — Many of the state's economic development programs are joint ventures among academia, business and industry, and government. The state recognizes that it no longer has the necessary resources to solve all of the state's economic needs. Further, the state recognizes that it cannot dictate agendas to the private sector, but must work with business and industry leaders in setting joint priorities. All four programs evaluated in this chapter involve some degree of partnership.

• Quasi-public agencies — A number of quasi-public agencies in Massachusetts carry out state economic development activities. The primary reason for this status is to give the agency greater flexibility, thereby avoiding legal constraints applied to state agencies such as civil service and construction laws. Second, it is thought that such status better insulates the agency from political decision-making and encourages business-industry relationships by removing the stigma of "public assistance." Quasi-public agencies include MTDC, BSSC, and MTPC.

• Innovators— The programs selected show a willingness to experiment with new ideas and imaginatively respond to state needs. MTDC, MCRC, and BSSC were first-of-a-kind programs.

• Programs with sufficient histories — Programs that have been in existence for a few years were selected. This allows for adequate observations and meaningful evaluations.

BAY STATE SKILLS CORPORATION

Legislative History and Organization

In the late 1970s, the leaders of high-technology industries advised state officials that Massachusetts' education and training systems were not producing a sufficient quantity of skilled workers. This labor shortage, especially of engineers, threatened the ability of high-technology firms to remain in the state. Discussion of this problem lead to the design of BSSC—a program funded by the state legislature to bring business and industry, academia, and government together to provide training and retraining in the state's high-growth occupations. Legislation to establish BSSC was advocated by the High

Technology Council and by EOEA Secretary Kariotis, who had once founded a high-technology firm of his own and was sensitive to the needs of the industry.

In 1980 legislation was submitted to the legislature; however, strong opposition killed the bill. The non-high-technology industries lobbied against BSSC because the funding was entirely earmarked for high-technology firms. Also, many critics believed that the program should be aimed at reducing high unemployment in economically distressed areas and among specific population groups: their position was strengthened by a report of the National Center for Jobs and Justice, released a day after the announcement of the BSSC legislation, which cited low minority employment in high-technology firms.

Despite initial defeat, Governor King decided to begin the program using existing state funds. He established a special pilot commission, operating out of EOEA, which between September and December 1980 awarded $500,000 in fifteen training grants.

In 1981, the governor refiled the BSSC legislation and dissipated opposition in two ways. First he pointed out that several commission grants had been awarded to non-high-technology projects. Second, he promised that the corporation would give priority in its programs to disadvantaged populations. As a result, BSSC was passed by the legislature in the summer of 1981. Its legislative mandate is to facilitate relationships among business and industry, labor, government, and education in expanding skills training consistent with state employment needs. Its primary activity is the awarding of grants to public and private nonprofit educational or training institutions which link up with private companies to conduct skills-training programs. The Corporation's current mission reads:

> BSSC is an economic development tool which works to provide education and industry partnerships for the skilled labor needs of high growth, emerging and traditional Massachusetts companies where knowledge-intensive training is necessarily.

Administration and Implementation

BSSC is a quasi-public agency governed by an eighteen-member board of directors. Fourteen of the members are appointed by the governor and must have experience in business and industry, skills training, education, labor organizations, or minority employment. Four are ex officio members from the state departments of Manpower Affairs, Education, Public Welfare, and the Board of Regents. Currently, the secretary of EOEA is the board chair. The corporation's staff budget totals $500,000.

While BSSC is technically a division of EOEA, the corporation is explicitly not subject to the supervision or control of that office. The corporation submits a separate budget request to the legislature, and state funds are appropriated through a separate line item in the budget.

BSSC grew from a $3-million program—the amount of the original 1981 funding—to a $6-million program in the span of about six months. At the close of 1985 the corporation was overseeing programs totaling about $13 million. In addition to state money, received a one-time grant totalling $750,000 in federal monies from the Department of Labor to fund training programs with the State's service delivery areas. This demonstration grant was utilized to improve private sector involvement in the JPTA system. BSSC also administers a program for training in occupations related to wastewater management.

BSSC describes itself as a "venture capital" organization for employment training. Grants are awarded on a competitive basis through a rolling request-for-proposals process. All grant programs require that participating businesses provide a match of cash or in kind, including contributions of equipment, facilities, and scholarships. Firms can take tax credits and deductions for their contributions. Applications for funding are submitted by the education or training institutions that will design the proposed program in conjunction with participating firms. Firms are not required to make hiring commitments, but it is hoped that in most cases the companies will hire program graduates. Applications are reviewed by the corporation's staff, and grant awards are made based on BSSC approval. By law, BSSC can fund proposals up to $200,000, but in order to maximize statewide distribution of funds, as well as obtain a strong mix of programs, proposals that average within the $50,000 to $100,000 range are favored. The following five types of grants programs are operated by the corporation.

• 50/50 matching grants program — This is BSSC's centerpiece program. Participating businesses must match grant funds provided from BSSC on at least an equal basis. The program is not restricted to specific client groups and training can take place in the classroom, laboratory or on the job. Grants are awarded for entry-level training and retraining programs for unemployed persons which run from six to twelve months as well as for skills training and advanced instruction. In 1985 BSSC sponsored forty-seven such programs.[17] In addition to its grant programs, since 1984 BSSC has conducted thirty-four Faculty-Industry Institute programs at Massachusetts universities. The programs, which last from one to two weeks, are designed to train faculty members in emerging technologies so they in turn can better prepare students for employment in the state.

• Targeted grant program — These grants function like those described above, but only a 20 percent match is required from business. In return, programs must be designed to serve at least one of four target groups: urban economically disadvantaged youth, public-assistance recipients, individuals dislocated as a result of Proposition 2 1/2, and individuals displaced from declining industries. The rationale for this program was that industry needed incentives to employ these populations. In 1985 BSSC ran four targeted programs.[18]

• Welfare programs — Funds are transferred from the Department of Public Welfare to BSSC for job training for Aid to Families with Dependent Children

(AFDC) recipients. This program is known as the ET Choices program and has received national praise for its success in placing AFDC recipients in jobs at a cost well below other job training options. BSSC ran eleven such programs in 1985.[19]

• Youth programs — This program supplies summer training for high school students. The matching-fund requirement is not applicable. BSSC ran nine such programs in 1985, eight of which involved computer training.

• Displaced homemakers — Five regional multipurpose centers, each with several satellite offices, across the state are available for persons needing to enter the labor market to achieve financial independence. The centers provide information, counseling, training, and placement services. The matching-fund requirement is not applicable, although each region has a private sector committing time and in-kind services.

GOAL ATTAINMENT AND EVALUATION

BSSC is universally well regarded in Massachusetts. Part of its success may be due to the corporation's willingness to critically evaluate its own activities and adjust its agenda to meet the varying economic needs of the state. In 1983 BSSC hired APT Associates, a Boston management consulting firm, to evaluate its performance, and in 1986 BSSC staff acknowledged the need for another outside evaluation. BSSC also closely monitors the performance of its grantees by conducting site visits and by requiring progress reports on a regular basis. Meaningful evaluation data on all aspects of BSSC are available and readily shared.

The 1983 APT report examined BSSC's general operations and evaluated twenty grant programs. The principal finding was that BSSC is a well-administered and extremely successful program by nearly all measures.[20] In 1986 this finding stills holds true. One of the original goals of BSSC was to foster new relationships between the public and private sectors, and private-sector participation in BSSC programs is still high. Since it began, over 900 companies have participated in one or more grant programs. These companies range from small local firms to major corporations and are located across the state. The flexibility of the grants programs allows for the diversity of regional economic needs, and most programs involve several firms to better insure job placement and occupation demand. In most cases, the private contributions well exceed the minimum requirements. The 50/50 Matching Grant Program averages about 150 percent in donations, while the Targeted Grant Program averages 50 percent. When firms were asked by APT Associates whether they would recommend BSSC to fellow businessmen, the response was overwhelmingly and enthusiastically yes.

Over 200 educational institutions have been involved with BSSC, including public and private two- and four-year colleges, universities, and community-based organizations, vocational-technical schools, and industry and trade associations. Job placement is extremely high. Eighty-seven percent of BSSC trainees get full-time employment in the private sector following graduation. The corporation even boasts a successful record of job placement for nontraditional workers—in 1985, for example, BSSC placed 250 welfare recipients in private-sector jobs.

Perhaps the greatest compliment BSSC has received is from the many states that have used BSSC as a model for their own skills-training agencies. Washington, Minnesota, Kentucky and Florida have their versions of BSSC well under way. In 1984, federal legislation was proposed to establish a U.S. Skills Corporation based on BSSC that would provide funding to states to set up skills-training programs. Unfortunately, the legislation eventually died, primarily because its prime sponsor, Senator Paul Tsongas from Massachusetts, left Congress suddenly.

Issues

The suitability of the corporation's role in serving disadvantaged populations has been an issue throughout its history. The APT evaluation found that the programs which serve the targeted individuals experienced relatively more enrollment and placement problems than other programs. The president of the High Technology Council has high praise for the corporation, but worries that the focus of the organization may be shifting away from the needs of the employers. The training of disadvantaged persons is questioned because JTPA, and the Department of Public Welfare are also in the targeted training business and the services of BSSC may duplicate administrative costs.

BSSC staff members agree that the 50/50 Matching Grant Program is the corporation's most appropriate activity, and they sometimes question the legislature's wisdom in broadening the scope of responsibilities given to them.[21] BSSC's promotion materials stress that its purpose is not to serve disadvantaged individuals, but rather to focus on employer needs. This approach, staff members argue, prevents the program from being stigmatized as serving "needy" groups, and therefore increases effectiveness.[22] They also believe that combining disadvantaged with nondisadvantaged groups in one system can improve service to the former without jeopardizing service to the latter.

Finally, Massachusetts officials are planning to reorganize its employment and training system and the potential role of BSSC, based on its successful record, may be greatly increased.

MASSACHUSETTS TECHNOLOGY DEVELOPMENT CORPORATION

Legislative History and Goals

The Massachusetts Technology Development Corporation was created as the result of a task force commissioned to evaluate the state's capital needs. In

1976, Governor Dukakis' Capital Formation Task Force concluded that there was indeed a "capital gap" and that the state needed to play a role in assisting economic development.[23] MTDC's enabling legislation was part of a comprehensive economic development program that included reforms and improvements in broad areas of economic development such as transportation, labor, taxes, energy regulation, as well as financial assistance. MTDC was established along with two other quasi-public-financing agencies: the Massachusetts Industrial Finance Authority, which caters to the needs of basic industries, and the Community Development Finance Corporation which focuses on depressed-area development.

MTDC succeeded the Massachusetts Science and Technology Foundation, which was created in 1972 to promote the development of high-technology industries. MTDC was originally intended to be funded with $10 million in state funds by the drafters of the legislation. However, when the budget was finalized in 1979, MTDC received an almost insignificant amount from the state and $2 million in federal funds from the Economic Development Administration (EDA).[24] It has since its inception received over $2 million from the state and another $1 million from the federal government.

Because the capital needs of the state have changed since the establishment of MTDC, the corporation's approach to financial assistance has changed as well. The 1978 federal capital gains tax legislation freed a substantial amount of capital for investment and thus reduced the national capital shortage. MTDC responded by shifting from early-stage and expansion financing to startup capital. Despite these changes, the objectives of the corporation have remained constant. As stated in their promotional brochure, MTDC's objectives are:

• to help create primary employment in technology-based industries;
• to attract and leverage private investment in Massachusetts companies;
• to foster the application of technological innovations where Massachusetts businesses are, or can be, leaders; and
• to nurture entrepreneurship among Massachusetts citizens, planting the seeds for long-term economic growth.

Administration and Implementation

MTDC's organization consists of an eleven-member board of directors and a staff of thirteen. The board represents members of the high-technology industry, state government, and academia. Its function is to give final approval on MTDC's investments and to establish policies for the corporation on direction of assistance and budgetary matters. The staff consists of the corporate officers, investment analysts, a public information officer, and support staff. Many of the officers and analysts have had previous banking experience.

MTDC operates three programs. While the Investment Program is the most visibly active, the Management Assistance and Financial Packaging Program has also been successful in helping new and expanding businesses. The

Management Assistance Program provides businesses counsel and review of initial business plans and assists with finding feasible capital sources. The Financial Packaging Program at MTDC assists new businesses in developing the best methods of presenting their investment opportunities to the private investors.

Under the the Investment Program, a company does not have to fill out a formal application; rather, it presents a written business plan. The investment analysts at MTDC then make an in-depth review of the proposal. To qualify for consideration a business enterprise must: (a) be located or agree to locate in Massachusetts; (b) be technology-based and its products sufficiently innovative; (c) produce a significant growth in employment; and (d) be able to demonstrate inability to secure capital from conventional sources on affordable terms.

MTDC envisions itself as filling a niche in Massachusetts' capital needs gap. The 1976 task force study concluded that sources for long-term capital were needed.[25] Within this area, MTDC, because of its low funding level, remains a lender of small proportion. MTDC can only invest up to $500,000 in any business, and typical loans and investments range from $100,000 to $250,000. This range makes MTDC unique as a financial source. Most private venture capital firms are not willing to contribute such a small amount to a business venture; MTDC can come in and complete a financial package.

Funding for MTDC is provided by both the state and federal governments. In 1979 MTDC received a $2-million grant from the EDA. In 1981 the corporation was awarded an additional $1 million under the Corporations for Innovation Development program of the U.S. Department of Commerce. The commonwealth of Massachusetts appropriated an additional $1 million to match the federal aid, and has made appropriations of over $750,000 in the years since 1981. The corporation has established both a revolving loan fund and a revolving equity investment fund. Since 1980 the corporation has recovered $1.8 million from both funds. The legislative intent was that MTDC would one day become self-sustaining from its investment returns and not require additional state appropriations.

Goal Attainment and Evaluations

In filling this niche in the capital markets, MTDC views itself as a success. Its measurement of success is based on money loaned, money leveraged, and the number of jobs created. MTDC has invested over $7 million in its six years of existence, claiming to have leveraged $5.25 private for every $1 MTDC for Massachusetts businesses. As well, the corporation credits its investments with the creation of 1,300 new jobs for the commonwealth, generating an additional estimated $2 million in tax revenues for the state.[26]

Although there has been no outside evaluation of MTDC's performance, the fact that the legislature appropriates substantial sums of money to the corporation each year may be interpreted as a show of support from the State

House. The corporation has been also used as a model for other state initiatives in economic development. It has won the acceptance and cooperation of private financial institutions, another measure of confidence and success.

MTDC staff members and others involved with Massachusetts' effort to encourage high-technology development attest that the corporation is successfully fulfilling the legislative mandate. Its investments may be nominal in relation to the total amount of capital loaned in the state, but they appear solid. The corporation gained $130,000 on its 1985 equity investments, with no losses from either fund.[27]

Issues

However successful the investments, should state money be used to finance this sort of economic development approach? Can this type of program successfully finance the fringe projects that would not otherwise be funded? These questions elicited a variety of responses from state officials.

Critics of the program feel that most of the projects that MTDC has loaned money to or invested in would have been funded by private financial groups anyway. They argue that the amount of money involved, though modest by investment standards, is nevertheless a substantial state expenditure. The corporation is therefore motivated to invest in businesses that can reasonably expect to succeed, not those that are considered risky or marginal.

Supporters of the program believe that the state can play a role in financing such enterprises and that additional sources of capital would stimulate innovation and growth. However, programs such as MTDC must be responsive to the changing needs of the state.

MASSACHUSETTS CAPITAL RESOURCE COMPANY

Legislative History and Goals

The Massachusetts Capital Resource Company was created in December 1977, also in response to the 1976 Capital Formation Task Force report and the lobbying efforts of Massachusetts' domestic life insurance companies. This initiative was a compromise between the state and the nine Massachusetts-based life insurance companies. The insurance group agreed to form MCRC in return for reduced state taxes on premium sales and investment income. At this time, state taxes on Massachusetts life insurance companies were the highest in the nation. MCRC was to be capitalized with $100 million over a ten-year period in order to expand the amount of long-term financing available to Massachusetts businesses.

The overall goal of MCRC, as articulated in the legislation, was to create employment opportunities within the commonwealth. The state legislature mandated that at least 1,000 jobs were to be created directly by MCRC's investments in the years 1979 and 1980, and at least 2,000 jobs were to be created in 1981 and all subsequent years. The organization was allowed to run as a private investment firm in all other respects.

Administration and Implementation

MCRC cannot be considered a state agency or even a quasi-state agency. The company was organized as a limited partnership whose only ties to the state are that it must report annually its job-creation achievements and that it is open to review by the Commission of Insurance. The organization consists of a nine-member board of directors representing four general partners and including the president of the corporation. The board has two standing committees, the executive committee and the investment committee. The company employs a staff of six executives and three support personnel.

MCRC's only function is to lend capital. The company is not to be in competition with other financial institutions; therefore, it must invest in the higher-risk business enterprises unacceptable to conventional capital sources. MCRC expects a market rate of return on its investments and offers a broad range of financing plans. Loans range from $200,000 to $2,000,000 and from senior debt through subordinated debt and equity capital to leveraged buy-outs.

The investment procedure requires submission of a feasible business plan, followed by a detailed evaluation of the business enterprise. All investment opportunities are presented by MCRC management to the investment committee for final approval. MCRC prefers to make subordinated debt investments, claiming that they are most sought after, and also the most difficult to obtain. MCRC has played a major role in supplying capital to the older, traditional industries as well as to the younger, technology-based industries—each type claims about half of the corporation's investments.

Attainment and Evaluation

MCRC's measurements of success include the rate of return to investor companies and to create a number of employment opportunities for the state. The company currently maintains at least a market rate of return on all investments and participated in twenty-four new financings in 1984, bringing its cumulative total to over $125 million. MCRC credits these investments with the creation or maintenance of 8,200 jobs, which well exceeds the 2,000 job-target set by the state.[28] In this regard, MCRC has fulfilled its legislative charge.

Issues

A company such as MCRC raises the same questions state-financed organizations do, yet a bigger issue with MCRC is whether similar institutions can or should be established in other states. The partners of MCRC do not believe that this program should be copied in other states because of their philosophical disagreement with the manner in which the partnership was formed. They believe that a state should not be able to direct an industry in such an important area of business as the investment of substantial sums of its own money. Another issue is whether Massachusetts made a wise maneuver in the compromise that established MCRC. With respect to the foregone tax revenues, it has been claimed that the state of Massachusetts more than financed the life insurance investment fund.[29] While the insurance companies may appear to be foregoing maximum returns with their investments in MCRC, their actual opportunity costs have been minimal.

CENTERS OF EXCELLENCE

Legislative History and Goals
The centers are joint industry, academia, and state government research endeavors, with Route 128 serving as role model. It is hoped that the centers will expand the growth of Boston and the Route 128 high-technology corridor to economically lagging areas of the commonwealth. Six centers for emerging technologies have been located across the state. Although all six are often referred to as "Centers of Excellence," in reality there are two similar governing entities, enacted in separate years and operating independently.

In 1981, during Governor King's administration, and in response to the need for a more highly trained work force, the legislature established a quasi-public agency, the Massachusetts Technology Park Corporation (MTPC). MTPC was mandated to create educational centers in developing areas of science and technology. The legislation stipulated that the first center focus on microelectronic technologies, and $20 million was appropriated to begin its construction. The Microelectronics Center's mission was to provide sophisticated instruction in microtechnology beyond that offered by Massachusetts' colleges and universities. The expense of the equipment required for much of this advanced training could not be borne by one institution alone. The Microelectronics Center will allow for shared usage of such equipment. MIT, desiring such a program, became deeply involved in the center's organization.

After the initial groundwork was laid for the Microelectronics Center, MIT and MTPC officials discussed the additional need for a state materials research center. MIT's department of Materials Science and Engineering was the largest program of its kind in the country, and Harvard had just been awarded a $1.2 million NSF grant for materials research. State officials were convinced that Massachusetts had the opportunity to capitalize on the strengths of these universities and lead the country in this technology. Legislation to establish and provide $20 million in funding for a Materials Research Center, under the governance of MTPC, was filed in 1984.

At the same time lawmakers were considering the Materials Research Center legislation, several politicians were lobbying for additional centers to be located in their districts. Also, the Dukakis administration had begun to explore the possibility of establishing several other centers across the state as part of a regional economic development plan. As a result, the Materials Research Center legislation was amended to include the Massachusetts Centers of Excellence Corporation (MCEC), an entity similar to MTPC but within the Executive Office of Economic Affairs. MCEC's mandate is the same as MTPC's—to create educational centers—and it has become parent of four such centers.

Although MCEC was created later than MTPC, in two cases MCEC provided a governing structure and boost for activities that had been developing independently. In the early 1970s the University of Massachusetts at Amherst prepared to apply for federal NSF funds to build a polymer science research center; before it could, the federal program was discontinued. However, the university continued to develop its polymer science department, and in 1983, a year before the establishment of MCEC, the school received a $6-million appropriation from the state legislature for use in building the facility. Plans for a biotechnology park in Worcester were also begun before MCEC. The Worcester Business Development Corporation had purchased, in 1982, land adjacent to the University of Massachusetts Medical School to build a biotechnology park. In contrast, the Photovoltaics Center and the Marine Science Center were initiated by MCEC.

Administration and Implementation

MTPC is a quasi-public agency under the executive secretariat of Manpower Affairs and is funded through a separate line item in the budget. MTPC has a twenty-three-member board of directors, appointed by the governor. Nine universities, both public and private, eleven industries, and three state offices are represented on the board. The board is required to meet quarterly; however, it and its several subcommittees meet more frequently. The board directly administers the Microelectronics and Materials Research Centers. The operating budget for FY 1987 exceeds $2 million, with public universities contributing almost $500,000 of that amount.

MCEC is a public agency under the executive secretariat of Economic Affairs and is funded primarily through that office. MCEC has a nine-member board of directors composed of three state officials, three industry representatives, and three public university representatives, all appointed by the governor. MCEC additionally has a technology board for each of its four centers, with membership weighted in favor of industry and academia. MCEC's annual operating budget for FY 1987 is $700,000, and $500,000 for each individual center.

The four technologies selected for Centers of Excellence are photovoltaics, biotechnology, marine science, and polymer science. These technologies were selected because there was:

- existing academic and industrial superiority;
- potential for stimulating economic growth and jobs;
- a dispersion of technologies across the state as well as a diversity, thereby reducing dependence on any one industry;
- potential for private-sector and federal support; and
- a tie to public universities.

The four Centers of Excellences differ in purpose and organization and are in various stages of development. The Photovoltaics Center in northern Massachusetts is primarily an export assistance center, and its activities are centered at Logan International Airport; The research component of this center is located at Lowell State University.[30] The Marine Science Center in southeastern Massachusetts is designed to develop commercial applications for the marine science research done by Harvard, MIT, and the Woods Hole Oceanographic Institute.[31] The Polymer Science Center in western Massachusetts is an advanced research institute.[32] The Biotechnology Center in central Massachusetts is primarily a technology park project, although incubator facilities are planned for the future.[33]

Goal Attainment and Evaluation

The centers are too new to fully assess their success. However, several indicators suggest a promising future for these projects. Foremost, the membership of all the boards is composed of the top industry executives and academicians in the state. The boards are meeting much more frequently than required, and members are very enthusiastic. This unusual degree of involvement reflects the seriousness of the endeavor.

Second, the centers further along in their development have proven to be effective magnets for private and federal dollars. In 1985, for example, the Polymer Science Center received a $10-million federal grant and the Photovoltaics Center received a $1 million federal grant. It is also expected that the activity associated with the Marine Science Center will encourage Congress to locate one of four national aquaculture centers in the state.

Third, the overall state goal for the centers is the development of new businesses and industries. One small spinoff industry from the Polymer Science Center has been established in Amherst and is hoped to be the first of many.

Finally, a secondary goal of the centers was to strengthen the public college and university system. Private educational institutions are very involved in these centers, and in the case of the Microelectronics and Materials Research Centers, seem to play a leading role. However, in all the centers state universities participate and the four Centers of Excellence are pivoted around programs at public universities. As a result, state universities have increased budgets and research capabilities.

The reaction from industry officials to the program has been generally positive, although most are reserving judgment for now.

Issues

Several industry leaders have questioned the way in which the state selected the technologies for development. State officials contend that the technologies were evaluated in round-table discussions between industry, academia, and state government leaders. The High-Technology Council argues that a better needs-assessment process should have been followed, and that the Photovoltaics and Marine Science Centers, for example, are based more on wishful thinking than on economic potential.

The ability of the state to encourage regional economic development is also questioned. The state's approach tries to blend social and technological goals in a common sense manner. A biotechnology company struggling to make a go of it will find rents lower in Worcester than it will in Cambridge. Firms engaged in marine sciences will be able to find workers more readily in southeastern Massachusetts than they will in the bustling Boston area. However, some industry leaders and the High-Technology Council argue that it will be extremely difficult to locate industry away from the existing science and technology infrastructure of Boston and Route 128.

Conclusions

The four programs discussed here illustrate the wide range of activities Massachusetts has undertaken to promote economic development through science and technology. Several conclusions can be drawn from this sample of initiatives.

The state is very much committed to the establishment of independent quasi-public entities. Many state officials believe this is an effective and flexible means of encouraging economic development. The quasi-public design is a result of the state's shift into activities traditionally undertaken by the private sector. The state recognized that these programs required different operating procedures from other state agencies because their activities are in areas that are quickly changing. State procedures, such as purchasing approval and hiring requirements, would prove too cumbersome and bureaucratic. Timely responses are needed for establishing training programs and financial packages for emerging technologies.

In 1985 the Senate Ways and Means Committee released a report questioning the establishment of additional independent authorities on the grounds that they have no formal coordinating organization and so may be subject to duplication and overlap of activities. However, several coordinating efforts have taken place. MCRC and MTDC refer clients to each other, and BSSC cooperates with the MCEC in setting up training programs at the Microelectronics Center.

These relationships are not formalized, however, nor are they overseen by one decision-making body.

Economic development efforts are not evenly distributed across the state. Although both the programs of MTDC and MCRC are available to all state individuals and businesses, few awards are granted to projects outside the Boston area. This is, in part, because they do not receive many applications from other areas of the state. The more rural, western areas cannot compete with or duplicate the existing high-technology infrastructure that is almost entirely contained within the Boston area. BSSC's program, however, has managed to extend grants to all areas of the state. Governor Dukakis, recognizing the need for regional economic development, has located the Centers of Excellence in economically needy areas of the state. Whether the state can successfully direct economic development to depressed areas, rather than leave such business decisions to the operation of a free market, remains to be seen.

Political maneuvering has, at times, skewed economic development agendas. The prime example is the existence of both MTPC and MCEC. The changeover of governors and the pork-barrel politics of the legislature have created several duplicative boards, administrators, and controlling authorities for the research and training activities.

Overall, however, the Massachusetts programs provide healthy and useful models for other states. BSSC, MTDC, and the Centers of Excellence are all replicable. As discussed earlier, MCRC may not be useful for other states because the specifics of its establishment may only be applicable for Massachusetts.

These four programs have been successful for several reasons. First, the state has been willing to experiment. MCRC, MTDC, and BSSC all were "invented" in Massachusetts. The state is willing to fund projects that come with no guarantees of success. MTDC and MCRC were established to fund activities deemed questionable by traditional lenders. Even though default might occur on some loans, it is believed that the benefits to the state in the long run will surpass the costs. There is also no guarantee for the Centers of Excellence program. Probably not all of them will prove successful; however, the state believes that those that do will more than compensate for any failure.

Second, Massachusetts recognizes the importance of cooperation among the different sectors. The state is committed to forging new partnerships between business and industry, government, and academia. Partnerships are deemed important for future economic growth. The state recognizes that it has limited resources and believes that it is reasonable to expect contributions from the private sector. The private sector benefits from these state initiatives and should bear some of the cost. Additionally this participation ensures that state efforts are directed to the needs of the private sector. Further, there is a new willingness among business leaders to work with government on projects. The membership of the various boards of these organizations includes some of the top CEOs in the state.

The state does not resist change. It realizes that many of its traditional industries are declining, and rather than merely postpone this decline, the state is funding worker retraining programs and emerging technologies. Even in this time of economic prosperity, the state is looking to its future economic needs and investing in programs that may not show a return for at least several years.

Finally, the state's long-term investment in education has provided skills training and opportunities for its citizens and put Massachusetts in the forefront of science and technology development. The public education system, at all levels, is well funded and innovative. The state capitalizes on the strengths of the private colleges and universities within its borders by providing financial aid to its residents to attend those institutions and by working in cooperative research endeavors such as those of the Centers of Excellence. BSSC provides customized job training for Massachusetts residents, including nontraditional workers. MCRC and MTDC provide financial support for many new college graduates who are attempting to establish new business enterprises. The result of these state efforts is a skilled, imaginative, and resourceful citizenry ready to meet the challenges of emerging technologies.

NOTES

1. Massachusetts State Senate Ways and Means Committee, *FY 1986 Budget Recommendations of the Senate Ways and Means Committee*, Boston, 1985, 2-13.
2. Marshall I. Goldman, "The Business of Attracting Industry,"*Technology Review*, (May-June 1984): 6.
3. Randy Fritz, "Choices for American Industry," report in progress, LBJ School of Public Affairs, University of Texas at Austin.
4. Massachusetts State Senate Ways and Means Committee, *FY 1986 Budget Recommendations*, 2-13.
5. Massachusetts State Senate Ways and Means Committee, *FY 1986 Budget Recommendations*, 2-15.
6. Nancy S. Dorfman, "High Tech Boom in Massachusetts," Massachusetts Institute of Technology, 1982, 3.
7. The High Tech Research Group, "Massachusetts High Tech: The Promise and Reality," Boston, 1983, 7.
8. National Science Foundation, *Federal Funds for Research and Development*, vol. 33, Washington, D.C., 1984, 31-34.
9. National Science Foundation, *Academic Science/Engineering R&D Funds—FY 1983*, Washington, D.C., 1985.
10. Dorfman, "High Tech Boom," 21.
11. Ibid., 22.
12. Fritz, "Choices for American Industry."
13. Ibid.

14. Massachusetts Department of Commerce, *Massachusetts: Creating the Future,* Boston, 1982, 24.
15. Interview with Senator John Olver, Massachusetts State Senate, Boston, October 1985.
16. U.S. Small Business Administration, Office of the Chief Counsel for Advocacy, *State Activities in Venture Capital, Early-Stage Financing, and Secondary Markets,* Washington, D.C., 1984, 35.
17. Twenty-five people were trained in manufacturing engineering. Private participants include Honeywell, General Electric, and IBM Corp. The education participant was Boston University. Private contributions totaled $268,000 and BSSC's contribution totaled $62,660.
18. Forty-five people were trained in data entry/word processing. Private participants include Altertext, BayBank, Kelly Services, Keystone Mass. Group, MONY, New England Telephone, Porter Square Personnel, Sommerville Hospital. The education participant was Sommerville Adult Education. Private contributions totaled $22,000 and BSSC's contribution totaled $80,196.
19. Eighteen people were trained in electro-mechanical drafting. Private participants include ALCO Electronic Products, Analog Devices, Digital Equipment Corp., and Raytheon Corp. The education participant was Women's Technical Institute. Private contributions totaled $16,050 and BSSC's contribution totaled $51,200.
20. APT Associates, Inc., *Business-Training Partnerships in Action: An Evaluation of the BSSC Program,* Cambridge, 1983, 4.
21. Interview with Maureen O'Hare, BSSC staff, Boston, January 1986.
22. Ibid.
23. Massachusetts Governor's Office, *An Economic Development Program for Massachusetts,* Boston, 1976, 16.
24. Interview with Robert Crowley, vice president, MTDC, Boston, January 1986.
25. Governor's Office, *An Economic Development Program for Massachusetts,* 16.
26. *Massachusetts Technology Development Corporation,* 7. Promotional brochure.
27. *Massachusetts Technology Development Corporation Annual Report,* Boston, 1985, 1.
28. *Massachusetts Capital Resource Corporation Annual Report* (Boston, 1984).
29. Cameron Huff, "A Preliminary Analysis of the Massachusetts Capital Resource Company," 1982, 25. Mimeograph.
30. The Photovoltaics Center is located in Lowell in northern Massachusetts. State officials claim that Massachusetts is one of three U.S. centers of photovoltaics research, with expected sales of $350 million in 1990. Most of the markets for photovoltaics are in Third World countries and the industry needs help in selling their products to these nations. As a first phase of this Center of Excellence, a combination of state agencies, led by the Energy Resources Department, commissioned a study of photovoltaics marketing needs and built an export assistance center at Logan International Airport. The second phase, in the planning stages, is to purchase production equipment for the University of Lowell to use in a photovoltaics training program. Beyond operational and an executive director's salary costs, this center has received $300,000 of state funds.

31. The Marine Science Center is located in North Dartmouth in southeastern Massachusetts. The goal of this center is to develop Southeastern Massachusetts University into a center of applied marine research in such fields as marine electronics, aquaculture, marine pharmaceuticals, and fishing. It is hoped that one day SMU will play a more major role in the commercial development of research emanating from the Woods Hole Oceanographic Institute, the Marine Biological Laboratory, MIT Labs and the Massachusetts Maritime Academy. There are plans to build a state research lab on the coast. Additionally the state has applied for federal selection as New England's regional aquaculture research center. No state funds, other than an executive director's salary, have been allocated.

32. The Polymer Science Center, located in Amherst in western Massachusetts, is the eighth-largest producer of plastic resins in the country. Two Massachusetts firms, General Electric and Monsanto, dominate the nation's industry. UMass-Amherst is already an internationally recognized center of polymer research. Late in 1985 a $10-million federal grant was awarded to the university for the building of a research facility. The primary activity of the Polymer Center is building a $24 million facility; it is not clear how the Center of Excellence designation will further this cause. Basic operational funds, an executive director's salary, and $6 million of state funds have been appropriated for this project.

33. The Biotechnology Center is located in Worcester in central Massachusetts. The Worcester Business Development Corp. has been working for years to develop a biotechnology park in Worcester, which would serve as a breeding ground for biotech/biomedical activity and would be close to the University of Massachusetts Medical School, Tufts Veterinary Medical School, the Worcester Foundation for Experimental Biology, and the Harvard University Primate Research Center. Biotechnology holds great promise for genetically engineering agricultural plants and the state is encouraging agricultural applications of this science. Completion of the park is scheduled for 1986. The state contributed $50,000 to the parks purchase, but otherwise has funded only a director's salary and general operating costs.

5

Although Minnesota may not be widely perceived as a locus of high technology, this sector is an important dimension of Minnesota's economic future. Control Data Corporation, 3M, and Cray Research maintain corporate headquarters in Minnesota. In addition, state government boasts over two dozen different programs dealing with high-technology development. This chapter first discusses distinguishing demographic and economic characteristics of the state and then introduces the conditions fostering high-technology interests within the state. After an overview of state programs, four specific programs are explored in greater depth to discern what ideas Minnesota has to offer in high-technology development.

Demographic and Economic Profile

POPULATION CHARACTERISTICS

In the last few decades, Minnesota's rate of population growth has slowed from 11.5 percent during the 1960s to nearly 7 percent in the 1970s. The national figure from 1970 to 1980 was 11.4 percent, putting Minnesota about 4 percent below the national growth rate (Table 5-1). A higher portion of Minnesota's population compared to the nation as a whole is rural—one-third of the state compared to one-fourth of the nation (Table 5-2). Minnesota has a predominately white population, with blacks comprising barely 1 percent of the total population in 1980 (Table 5-3). Concerning migration, Feeney states that "in the last decade slightly more people moved into Minnesota than moved out—worth noting because Minnesota has traditionally been a supplier of people to the rest of the country."[1]

Other significant population changes in Minnesota involve education, age, and migration. Education levels in Minnesota have improved since 1960; median years spent in school have increased from 10.6 years in 1960 to 12.6 years in 1980. The largest increase came in the share of the population completing four or more years of college (Table 5-4). In addition, Minnesota has the lowest high school dropout rate in the nation.[2] The age distribution of Minnesota's population has shifted in recent years, paralleling national shifts. In 1970, the bulk of the state's population was 19 years old or younger; by 1980, most people were between 20 and 44 years old (Table 5-5).

— This chapter was written by Sidney Bailey Hacker
and Robert D. Sommerfeld.

TABLE 5-1

Population of Minnesota and Percentage Change
Compared to the United States, 1970, 1980, and 1984
(in 1,000s and %)

	Minnesota	Minnesota Change	U.S. Change
1970	3,806	—	—
1980	4,076	7.1	11.4
1984	4,162	2.1	4.1

Source: U.S. Dept. of Commerce, Bureau of the Census, *Current Population
Reports, Local Population Estimates*, Series P-26, No. 84-52-C, p. 11; idem,
1980 Census of Population, vol. 1, ch. A, part 25, p. 27.

TABLE 5-2

Urban and Rural Composition of Minnesota
Compared to the United States, 1970 and 1980
(%)

	1970		1980	
	Minnesota	United States	Minnesota	United States
Urban	66.5	73.6	66.9	73.7
Rural	33.5	26.4	33.1	26.3

Source: U.S. Department of Commerce, Bureau of the Census, *1980 Census of
Population*, vol. 1, ch. A, part 25, p. 27.

TABLE 5-3

Racial Distribution of Minnesota
Compared to the United States, 1980
(%)

	Minnesota	United States
White	96.6	87.5
Black	1.3	11.1
Other	2.1	1.4

Source: U.S. Department of Commerce, Bureau of the Census,
Statistical Abstract of the United States, 1985, p. 31.

TABLE 5-4
Educational Levels in Minnesota
Compared to the United States, 1980
(%)

	Minnesota	United States
Elementary school (less than 5 years)	1.2	3.6
High school	73.1	66.5
College (4 or more years)	17.4	16.2
Median years of school completed	12.6	12.5

Source: U.S. Department of Commerce, Bureau of the Census,
1980 Census of Population, vol. 1, ch. C, part 25, p. 61.

TABLE 5-5
Age Distribution in Minnesota
Compared to the United States, 1970 and 1980
(%)

Age Group	1970		1980	
	Minnesota	United States	Minnesota	United States
0-19	40.0	37.8	32.8	32.0
20-44	30.1	31.7	37.3	37.2
45-64	19.2	20.6	18.2	19.7
65+	10.7	9.8	11.8	11.3

Source: U.S. Department of Commerce, Bureau of the Census, *1980 Census of Population*, vol.1, ch. B, part 25, p. 27; idem,*1970 Census of Population*, vol. 1, ch. B, part 25, p. 69.

THE ECONOMY OF THE STATE

From 1967 until the early 1980s Minnesota state government worked to relieve the local property tax burdens of its citizens and make taxation generally more equitable. A large program of intergovernmental revenue transfers collectively known as the "Minnesota miracle" were financed through heavy state income taxation. The transfer payments reached their apex in 1979 when an omnibus bill passed the state legislature that both lowered income tax rates and increased transfer payments. This was possible because the personal incomes of Minnesotans were rising very quickly. As business boomed, personal income rose and revenue from income taxation increased automatically.

However, in the early 1980s Minnesota's economy slumped. Minnesota is becoming an increasingly export-based economy. Therefore, it is very sensitive to downturns in the national economy and changes in the trade balance of the nation as a whole. A high dollar, a national trade imbalance, and the growth of the federal deficit probably affected Minnesota's economy more than other states.[3] Two important Minnesota industries, agriculture and taconite iron ore mining, were hit particularly hard. As the economy slumped, personal income lowered and state income tax revenues decreased. The state government's overreliance upon income taxation led to a series of fiscal crises in state government and contributed to the political downfall of then Republican Governor Albert Quie.

Minnesota's economic health improved as the rest of the nation recovered from the recessionary years of the early 1980s. However, the experiences of 1980-1983 changed state government. The new governor, Governor Rudy Perpich, has worked to decrease the reliance of state government upon income taxation. Local property taxes are rising as intergovernmental transfer payments decrease. Perpich also wants to diversify Minnesota's economy; hence, he emphasizes promoting high-technology innovation and international marketing skills in Minnesota businesses.

Because the Twin Cities are so obviously prosperous it is tempting to simply bifurcate Minnesota into two basic economic parts—a booming metropolitan area and an economically depressed rural region. However, this is an oversimplification. Only the northeastern corner of Minnesota, with its terminally ill iron ore industry and its many depressed pulp and paper mills, can truly be called depressed. Other rural areas in Minnesota have suffered from falling agricultural prices, but most regions have diversified their economies in the last ten years. In particular, the central region of Minnesota has gained three times as many manufacturing jobs as any other region in Minnesota.

The far west of Minnesota that borders the Dakotas is more heavily dependent upon agriculture than any other area in Minnesota, yet even there the manufacturing and service sectors have grown to replace some lost farm jobs. In summary, Minnesota has a slowly diversifying economy except for the northeastern sector. In the last thirty years, agricultural employment has already severely declined in Minnesota. If agricultural prices do not suddenly decline once more, Minnesota will probably remain economically healthy.

The metropolitan region of Minneapolis and St. Paul and the rest of Minnesota are intrinsically linked politically and economically. The state government has felt the political pressures of rural legislators, and the state is trying to aid farmers with programs to increase the efficiency of farming via high technology. Bank failures or slumping business activity in rural Minnesota can still affect finance, manufacturing, and wholesaling in the Twin Cities despite Minnesota's desire to develop national and international markets for its goods and services.[4]

Table 5-6 emphasizes Minnesota's general economic health. Between 1972 and 1982 only two sectors, mining and transportation, experienced negative growth. Every other sector expanded its employment by at least 10 percent. Like the rest of the nation, Minnesota's economy had high service sector growth, fueled perhaps by the economic expansion of the Twin Cities as evidenced by 46 percent employment growth in the finance and insurance sector.

More detailed analysis of employment trends in Minnesota's manufacturing industries is provided in Table 5-7. Nondurable manufacturing employment dropped between 1972 and 1982 because of agricultural and forestry product slumps. Durable manufacturing employment rose more than 25 percent despite declines in primary metals and transportation equipment — two industrial sectors that were probably affected by downturns in the automotive industry. Minnesota manufacturing employment should be fairly resilient if Minnesota industries can maintain technological advantages. Over 49 percent of Minnesota's manufacturing employment came from fairly sophisticated industrial sectors, that is, nonelectrical machinery, electrical equipment, fabricated metals, and instruments.

TABLE 5-6

Nonagricultural Employment and Share by Sector in Minnesota, 1972, 1977, and 1982, and Percentage Change between 1972 and 1982
(employees in 1,000s, shares, and changes in %)

	1972 Emp.	Share	1977 Emp.	Share	1982 Emp.	Share	1972-1982 Change
Mining	13.8	1.0	12.9	.1	9.5	.1	-31.2
Construction	61.5	4.5	68.7	4.3	59.7	3.5	- 2.9
Manufacturing	310.2	22.9	339.3	21.2	346.3	20.3	11.6
Transportation & public utilities	86.3	6.4	92.4	5.8	94.9	5.6	10.0
Wholesale & retail	332.4	24.6	403.5	25.3	430.9	25.2	29.6
Finance & insurance	67.2	5.0	82.2	5.1	98.2	5.7	46.1
Government	246.2	18.1	286.3	17.9	288.8	16.9	17.3
Services	239.6	17.7	312.0	19.5	380.6	22.3	58.8
Total	1357.1		1597.3		1708.7		25.9

Source: U.S. Department of Commerce, Bureau of the Census, *1982 Census of Manufactures, Geographic Area Series, Minnesota*, p. 8; idem, *1977 Census of Manufactures, Geographic Area Statistics*, pp. 24.5-24.6.

TABLE 5-7

Manufacturing Employment and Share by Industry in Minnesota,
1972, 1977, and 1982, and Percentage Change between 1972 and 1982
(employees in 1,000s, shares, and changes in %)

	1972		1977		1982		1972-1982
	Emp.	Share	Emp.	Share	Emp.	Share	Change
Nondurable							
Food/kindred	45.6	17.3	42.7	14.2	41.0	13.5	-10.0
Tobacco		none		none		none	
Textile	2.1	.8	2.5	.8	2.0	.7	- 4.8
Apparel	6.9	2.6	5.7	1.9	—		
Paper products	18.1	6.9	12.7	4.2	13.3	4.4	-26.5
Printing/ publishing	21.9	8.3	28.9	9.5	34.8	11.4	58.9
Chemicals	6.3	2.4	6.2	2.0	6.5	2.1	4.8
Petroleum refining	1.6	.6	1.6	.5	—		
Rubber & plastic	7.7	2.9	10.6	3.5	12.6	4.1	63.6
Leather	—		2.1	.7	1.8	.6	
Total nondurable	110.2	41.8	113.0	37.5	112.0	36.8	-12.0
Durable							
Lumber & wood	9.2	3.5	12.8	4.2	10.2	3.4	10.9
Furniture & fixtures	4.2	1.6	4.0	1.3	3.8	1.2	- 9.5
Stone, clay, glass	7.1	2.7	11.7	3.9	9.8	3.2	38.0
Primary metal	7.1	2.7	7.4	2.5	6.2	2.0	-12.7
Fabricated metal	32.8	12.4	30.3	10.0	30.9	10.2	- 5.8
Nonelectric machinery	55.0	20.9	64.1	21.3	71.0	23.3	29.1
Electrical equipment	18.3	6.9	29.0	10.0	30.5	9.9	66.7
Transportation equipment	9.8	3.7	8.0	2.7	6.2	2.0	-36.7
Instruments	9.8	3.7	13.8	4.6	17.8	5.8	81.6
Miscellaneous	—		7.4	2.5	6.0	2.0	
Total durable	153.3	58.1	188.5	62.5	192.4	63.1	25.5
Total mfg.	263.5	99.9	301.5	100.0	304.4	99.9	15.5

Source: U.S. Department of Commerce, Bureau of the Census, *1982 Census of Manufactures, Geographic Area Series, Minnesota,* pp. 8-13; idem, *1977 Census of Manufactures, Geographic Area Statistics,* pp. 24.10-24.17.

Minnesota residents receive slightly more per capita income than the average American (Table 5-8). Moreover, there are significantly fewer people below the poverty level in Minnesota than the average for the nation (Table 5-9). This may be because there are no significant racial minority groups in the Twin Cities area. Minnesota's poor are rural poor. There are more farmers in Minnesota than in most other states, while there are fewer operators and laborers (Table 5-10).

TABLE 5-8
Per Capita Income and Percentage Change in Minnesota
Compared to the United States, 1970, 1980, and 1984
(in $ and %)

	Minnesota	Change	United States	Change
1970	3,893	—	3,945	—
1980	9,688	148.9	9,494	140.7
1984	13,247	36.7	12,789	34.7

Source: U.S. Department of Commerce, Bureau of Economic Analysis, *1984 Survey of Current Business*, p. 18; idem, Bureau of the Census, *Statistical Abstract of the United States, 1984*, p. 457.

TABLE 5-9
Individuals below the Poverty Level in Minnesota
Compared to the United States, 1970 and 1980
(%)

	Minnesota	United States
1970	8.2	13.0
1980	7.0	12.1

Source: U.S. Dept. of Commerce, Bureau of the Census, *1980 Census of Population*, vol. 1, part 25, p. 397; idem, *1970 Census of Population*, vol. 1, part 25, p. 355.

TABLE 5-10
Occupational Structure in Minnesota for Employed Persons
Sixteen Years and Over Compared to the United States, 1980
(workers in 1,000s and %)

	Minnesota		United States	
	Workers	Percentage	Workers	Percentage
Managerial & professional	434.5	23.0	22,151.6	22.7
Technical, sales & admin.	567.9	30.1	29,593.5	30.3
Service	264.6	14.0	12,629.4	12.9
Farming, forestry & fishing	106.9	5.7	2,811.3	2.9
Production, craft, & repair	212.9	11.3	12,594.2	12.9
Operators & laborers	298.7	15.8	17,859.3	18.3
Total	1,885.5	100.0	97,639.3	100.0

Source: U.S. Dept. of Commerce, Bureau of the Census, *1980 Census of Population*, vol. 1, part 25, pp. 397-399.

HIGH-TECHNOLOGY SECTOR

The recession in the early 1980s was the impetus for the creation of many state programs to promote high-technology growth. Northern Minnesota counties were the hardest-hit victims of the recession. In 1982, 14,000 of the 15,000 hourly workers employed on the Mesabi iron ore range were laid off. Minnesota iron ore mining was decimated because of the increasing popularity of small cars, the discovery of other taconite iron ore ranges in the Third World, and the use of continuous-casting technology in steel production.[5]

As the market for taconite steel fell through, Minnesota's economy also experienced a decline in agricultural and forestry industry profits. However, Minnesota's population has been well served by a superior public school system. While the University of Minnesota's main campus at Minneapolis may not be a world-class institution, for the last few years the legislature has been putting millions of dollars into the university system to aid high-technology research. In 1984, the Supercomputer Institute alone received over $6 million in state aid. However, the Minnesota High Technology Council believes that high-technology growth may be curtailed by a lack of qualified engineers and scientists graduating from Minnesota's universities.[6]

In the near future Minnesota will probably have to concentrate upon developing home-grown high-technology companies. The very high personal and corporate income taxes of Minnesota make the relocation of out-of-state companies to Minnesota very unlikely.[7] The challenge to Minnesota is to develop stable high-technology industries that can gain a price advantage through innovation to overcome the naturally high costs of doing business in a state with high taxes, extensive unionization, and hefty transportation costs.

Most of Minnesota's high-technology employment is in two sectors—office/computing machine manufacturing and instruments (Table 5-11). Almost one half of all high-technology jobs are office/computing machine industry jobs. Moreover, four of the seven industries surveyed had less than 500 employees each. High-technology employment is a substantial portion of Minnesota manufacturing employment and the computer industry is a substantial part of Minnesota's high-technology sector.

Table 5-12 demonstrates the importance of private-sector R&D in Minnesota. Minnesota receives far more of its R&D dollars from industry and nonprofit sources than other states. Seventy percent of the relatively meager amount of federal R&D funds that find their way to Minnesota are Defense Department dollars (Table 5-13). It is not surprising that Minnesota is not a predominant center for R&D nationally since it has a small population and consequently a small number of scientists and engineers (Table 5-14).

TABLE 5-11
High-Technology Manufacturing Employment
in Minnesota and Percentage Change, 1972, 1977, and 1982
(employees in 1,000s, change in %)

	1972		1977		1982
	Emp.	Change	Emp.	Change	Emp.
Drugs	.2	150.0	.5	0.0	.5
Industrial organic chemicals	—	—	—	—	.2
Office/computing machines	19.0	24.2	23.0	42.4	33.6
Electronic components	4.1	56.1	6.4	15.6	7.4
Aircraft & parts	.2	100.0	.4	25.0	.5
Missiles/space vehicles	—	—	—	—	—
Instruments	9.8	40.8	13.8	28.9	17.8
Total high-tech emp.	35.2	44.4	51.4	31.5	67.6
All manufacturing	263.5	14.4	301.5	1.0	304.4
Percentage of high-tech	13.5		17.0		22.0

Note: Statistics for some industry groups are withheld to avoid disclosing figures for individual companies. Also, the above table does not account for auxiliary employment in Minnesota manufacturing sectors which accounted for nine percent and twelve percent of manufacturing jobs in 1977 and 1982, respectively. Auxiliary employees include design engineers, production planners and administrative personnel who provide support services to the company as a whole. Minnesota's large percentage of auxiliary manufacturing employment may reflect the preponderance of corporate headquarters in the state.
Source: U.S. Department of Commerce, Bureau of the Census, *1982 Census of Manufactures, Minnesota State Report* , pp. 8-13; idem, *1977 Census of Manufactures, Geographical Area Statistics*, pp. 24.10-24.17; idem, *1972 Census of Manufactures, Geographic Area Statistics*, pp. 24.8-24.12.

TABLE 5-12
Federal Obligation for R&D by Performer in Minnesota
and Share Compared to the United States, 1983
($ million and %)

Performer	Funds	Share	U.S. Share
Federal facilities	27.3	6.1	27.1
Industry	316.9	70.7	49.1
Universities	75.0	16.7	18.8
State & local government.	1.8	0.4	4.5
Nonprofit	27.4	6.1	0.5
Total	448.2	100.0	100.0

Source: National Science Foundation, *Federal Funds for Research and Development*, vol. 33, 1984, p. 142.

106

TABLE 5-13
Share of Federal Obligations for R&D in Minnesota
by Agency Source Compared to the United States, 1983
(%)

Agency	Minnesota Share	U.S. Share
Agriculture	3.1	2.2
Commerce	0.1	0.9
Defense	71.2	61.0
Energy	1.2	12.0
Health & Human Services	17.6	11.5
Interior	2.2	1.0
Transportation	0.3	0.9
EPA	1.3	0.6
NASA	0.5	7.0
NSF	2.5	2.8

Source: National Science Foundation, *Federal Funds for Research and Development*, vol. 33, 1984, p. 150.

TABLE 5-14
Employed Scientists and Engineers
in Minnesota, and Percentage of United States Total, 1982
(in 1,000s and %)

	Minnesota	United States
Scientists	29.3	2.1
Engineers	32.2	1.7
Total	61.2	1.9

Source: National Science Foundation, *U.S. Scientists and Engineers 1982*, 1984, p. 81.

Science and Technology Policy

HISTORICAL ACCOUNT

Minnesota began funding scientific research as early as 1911, when the state legislature established a research facility at the University of Minnesota now known as the Mineral Resources Research Center. This early commitment of state funds to promote economic growth via research and development is an example of the close relationship between the private and public sectors in Minnesota. Seventy years later, private businessmen have important roles to play in Minnesota's high-technology policy through their participation in, and sometimes control of, economic priority-setting bodies like Minnesota Wellspring, Minnesota Business Partnership, and the Minnesota High Technology Council.

Two men in particular have taken the lead in formulating high-technology development policy in Minnesota. William Norris, the single most important private actor in policymaking, is the former chief executive officer of the Control Data Corporation. Norris has been particularly influential in devising the original 1981 and 1982 state programs. Governor Rudy Perpich, the most important public-sector actor, adopted high-technology development as a campaign platform in 1981. Perpich's leadership fostered the creation of several more programs in 1983.[8]

Minnesota appears to have enthusiastically adopted high-technology development as a key policy issue. Much of the substance of the state's recent efforts can be traced to a 1981 report from the Task Force on Technology Intensive Industries. The task force was appointed by the commissioner of the Minnesota Department of Economic Development, with representatives from several high-technology corporations and the University of Minnesota's Institute of Technology. The report from the task force emphasized the importance of high-technology industry "working in harmony with other parts of the economic system—parts that include state government, educational institutions, tax policies, the public regulatory policies, business leaders, labor leaders, and many more."[9] The report goes on to state that Minnesota should not only be adequate but "superior in providing the conditions necessary for continued growth of our technology intensive industries" due to the stiff competition from the Sunbelt and New England. The tone of the report is urgent; the message is that something drastic needs to be done immediately. Specific suggestions of the task force include improving the state education systems, improving technology development and transfer, reforming tax structure and policies, and improving understanding of business and industry's role in society.

Minnesota offers over two dozen high-technology programs spanning a range of institutions and a variety of structures. But while there may be an abundance of enthusiasm in Minnesota, there is also a marked lack of coordination. The Governor's Office of Science and Technology (GOST) began to address this issue toward the end of 1985. An ad hoc advisory committee to GOST was appointed to develop guidelines to deal with the problem. A more formal committee, the Governor's Technology Coordination Committee, was created to consider statewide strategies for the economic future of Minnesota.[10]

Not only coordination within the state but coordination among northern states is emerging as an issue for Minnesota. Border concerns are particularly important. Of the five metropolitan statistical areas in the state, only two lie entirely within it—Rochester, home of the Mayo Clinic, and St. Cloud. Duluth and Minneapolis-St. Paul are shared with Wisconsin, while Fargo-Moorhead is shared with North Dakota.

Minnesota's relationships with its neighboring states reflect Governor Perpich's relationships with the governors of Wisconsin and South Dakota. In an effort to avoid battling other northern states in the same economically strained situation as Minnesota, Governor Perpich made a pact in 1983 with Governor Tony Earl of Wisconsin to help each other's states in education and in business.[11] On the western border, though, the relationship is not as friendly. According to one author, Governor William Janklow of South Dakota and Governor Perpich are "fighting an open and bare-knuckles border war over corporate recruiting."[12] Perpich declared a no-raid policy for Minnesota, prohibiting government and business leaders from recruiting, unsolicited, out-of-state corporations. Janklow, on the other hand, has sent several raiding parties into Minnesota to lure companies into South Dakota.[13]

HIGH-TECHNOLOGY POLICY

Minnesota's programmatic efforts to develop high-technology within the state incorporate three main objectives: improvement of the University of Minnesota, incubation of high-technology businesses, and private-sector involvement in policymaking.

Improvement of the University of Minnesota

There are nine different technology development centers in the University of Minnesota system. Some are quite old, like the Mineral Resources Research Center, the Agricultural Extension Service, and the Particle Technology laboratory, founded in the mid-1950s. Others, like the Microelectronics Center and the Supercomputer Institute are high-profile, new programs with budgets between $2.5 and $6 million per year.

Incubation of High-Technology Businesses

Only one of the many small business incubation services in Minnesota receives public funding—and even this service receives St. Paul funds, not state government dollars. The Control Data Corporation runs nine Business Technology Centers throughout Minnesota. Small businesses should be able to find adequate capital funding since Minnesota is the seventh largest source of venture capital in the nation.[14]

Encouragement of Private-Sector Involvement in Policymaking

The oldest organization founded to specifically link the private business community with public policymaking concerns is the Minnesota Business Partnership (MBP). The MBP is a unique example of the relationship between business and government in Minnesota. It was founded in the late 1970s by a number of chief executive officers. The MBP realized that government must be an equal partner in shaping the economy of Minnesota—that the "free market" is a thing of the past. Also, business people must realize that they have a social responsibility to assure the continued economic health of the greater community—being solely concerned with private profit-making is a dangerous thing.[15] While MBP does not concentrate upon high-technology growth, but rather concerns itself with Minnesota's general economic health, a similar organization, the Minnesota High Technology Council, is primarily concerned with high-technology matters. It is particularly concerned with the state of high-technology educational services. Both organizations have overlapping memberships and share basic societal concerns.

Minnesota Wellspring is another example of nongovernmental interest co-opting into policymaking. This economic advisory council was also founded in the recession of the early 1980s. Its main feature is the combination of four separate interest groups into one planning body. Labor, the business community, state government officials, and academics share control of the Wellspring, although it is chaired by Governor Perpich.

MAJOR STRATEGIES

Minnesota has employed a variety of strategies to implement the state's high-technology development objectives. These strategies include policymaking mechanisms, business incentives, training and incubation, university training and research, university-industry relations, and research activities of state agencies. Specific components are listed below.

Policymaking or Coordinating Mechanisms
 • Office of Science and Technology — Created in 1983, this office attempts to coordinate other government high-technology programs and devise long-term goals.
 • Minnesota Business Partnership — Private organization, discussed above.
 • Minnesota Wellspring — Public and private program, discussed above. Receives no direct state funding, although it is housed in state office space and the salaries of its executive director and his assistant are paid by the state. Collects membership fees and donations.
 • Minnesota High Technology Council — Private organization, grew out of a University of Minnesota Institute of Technology advisory committee. Its main purpose is to encourage educational improvements that can improve the technological skills of Minnesota's work force.

Business Incentives for Technological Innovation
 • Technology transfer tax credit — Allows up to 30 percent of net value of technology transferred to be credited for qualified small businesses locating in the High-Technology Corridor project area.
 • Contribution tax credit — Allows 50 percent of first $50,000 contributed to a small business assistance office/innovation center to be credited.

Training and Incubation
 • Business Technology Centers — A Control Data Corporation incubation service run for profit.

• Help-Start-A-Company — A Minnesota Business Partnership program to loan out experienced executives to small companies.

• Minnesota Educational Computing Corporation (MECC) — Not-for-profit public corporation that distributes and develops educational software nationwide. MECC was originally a state-funded agency that regulated computer acquisitions in Minnesota's public school system.

• Total Information Services (TIES) — Has a purpose similar to MECC, but is operated on a smaller regional scale. It is run by a joint board representing fifty-three school districts and intermediate-level vocational schools to distribute software only within the state.

University Training and Research

• University of Minnesota's Technology Research Centers — Concentrates university technical resources in particular areas. Among the centers are the Natural Resource Research Institute (located in Duluth), the Microelectronic and Information Sciences Center (Minneapolis), and the Supercomputer Institute (Minneapolis).

University-Industry Relations

• University Research Consortium — A private corporation that markets the consulting services of university faculty members.

• Microelectronic and Information Sciences Center — Receives a significant portion of its funding from private grants to perform contractual research.

• Minnesota High Technology Corridor — Enterprise zone development that will geographically link the Minneapolis campus of the University of Minnesota campus and downtown Minneapolis. The Supercomputer Institute will be housed there. The Corridor has received over $6 million in funding and land grants from the University and the City of Minneapolis. No target date for completion has been set yet.

Research Activities of State Agencies

• Office of Science and Technology — Responsible for providing state assistance to promote the development of medical technology.

• Agricultural Extension Service — Run out of the university system, attempts to perform basic research as well as consulting work. The agency operates a data base for agriculture in the state called EXTEND.

Program Assessments

The following four programs were more closely evaluated: The Governor's Office of Science and Technology (GOST), Microelectronics and Information Sciences Center (MEIS), Minnesota Educational Computing Corporation (MECC), and Minnesota Wellspring. These programs were chosen from among thirty other public-private partnerships, trade organizations, educational organizations, incubator services, and government agencies that in some way affect high-technology in Minnesota. Criteria used in the selection process included the age of the program, the overall significance of the program, and its uniqueness in comparison to other programs nationwide. The goal was to present to the reader an enlightening mix of different types of programs.

Conclusions are based upon inspections of publicly available documents about the respective programs, telephone interviews, and personal interviews. The interviews concentrated upon high-level administrative personnel and staff. Unfortunately, no internal evaluations of the four programs were available, nor any comprehensive independent evaluations.

MICROELECTRONIC AND INFORMATION SCIENCE CENTER

The Microelectronic and Information Science Center (MEIS) is a program of the University of Minnesota. This section describes MEIS's history, goals, and functioning, as well as issues and questions related to MEIS as a model program for the development of science and technology.

Legislative History and Goals

The Microelectronic and Information Science Center, like several other high-technology programs in Minnesota, is the product of a William Norris idea. Norris, by his own admission an ardent believer in cooperative research among universities, industry, and government, cites MEIS as a prime example of how cooperation can work successfully to "create and transfer new knowledge more efficiently and to better train more people in critical disciplines."[16]

In 1980, four companies—Control Data Corporation, Honeywell, Inc., Sperry Corporation, and 3M—approached the Institute of Technology at the University of Minnesota with a proposal for a Microelectronic Information Sciences Center. With the proposal came contributions from the companies totaling $6 million. By the following year, MEIS was formed and reviewing research proposals at the University of Minnesota. The state did not provide any funding until the 1983-1985 biennium, but state fiscal support has continued since then.[17]

Wallace Lindeman, director of MEIS, claims that current conditions require cooperation between business and academia. Laboratory equipment is so expensive and science is becoming such a complex discipline that cooperation offers a means of efficiently and effectively channeling limited resources.[18] MEIS exists to bridge the gap between the University of Minnesota and high-technology industry in the state by advancing cooperative research. MEIS also recruits and trains graduate and postgraduate students in the microelectronic and information sciences.[19]

The objectives of the MEIS-sponsored research are "the nucleation of strategic research interests" and the launching of "research programs of international recognition" to promote the University of Minnesota and the state as a whole as international competitors in high-technology research and

112

development.[20] The attraction of substantial private matching funds is seen as the key to achieving MEIS's research objectives.

Administration and Implementation

MEIS is one of nine Centers of Excellence within the Institute of Technology at the University of Minnesota. Its staff consists of a director, an associate director, two secretaries and two part-time staff members. When MEIS was formed, an advisory council was created to review proposals and make awards. However the advisory council, composed of industry and university representatives, was a part of the university rather than an objective, independent board. Subsequently, the council removed itself from the university to gain independence. The advisory board is now known as the Minnesota High Technology Council (MHTC) and has been successful as a lobbying group for improved education in the state, especially science and technology related education. MEIS's advisory council was replaced by the Management Board and the Technical Coordinating Committee, both of which have representatives from each sponsor corporation as well as from the university.

In 1985, the sponsoring companies had expanded from the four founding companies to include four associate sponsors: ADC Telecommunications, Inc., Cray Research, Inc., VTC Incorporated, and Zycad Corporation. The four founding corporations remained the center's only source of funding until 1983, when the state allocated $1.2 million through 1985, and another $1.35 million from 1985 to 1987. MEIS was able to obtain $6 million from other sources in 1985.

MEIS has spent its money in a variety of ways other than direct grants for research. In 1983 MEIS sponsored a visiting professorship and a special course in the Department of Chemical Engineering and Materials Science. MEIS has also sponsored a series of seminars in the Department of Chemistry involving physicists, materials scientists, engineers, and chemists. In the Department of Computer Sciences, MEIS has funded the development of courses in artificial intelligence. Funds were provided for modifications of the electrical engineering building and for maintenance of the laboratory in that building. Many different departments of the University of Minnesota have benefited from MEIS funding.[21]

MEIS relies on the lobbying efforts of the dean of the Institute of Technology (IT) and the university president to obtain funding from the state legislature. However, MEIS is administratively and functionally separate.[22] IT helps coordinate faculty members from the different departments for the cooperative research funded through MEIS; the university administration channels the state appropriation to MEIS. Those funds are applied to research projects—four major programs receive $300,000 each and six to eight "seed fund" projects receive $20,000 each. The smaller projects require more money than the $20,000 granted by MEIS; therefore, the faculty members must find matching funds.

Assessment of Goal Attainment

MEIS's basic function is to fund research projects dependent upon cooperation among faculty members from different disciplines and industry researchers. MEIS hopes these cooperative efforts will place Minnesota on the cutting edge of technological discovery. MEIS must attract funding and brain power and coordinate projects with industry scientists. How can MEIS's effectiveness be measured?

Before this question can be addressed, an explanation of MEIS's three-to-five-year program cycle is necessary. The process begins with proposals of research projects and arrangements for entering graduate students to participate as research assistants. The research proceeds and the students progress through their course work. At the end of the cycle, the students graduate and the research begins to yield results. The new PhDs enter the workplace and generate new ideas for cooperative research, which in turn attract and involve new students, and the cycle repeats.

The first MEIS projects were funded in 1982, so in 1986 MEIS was still in its first cycle. The first round of doctoral students (numbering seventeen) graduated in 1986. MEIS had published thirty-four technical reports by 1985, but there were no claims of marketable products attributable to the research funded at that date.

Lindeman believes that for MEIS to support the caliber of research necessary to gain national and international ranking, the state must commit a minimum of $5 million to the center. The 1985-1987 figures fall far short of that amount. If MEIS is to recruit out-of-state graduate students to its program, then it must compete with Stanford, Berkeley, and MIT. In order to compete, MEIS must have funding to provide competitive fellowships, salaries, and state-of-the-art equipment.[23] At present, MEIS is not nationally competitive in any of these arenas.[24]

The basic function of industry-university research support is bridging the gap between academic and industrial scientific activities. If MEIS is meeting this goal, then industry scientists should be found performing experiments with professors in university laboratories and professors should be doing the same in private laboratories.

This is not quite the case. Some industry involvement exists. Industry representatives serve on MEIS management and advisory boards; however, their opinions are secondary to those of the university representatives.[25] Some industrial facilities are open to faculty members, and there is at least one case of faculty use. Two scientists from Honeywell are actively involved in advising researchers in a MEIS research project at the university. During the summer, students serve internships with sponsor companies. Industry-university interaction exists, but true cooperative research remains the exception rather than the rule for MEIS.[26]

Among strategists of Minnesota's high-technology development, MEIS is seen as an important university-industry link.[27] However, no single group has made the development of MEIS a primary goal. MHTC continues to lobby for MEIS and is very supportive of the center's work, but MEIS is just one of several programs MHTC is promoting in the legislature. The University of Minnesota is the flagship college of the state and the only state university; MEIS does not appear to be the flagship program of the Institute of Technology.[28] The research performed through the medical school at the university gains more attention than MEIS, probably because the medical research has resulted in several marketable medical instruments. MEIS's research differs in nature from medical research because MEIS's researchers are not also practitioners. The lack of marketable results may account for MEIS's low priority on policymakers' agendas.

Issues and Questions

MEIS is a young program in need of greater funding; however, MEIS's model has potential for establishing significant university-industry links in states other than Minnesota. MEIS is not a university department, but a consortium that coordinates researchers and resources with a minimum of staff. Several programs have adopted the MEIS structure. Lindeman claims that the Colorado Advanced Technology Institute was modeled after MEIS. MEIS is also the model for a broader consortium recently established in Minnesota known as the Minnesota Technology Development Institute (MTDI). MTDI is a regional coordinating entity, bringing together resources from nine midwestern states.

The MEIS model is spreading; the concept is a solid one. However, MEIS has several obstacles to overcome. MEIS requires cooperative research among university faculty members from different departments. Often, faculty members resist working on projects in which credit must be shared with others. If an exceptionally competitive atmosphere exists, cooperative research may be almost impossible to foster.

Cooperative research between industry scientists and university researchers may also prove difficult to establish. Industry researchers are under pressure to create marketable results within a reasonable amount of time, while academic scientists are more interested in the long-term quest for knowledge. Tangible products may not be a priority with university scientists. The goals of the two groups differ and are not always easily reconciled or coordinated.

MEIS must continue to obtain support in terms of funding and participation from the private sector. Minnesota has a history of widespread involvement of the private sector in state policy issues. Populist politics in Minnesota is unique because Minnesotans become involved to enhance government's role, not limit it. Attitudes change with time, but the attitude in Minnesota has fostered deep private investment in cooperative efforts. Can Minnesota's level of involvement be duplicated elsewhere?

MINNESOTA EDUCATIONAL COMPUTING CORPORATION

Minnesota Educational Computing Corporation (MECC) is a state-owned, nonprofit corporation that produces software and educational courseware (packages of software and curriculum materials) for kindergarten through twelfth-grade students.

History and Goals

When MECC was created in 1972 by the Minnesota legislature, the initials stood for Minnesota Educational Computing Consortium, and the officials were charged with providing computer educational services and enhancing educational opportunities throughout the state. MECC is the nation's oldest producer of instructional software for microcomputers.[29]

In the early 1970s, small personal computers were not on the market, only large mainframe computers; therefore, computer procurement involved large sums of money. MECC was able to evaluate school needs and find the most appropriate and adaptable computer system for each school district. MECC was cast in a regulatory role for the state due to the consortium's expertise in computers. By 1975, 95 percent of Minnesota's school districts had access to mainframe computers through remote terminals as a result of MECC's activity.

Even though MECC was producing educational courseware, its regulatory role absorbed the majority of its time and energies. However, as the less expensive, less complicated personal computers evolved, MECC's expertise became less important; the consortium's regulatory role evolved into a brokerage role. School districts put in their requests and MECC procured and distributed the hardware.

Coincidental with MECC's movement away from a regulatory role was its expansion in courseware development. In 1978, MECC created its first software for microcomputers, and by 1985, MECC's catalogs advertised over 300 software products. With product expansion came client-base expansion. By 1980, MECC's products were available beyond Minnesota's borders, and in its 1984-1985 annual report, MECC boasted 220 institutional members in forty-nine states and on six continents.[30] In-service training, a consulting "help line" and an annual conference for computing professionals and educators have become part of MECC's offerings. Software packages for school administrators in accounting, payroll, and budgeting are among the newest MECC products along with educational products tailored for home use.

MECC expanded from a 2-staff office in 1973 to a 123-staff corporation by 1985. In May 1984, MECC converted from state consortium status to state corporation status as a result of its substantial success. The conversion means that MECC no longer receives state funds. As a state corporation, MECC is no longer subject to the state's bureaucratic hiring and purchasing policies. Any profits MECC generates go not into the state treasury but directly back into MECC. However, the governor appoints MECC's board of directors. MECC must now compete for state contracts through Minnesota's Department of Education. Since 1984, MECC has won five of the seven contracts for which it has bid.

Despite the fact that corporation status places MECC in a more competitive environment, Richard Pollak, the director of special projects, believes the move was necessary for MECC's continued growth.[31] MECC was not at liberty to hire particular individuals without observing tedious government-required procedures. In a field as specialized and individualized as software development, the state's somewhat prosaic hiring practices meant lost opportunities in acquiring important talent. Purchasing requirements were just as cumbersome, in that any purchase over $50 was subject to the competitive bidding process. And for a consortium that is product-focused (as contrasted to service-focused), time is money. The cumbersome purchasing procedures were an obstacle to MECC's growth.

MECC's considerable success as a state-funded entity posed political problems that further spurred a change in MECC's formal relationship to the state government. Legislators (and others) began to wonder if MECC's success and growth were due to overfunding; businesses felt that MECC's protected status as a state-funded office created an unfair competitive edge in the instructional software development arena.[32]

Administration and Implementation

In FY 1985-1986, the Minnesota Educational Computing Corporation was not yet two years old but still thriving despite the absence of all state funds. It employed 108 full-time and 12 part-time persons and operated with an annual budget of $7.2 million.

A nine-member board of directors appointed by the governor of Minnesota oversees MECC. The president coordinates MECC's five divisions: software, which designs and develops classroom software; marketing, which analyzes educational trends and devises marketing strategies; administration, which oversees MECC's internal operations and administrative computing applications; services, which provides client support and quality assurance; and special projects, which explores emerging technological trends in computing and education.

MECC distributes its products through a variety of packages tailored to clients' resources and levels. Institutional memberships allow a state or school district to purchase courseware systems and legally reproduce them for one year. Catalog sales allow for direct single-item purchases, and dealers and distributors afford broader public access to MECC's products on a retail basis.

Attainment of Goals

To better assess MECC's attainment of its goals, it is important to review the corporation's objectives. According to MECC's president, the goals are "superior service to customers, corporate growth, and improvement of educational computing in Minnesota, across the country, and around the world."[33] MECC measures its own success by whether or not it remains self-sustaining. If product sales remain high enough to support or even expand the corporation, then MECC will know it is adequately servicing its customers. And the more customers, the greater the proliferation of its educational software. MECC appears to be meeting its goals. Its budget expanded $1.2 million in two years (from 1984 to 1986).

In terms of MECC's particular mandate—to enhance computer education and equality of education throughout the state—the expansion from two staff persons to over sixty times that number is a robust indicator of its success. However, assessments of MECC's impact on the overall development of high technology in Minnesota are less straightforward. If MECC's role in the strategy is enhancement of the state's educational infrastructure, then Minnesota's high national rank in terms of high school graduates is an indicator of MECC's effectiveness. No direct evidence like comparative scores on computer literacy exams is available, but given its length of service—over a dozen years—MECC is likely to have had a positive impact on the quality of primary and secondary education in the state.

However, if MECC's role in Minnesota's high-technology development strategy is the active shaping of educational policy around emerging technological and industrial needs, then it has not been successful. Several different groups in Minnesota actively develop strategy for the state's economic development, targeting high technology as a promising sector; MECC is not one of those groups. When asked to evaluate MECC's impact on high-technology development in the state, Herb Johnson, chairperson of the Minnesota High Technology Council (MHTC) was not familiar with the program. Johnson's comment carries special significance because one of MHTC's fundamental purposes is to improve primary and secondary public education.[34] When Cindy Christ, the associate director of the Governor's Office of Science and Technology, was asked to list the five most significant programs in terms of their role in the development of high-technology in Minnesota, MECC was not on the list.[35] When a legislative analyst researching economic development programs for the Minnesota House of Representatives was asked for an "outsider's" evaluation of MECC, he had only cursory awareness of its existence and did not relate it to the active development of high-technology.[36]

One possible reason for MECC's low profile could be its lack of impact on the quality of education in the state, but the evidence presented on MECC's length of service and range of client base—all 423 school districts in Minnesota—indicates otherwise. Another possible reason for MECC's low profile is its function as a provider of educational tools and not as a lobbying force in the legislature. MECC is not involved in educational *policy*, but in educational *products*. Noneducators like Herb Johnson and Cindy Christ have little cause to be familiar with MECC. Therefore, its impact on the state may be more subtle than other high-technology programs. Its asset as a program may be more in terms of improvement of Minnesota's image nationwide, especially within the education community. Because it distributes its products nationally, MECC provides an understated means of associating Minnesota with the cutting edge of educational technology. MECC advances Minnesota's reputation as a "brain state." Widespread computer technology in public schools may increase Minnesota's attractiveness to executives with young families. The resulting expanded, improved labor pool is more attractive to potential immigrating corporations.

Issues and Questions

How well does MECC serve as a role model for high-technology development? In terms of funding, the example of a state-funded agency that is so successful that it becomes self-sustaining in eleven years is one that other states would want to pattern their own programs after. Legislators would be much more willing to fund small consortia if they anticipated self-sufficiency as an eventual outcome.

But a weakness in the funding aspect of MECC is the nature of the corporation's client base, that is, public schools. Public schools usually have scant resources that become even more limited during periods of economic contraction. Product prices must remain affordable to public schools, yet MECC must be able to cover the costs of product development. If production costs increase, but school budgets do not, MECC could experience a decline in demand, resulting in an inability to remain self-sustaining.

Regarding short-term impact, a program such as MECC may not serve as a means of overtly attracting other high-technology firms to a state and so may not appeal to policymakers. The immediate effects of such a program are neither quickly apparent nor easily measurable. Long-term prospects are more promising. In an age when computers are as common as typewriters, a computer-literate work force can only enhance a state's attractiveness to prospective high-technology companies. Likewise, a superior public-school system may facilitate recruitment of talented professionals with young children.

Finally, in terms of product, can similar programs set up in other states compete with MECC? Has it, with at least 33 percent of all courseware sales, cornered the market on educational software?[37] MECC is the largest distributor of educational software in the nation and invests 60 percent of its resources in new product development so that its clients will renew their yearly contracts.[38] Imitative programs may find the competition prohibitive.

Improved public education is a solid goal for economic development; as a long-term educational program, MECC has potential. However, as a long-term high-technology development program, MECC shows no direct impact on state industrial growth.

MINNESOTA WELLSPRING

Legislative History and Goals

In a document entitled *Minnesota Wellspring: A Call for Action*, 1986, Wellspring is described as "an alliance of business, labor, government, education, and agriculture, formed to strengthen Minnesota's economy through effective public policies and public/private cooperation."[39] This alliance consists of prominent state leaders in all the aforementioned sectors who meet periodically to discuss the reports of various Wellspring research committees or task forces. These leaders issue policy recommendations primarily directed to the legislature.

Wellspring was formed in 1981. In that year Minnesota was suffering from the recession of the early 1980s. Farm prices were dropping, and some basic Minnesota industries such as pulp and paper processing, grain processing, and taconite iron ore mining were declining. Nineteen eighty-one was also a bad year for state government. Governor Albert Quie and the legislature had overestimated tax revenues, so there was a large budget deficit. It is impossible to conclude that any of these factors were directly causal, but as a whole they created an environment of concern that readied Minnesota for the role of Wellspring.

Staff members at Wellspring report that one of the most important factors that won respectability for Wellspring was the evident cooperation of the original co-chairs, Raymond Plank and David Roe. Raymond Plank is the chairman and chief executive officer of the Apache Corporation and a prominent political conservative. David Roe was the president of the Minnesota AFL-CIO. These two have very different political backgrounds and were respected representatives of distinct and sometimes antagonistic groups.[40]

Wellspring demonstrated its stability when the original honorary chairman, Governor Quie, left state office in 1982. The new governor, Rudy Perpich, accepted the post of honorary chairman immediately. It was important to Wellspring that the governor of Minnesota demonstrate approval of Wellspring's place in policy formulation by serving as its honorary chairman. Wellspring staffers are confident that even if Governor Perpich should lose his reelection bid in 1986, the new governor will also have to recognize Wellspring's importance and serve as its honorary chairman.[41]

Wellspring is concerned about the general economic health of Minnesota and does not limit its activities to the promotion of new industries like advanced-technology companies. During its five-year existence Wellspring has issued policy recommendations and published research on the farm crisis, hostile corporate takeover bids, the promotion of economic innovation, tax reform, community-based economic development centers, venture capital formation, energy production, and education. However impressive this list appears, it is crucial to realize that there are many issues on which Wellspring takes no stand for fear of dividing its diverse membership. For instance, Wellspring sought only to inform the general public about, not lobby for or against, the governor's study commission's report on tax reform in 1985. Wellspring formed COMPETE (Citizens of Minnesota Proposing Equitable Tax Enactment) to set up a speaker's bureau and disseminate information about the proposed income tax cuts, but professed neutrality about the the issue itself.[42]

Administration and Operation

Wellspring has only three nonvolunteer staff members. These are Edward Hunter, the executive director, his assistant, and one secretary. All three are state employees loaned to Wellspring free of charge. Mr. Hunter is a member of the State Planning Agency, and his involvement in Wellspring helps coordinate Wellspring's economic development plans with future state government initiatives.[43]

The executive director helps set a general agenda for Wellspring to consider. Periodically, Wellspring's forty-member board of directors meets to consider the reports of commissions and task forces. This was the primary method of decisionmaking at Wellspring until 1983. In that year a small (ten-member) policy board was formed to supplement the board of directors. This policy board is now the primary forum for decisionmaking. However, since so many different interest groups are represented within its membership Wellspring is far from dictatorial.[44]

Probably the most active and visible members of Wellspring are its co-chairs; these are two volunteers who are elected to manage the operations of Wellspring along with the executive director. In 1985 two new co-chairs were elected to succeed Plank and Roe. One is the chief executive officer of a local telecommunications firm who has served as chairman of the Minnesota High Technology Council. The credentials of the other new co-chair combine the fields of labor organization and education—he has been the executive secretary for the Minnesota Federation of Teachers and an elementary school teacher.[45]

Over half of Wellspring's roughly $200,000 budget comes from grants by the State Planning Board. After funneling back this grant money to pay its borrowed state employees, Wellspring has only $100,000 a year to spend on publications, the sponsoring of public events, and research.[46] In 1986-1987 Wellspring will seek to expand its staff while also achieving a greater degree of independence from state government. Some people appear to view Wellspring as being biased because of its close ties to the state. The consortium also hopes to obtain a general grant of $50,000 from the state legislature in FY 1986-1987. Part of that money will be used to make the executive director a full-time employee of Wellspring. Since the present executive director is also a member of the State Planning Agency, he can only devote part of his time to Wellspring. Wellspring's goal is to demonstrate that it is an independent institution beyond the pale of public-sector activities.[47]

Attainment of Goals

Wellspring is in a transitional phase. Its first five years centered around demonstrating its worth to other policymakers in the state.[48] In the future, Wellspring will try to develop a tighter focus upon its policy recommendation work by concentrating its lobbying and research efforts on a few specific issue areas.

Wellspring has two main limitations. First, it cannot investigate and lobby for controversial issues that may split the consortium. Recognizing this weakness, Wellspring is attempting to make its policy agenda more specific. It is hoped that with a narrower field of interest, discussions can become more focused and technical so that friction between the various interest groups will lessen. A more focused agenda may also increase the lobbying influence of Wellspring.[49]

Wellspring's other major limitation is its close connection with state government. This creates a perceptual problem—people do not feel that Wellspring is independent of the State Planning Board. However, this problem does not seem to decrease Wellspring's ability to attract vital private-sector leaders like William Norris, Chuck Denny, and Raymond Plank into its ranks.[50] Perhaps some hard-core cynics believe that Wellspring is only an arm of the State Planning Board, but it has an impressive record of getting its ideas accepted by the legislature, such as the Midwest Technology Development Institute.[51]

Issues and Questions

Wellspring faces limitations in terms of both funding and staff. All participants in Wellspring are volunteers except for those state employees who must balance their work for Wellspring with their other state government jobs.[52] Half of Wellspring's funds come from the State Planning Board. Wellspring is seeking to double its private fund-raising and obtain a $50,000 annual membership fee from state government.[53]

Given that Wellspring has no specific clientele base, it can best be assessed by examining its success or failure in having its policy recommendations adopted and the degree of cooperation it has created among its member interest groups. As noted above, Wellspring's policy recommendations have had a significant impact upon state policymaking. It is more difficult to determine the degree of cooperation Wellspring has fostered. However, from evidence at hand it can be concluded that the program's continued existence and steady growth are indicative of interest-group cooperation. The smooth transition of co-chairs in late 1985 also seems to indicate consensus among the membership.

GOVERNOR'S OFFICE OF SCIENCE AND TECHNOLOGY

Legislative History and Goals

The Governor's Office of Science and Technology was created in 1983 by Governor Rudy Perpich. Despite its name, GOST only operated under direct gubernatorial control for the first six months of its existence. Since October 1983 it has been located in the the state Department of Energy and Economic Development. The purpose of the office is to serve as "the permanent locus within state government for the coordination and development of technology initiatives and policy recommendations."[54] Though this description seems to imply that GOST is a decisionmaking center for all state technology development programs, it does not actually perform this function.

GOST appears to have two main objectives. First, it acts as a clearinghouse for inquiries about the role of science and technology in Minnesota. Second, it maintains close ties with public and private economic development organizations, the scientific community, and trade organizations in advanced-technology industries. Interacting with organizations like the Minnesota High Technology Council, the Minnesota Business Partnership, and Minnesota Wellspring enables GOST to promote and evaluate technologically driven growth in Minnesota.

GOST's primary political support comes from Governor Perpich and Democratic legislators in the state Senate. However, GOST has political opposition in the state House of Representatives, where Republican conservatives have attempted to cut its budget in the 1985 legislative session and eliminate it altogether in 1986.[55]

As its name implies, GOST is not only concerned with high-technology. GOST seeks to improve all sectors of Minnesota's economy by promoting the application of science and technology to traditional, not just emerging, industries.[56]

Administration and Operations

Not counting the staffs of the above subsidiary organizations, GOST employs four full-time workers, three professionals and one clerk. With this small staff GOST writes and distributes numerous pamphlets and booklets—some simply public-relations material and some invaluable guides to Minnesota's high-technology sector. GOST's main purpose is not to perform independent research projects that make policy recommendations on state government programs. GOST is a coordinating and outreach program. The database on "technologically intensive" businesses in Minnesota is indicative of GOST's somewhat dull, but useful goals—to inform rather than advise, and to communicate with rather than lead.[57]

During the 1986 legislative session it became evident that the state would have to cut appropriations made the previous year in order to avoid a deficit. GOST, like all offices in the state department of Energy and Economic Development, was forced to shave its operating budget by 10 percent. However, GOST and other technology development programs were spared substantial budget cuts, unlike other parts of the Department of Energy and Economic Development.[58]

Assessment of Goal Attainment

GOST's work as a publicity generator and information gatherer are important. GOST is also valuable because it provides quick and easy access for entrepreneurs to state government. Its efforts to establish close ties with the private high-technology development organizations is appreciated by Minnesota businessmen because GOST is tangible evidence that Governor Perpich is concerned about economic growth in advanced-technology sectors.[59]

Conclusions

The four programs presented in this study illustrate Minnesota's efforts to encourage private-sector involvement in high-technology development strategies and programs. In some cases, the programs were initiated by business and then adopted by state government; in others, the programs were state-initiated but became less state-controlled over time. The majority of Minnesota's public and private endeavors in high-technology development are directed at creating and fostering home-grown companies. People in Minnesota have a sense of being isolated from the rest of the nation and are aware of the difficulty of attracting companies away from New England and the Sunbelt. Minnesota has adopted strategies that encourage technology transfer and provide a better-trained labor force.

There is no program coordination in Minnesota. The programs were not created as components of a central strategy; rather, they are products of timely ideas. The only area of overlap, however, is in policymaking bodies, such as Wellspring and GOST. Much of the private-sector energy and enthusiasm is channeled into planning Minnesota's economic future. The effects of overlap and lack of coordination are minimized by the presence of the same individuals on several different boards overseeing the various programs. GOST works to enhance the existing informal communication system among programs by providing a single, common representative on as many boards as possible.

Geographic impact is an important dimension of Minnesota's high-technology programs. Minnesota is divided into two states—the metropolitan area of the Twin Cities, including surrounding towns and suburbs, and the greater-Minnesota area. MECC is the best example of a program serving the entire state. Virtually all Minnesota school districts subscribe to MECC, so that even the rural areas are being exposed to educational software. Communities outside the Twin Cities do not benefit directly from increased funding of MEIS research. All the industries involved in cooperative research are in the metropolitan sector. Wellspring's focus is statewide due to its five-part coalition; because of the coalition, Wellspring's goals must remain sensitive to the rural sector. The Office of Science and Technology does not omit rural high-technology programs from its list of state resources; however, the majority of people interested in the information GOST has to offer are from the Twin Cities. Out of the four programs evaluated, at least two affect the rural as well as the urban regions of the state.

Frequently, a young program in Minnesota will separate itself from its institution of origin in order to impact and respond more dynamically to changes in state policies. In each case, the move away from the founding institution has been to allow the program greater flexibility in function and purpose. State government would transform an idea into a cohesive group working on some aspect of high-technology development. But the state has not had to maintain support and responsibility for the incubated programs in at least two cases. Once the group develops a strong identity and sense of purpose reaching beyond the institution to which it was originally connected, the group becomes independent.

A common feature of Minnesota's programs is dependence upon volunteer time. The time and energy of volunteers provide direction and substance to high-technology development programs. MEIS must rely on industry scientists to become involved in cooperative research in capacities more active than advisory. Wellspring's task forces are all comprised of volunteers. State government is not the prime mover for technology development in Minnesota's economy. Of the four programs analyzed above, only the Governor's Office of Science and Technology can legitimately be called a state office.

Minnesota's programs also share the handicap of newness. All four programs have been in their current structure for less than ten years. They are still experimental; none has been tried and tested by environmental changes (with the exception of MECC). Each program has done little research, if any, on the effectiveness of its own strategy for developing high technology; even so, the strategies remain in place.

Overall, high technology remains on the policy priority list in Minnesota. Loss of significant industries in the state, such as farming and mining, the presence of several high-technology company headquarters, the flow of ideas from the private sector, and the election of a high-technology-oriented governor have provided the momentum for the development of high-technology industry in Minnesota. This momentum has found expression in a variety of programs, but concrete, measurable impact has yet to emerge as the result of these programs' existences.

NOTES

1. Donald T. Feeney, "Minnesota," *American Demographics* 6 (Fall 1984): 36.
2. James Rowen, "Midwest Survival of the Fittest," *Across the Board* 20 (June 1983): 22.
3. Minnesota Council of Economic Advisors, hereafter CEA, *Economic Report to the Governor, 1986.*
4. CEA, *Economic Report, 1986.*
5. "Iron Mining Sinks on the Mesabi," *Business Week* (July 26, 1982): 28. Also, see Peter J. Kakela, "Factors Influencing Mine Location: An Iron Ore Example," *Land Economics* 58, 4 (November 1982): 524-536, for an excellent discussion about how taconite iron ore mining went bust, boomed, and went bust again in Minnesota in the space of about fifteen years. The author makes clear how insignificant state economic incentive policies were in the face of a sudden technological change in iron ore extraction.
6. Wilbur Maki and Hossein Akhavipour, *The Role of Technology Intensive Industry in Minnesota*, Minnesota High Technology Council, December 1984. Pamphlet.
7. "The Lower Cost of Backaches," *Forbes*, November 1983, 95. However, it is encouraging to note that through the efforts of Governor Rudy Perpich and like-minded individuals the Minnesota state legislature made substantial income tax rate cuts in 1985.
8. Interview with Charles M. Denny, president and chief executive officer, ADC Telecommunications, Minneapolis, January 13, 1986; interview with Herbert C. Johnson, chairman, MHTC, Minneapolis, January 17, 1986.
9. See *Report to Commissioner of Economic Development on Technology Intensive Industry in Minnesota and its Future*, St. Paul, January 1981, 1-14.
10. Telephone interview with Cynthia Christ, assistant director, Office of Science and Technology, December 11, 1985.

126

11. Rowen, "Midwest Survival of the Fittest," 22.
12. Ibid. The situation has cooled somewhat since this article was written. According to an April 11, 1986, letter from Jayne Khalifa, director of the Governor's Office of Science and Technology, the battle with Janklow is no longer an issue.
13. Interview with Christ, St. Paul, January 13, 1986.
14. Organization for Economic Cooperation and Development, *Venture Capital in Information Technology,* Paris, 1985, 19.
15. Judson Bemis and John A. Cairns, "In Minnesota, Business Is Part of the Solution," *Harvard Business Review* (July-August 1981): 85-93.
16. William C. Norris, "Cooperative R&D: A Regional Strategy," *Issues in Science and Technology* 1, 2, Winter 1985: 92-102.
17. Ibid.
18. Interview with Dr. Wallace Lindeman, director, MEIS, Minneapolis, January 14, 1986.
19. Ibid.
20. IT, *MEIS Program Review,* 11.
21. IT, *MEIS Program Review,* 5-10.
22. Interview with Lindeman.
23. Ibid.
24. In a letter from Lindeman, April 11, 1986, he states that the exception to this statement is MEIS's fellowships, which *are* nationally competitive.
25. Interview with Dr. Martha Russell, associate director, MEIS, Minneapolis, January 17, 1986. Lindeman states, in a letter dated April 11, 1986, that the industry representatives' opinions are given equal weight.
26. Lindeman states that "at the moment a truly cooperative program utilizing both university and industry personnel and faculties is being organized." Letter dated April 11, 1986.
27. Interview with Denny.
28. Interview with Dr. Margaret Dewar, Humphrey Institute, University of Minnesota, Minneapolis, January 16, 1986; interview with Denny.
29. Minnesota Educational Computing Corporation, *MECC Report, 1984-85,* St. Paul, 1986, 4.
30. *MECC Report,* 5.
31. Interview with Richard Pollak, director of special projects, MECC, St. Paul, January 15, 1986.
32. Interview with Pollak; telephone interview with Christ, December 5, 1985.
33. *MECC Report,* 3.
34. Interview with Johnson.
35. Interview with Christ, St. Paul, January 17, 1986.
36. Interview with Doug Wilson, legislative analyst, Minnesota House of Representatives, St. Paul, January 17, 1986.
37. *MECC Report,* 6.
38. Interview with Pollak.
39. Minnesota Wellspring, *Minnesota Wellspring: A Call for Action, 1986,* St. Paul, 1985.
40. Interview with Lis Christianson, assistant to executive director of Wellspring, St. Paul, January 13, 1986.
41. Ibid.
42. Ibid.
43. Ibid.

44. Ibid.
45. Minnesota Wellspring, *Minnesota Wellspring Update, October 1985.* Pamphlet.
46. Minnesota Wellspring, *Minnesota Wellspring Recommended Annual Budget Revised May, 1984.* Photocopy.
47. Minnesota Wellspring, *A Call for Action,* 1986.
48. Interview with Christianson.
49. Ibid.
50. Ibid.
51. Interview with Christ. Ms. Christ gave us information about Wellspring's legislative record.
52. Interview with Christianson.
53. Minnesota Wellspring, *A Call for Action, 1986.*
54. Governor's Office on Science and Technology, *High Technology in Minnesota: A Directory of Programs, Policies and Services,* St. Paul, August 1985.
55. Interview with Wilson.
56. Interview with Jayne Khalifa, director, Governor's Office of Science and Technology, and Christ, St. Paul, January 13, 1986.
57. Ibid.
58. Telephone interview with Christ, April 15, 1986.
59. Interview with Denny.

6

New York has been active in the area of technology policy since 1963 when the New York State Science and Technology Foundation (NYSSTF) was created by the legislature. NYSSTF differs from most governor's or legislature's science and technology advisory board in its operations. The NYSSTF programs (described later in this chapter) are comprehensive, innovative, and more ambitious than most other states' science and technology programs. Policymaking, politics, economics, and the attractiveness of high-technology are intertwined in the history and functioning of New York's science and technology policy. The wide range of educational institutions, infrastructure resources, existing industries, and supporting activities make New York a fertile environment for economic growth. Recognizing these advantages, New York's policymakers believe high-technology industry development represents the best opportunity for the state to capitalize on existing resources and to participate fully in the emerging economy. The NYSSTF is designed and functions as a "catalyst for the development of new technologies, wherein scientific discoveries evolve into commercially viable processes and products, and thus benefit the economy of the entire state."[1] Later in this report, several New York programs will be profiled. It is useful to begin with a comparison of the state's demographic, economic, and high-technology industry characteristics to those of the nation.

Demographic and Economic Profile

POPULATION CHARACTERISTICS

In 1970, nearly 10 percent of the entire population of the United States lived in New York. Although that percentage had dropped by 1980, New York is still the second most populous state in the nation. While the country's population grew by 11.4 percent in the 1970s, New York's population declined by 3.7 percent. And even though New York's population has again been growing in the early 1980s, its increase of 1 percent lags behind the nation's 4 percent between 1980 and 1984 (Table 6-1). The age distribution of New York reflects a slightly younger population than that of the nation. (Table 6-2).

— This chapter was written by Harald Fischer and Amy Miriam Peck.

TABLE 6-1
Population of New York and Percentage Change
Compared to the United States, 1970, 1980, and 1984
(in 1,000s and %)

	New York	New York Change	U.S. Change
1970	18,237	—	—
1980	17,558	-3.7	11.4
1984	17,735	1.0	4.1

Source: U.S. Department of Commerce, Bureau of the Census, *1980 Census of Population,* vol. 1, part 34, p. 29.

TABLE 6-2
Age Distribution in New York
Compared to the United States, 1970 and 1980
(%)

	1970		1980	
Age Group	New York	United States	New York	United States
0-19	35.3	37.8	30.3	32.0
20-44	31.8	31.7	36.1	37.2
45-64	22.1	20.6	21.2	19.7
65+	10.8	9.8	12.3	11.3

Source: U.S. Department of Commerce, Bureau of the Census, *1980 Census of Population*, vol. 1, part 34, p. 79.

TABLE 6-3
Urban and Rural Composition of New York
Compared to the United States, 1970 and 1980
(%)

	1970		1980	
	New York	United States	New York	United States
Urban	85.7	73.6	84.6	73.7
Rural	14.3	26.4	14.3	26.3

Source: U.S. Department of Commerce, Bureau of the Census, *1980 Census of Population*, vol. 1, part 34, p. 29.

TABLE 6-4
Racial Distribution in New York
and the United States, 1980
(%)

	New York	United States
White	79.5	83.1
Black	13.7	11.7
Other	6.7	5.1

Source: U.S. Department of Commerce, Bureau of the Census, *1980 Census of Population*, Vol. 1, Part 34, p. 71.

In 1980, 84.6 percent of New York citizens, or 10.9 percent more than the national average, lived in urban areas, largely in New York City (Table 6-3). A relatively large number of minorities live in New York; the state has 2 percent more blacks than the nation, and 1.5 percent more members of other minorities—mostly Chinese, Filipino, Japanese, and Indian (Table 6-4). Most minorities live in New York City.

Educational Structure and Manpower Resources
Although New York is the home of some of the best academic institutions in the world, a 1982 study conducted by the Batelle Columbus Laboratory identified a number of spot shortages, especially in the various fields of engineering.[2] These shortages are not due to the quality of the state's academic institutions; rather, one problem lies in the "brain drain" that afflicts the area.[3] Factors such as the opportunity to live and work in more pleasant climates, a high rate of personal income tax in New York, and perhaps the environment of some cities in the state foster this condition.[4] At present New York State seems to be well endowed in terms of the professional and technical capabilities needed to support high-technology industries: it possesses an excellent pool of craftsmen and skilled workers as well as a sufficient number of technical personnel.[5] But according to the Batelle study, these skilled workers are moving closer to retirement and are not being replaced through current training programs.[6]

THE ECONOMY OF THE STATE

The dominant economic sector in New York, as measured in relative employment shares, shifted from manufacturing, the largest sector in 1972, to services, which had the largest percentage of employees in 1982 (Table 6-5). The relatively high share of the finance, insurance, and real estate sector (9.2 percent) reflects that New York State, especially New York City, is the world's financial center.

132

TABLE 6-5
Nonagricultural Employment and Share in New York State by Sector,
1972, 1977, and 1982, and Percentage Change between 1972 and 1982
(employees in 1,000s, shares and changes in %)

| | 1972 | | 1977 | | 1982 | | 1972-1982 |
	Emp.	Share	Emp.	Share	Emp.	Share	Change
Mining	7.0	0.1	6.9	0.1	6.4	0.1	- 8.5
Construction	272.3	3.8	190.2	2.7	213.8	2.9	-21.4
Manufacturing	1,602.2	22.7	1,459.6	21.2	1,361.8	18.8	-15.0
Trans.	472.8	6.0	425.3	6.2	421.9	5.8	- 1.3
Wholesale & retail	1,445.0	20.5	1,427.6	20.8	1,454.3	20.1	0.6
Finance & insurance	591.3	8.4	577.8	8.4	670.5	9.2	13.3
Government	1,243.9	17.6	1,270.8	18.5	1,289.7	17.8	3.6
Services	1,404.0	19.9	1,499.5	21.8	1,815.8	25.1	29.3
Total	7,038.5	100.0	6,857.6	100.0	7,234.1	100.0	2.7

Source: U.S. Department of Labor, Bureau of Labor Statistics, *Employment, Hours, and Earnings, States and Areas, 1939-82*, vol. 2, pp. 30-53.

The national recession of the 1970s was particularly severe in New York State: between 1972 and 1982, total state employment increased by only 2.77 percent, whereas total national employment increased by 22.3 percent. Moreover, the increase in New York was considerably slower than the nation as a whole in every sector—in fact, three sectors that increased nationally showed a decline in New York: mining, construction, and transportation. It should be noted, however, that the most serious decline occurred in the middle of the past decade—an absolute decline of 2.57 percent in total employment between 1972 and 1977—while the 1977-1982 period showed growth (5.49 percent).

The manufacturing industries in New York are relatively balanced, with no specific industrial concentration or specification in any one industry (Table 6-6).

Those with the highest employment shares in 1982, that is, printing/publishing (13.2 percent), electrical equipment (12.6 percent), and electrical machinery (10.8 percent), with the exception of the apparel industry (13.4 percent), are relatively high value-added industries, a sign of relative sophistication.

But the growth rates of these industries reflect the same weak economic development mentioned above: only one industry, measuring instruments, grew significantly (16.1 percent) between 1972 and 1982. Two industries, printing/publishing and electrical equipment, were almost stagnant (1.8 and -0.1 percent, respectively), and all other industries took steep or even very steep falls in terms of absolute employment.

TABLE 6-6

Manufacturing Employment and Share by Industry in New York State,
1972, 1977, 1982, and Percentage Change between 1972 and 1982
(employees in 1,000s, shares and changes in %)

	1972 Emp.	Share	1977 Emp.	Share	1982 Emp.	Share	1972-1982 Change
Nondurable							
Food/kindred	92.3	6.1	75.2	5.4	66.1	5.2	-28.2
Tobacco	—	0.3	0.2	—	—	—	—
Textile	55.6	3.6	43.0	3.1	28.7	2.2	-48.3
Apparel	247.3	16.3	214.4	15.4	171.5	13.4	-30.6
Paper products	50.7	3.3	46.1	3.3	48.7	3.8	-19.1
Printing/ publishing	164.9	10.9	154.3	11.1	168.0	13.2	1.8
Chemicals	53.1	3.5	51.6	3.7	48.7	3.8	- 8.2
Petroleum refining	—	2.0	0.1	2.1	0.2	—	—
Rubber & plastic	37.1	2.4	34.5	2.4	32.7	2.5	- 8.2
Leather	39.8	2.3	29.3	2.1	24.4	1.9	-38.9
Total nondurable	740.8	49.0	651.1	47.0	583.2	43.3	-21.3
Durable							
Lumber & wood	17.6	1.1	14.8	1.0	—	—	—
Furn, & fixtures	28.3	1.8	24.2	1.7	22.9	1.8	-19.0
Stone, clay, glass	36.0	2.3	31.2	2.2	26.5	2.0	-26.3
Primary metal	56.4	3.7	53.3	3.8	37.9	2.9	-32.8
Fabricated metal	92.9	6.1	83.0	6.0	76.5	6.0	-17.6
Nonelectric machinery	135.1	8.9	133.3	9.6	137.6	10.8	- 1.8
Electrical equip.	161.0	10.6	148.6	10.7	160.8	12.6	- 0.1
Trans. equip.	69.8	4.6	73.5	5.3	57.4	4.5	-17.7
Instruments	96.4	6.3	100.6	7.2	112.0	8.8	16.1
Miscellaneous	79.1	5.2	70.0	5.0	57.0	4.4	-27.9
Total durable	772.6	51.0	732.8	52.9	688.6	56.6	-10.9
Total mfg.	1,513.4	100.0	1,509.9	100.0	1,271.6	100.0	-15.9

Note: Some statistics are withheld to avoid disclosing data for individual companies.
Sources: U.S. Department of Commerce, Bureau of the Census, *1982 Census of Manufactures, Geographic Area, New York*, pp. 10-18; idem., *1977 Census of Manufactures, Geographic Area Statistics*, pp. 33.12-33.21.

In New York State, more people are employed in managerial and professional occupations and in technical, sales, and administrative support occupations than on the average in the nation (Table 6-7). Correspondingly, the number of people working in production, craft, and repair occupations and as operators and laborers is lower than the national average.

TABLE 6-7

Occupational Structure in New York State
for Employed Persons Sixteen Years and Over
Compared to the United States, 1980
(workers in 1,000s and %)

	New York Workers	Share	U.S.Workers	Share
Managerial and professional	1,911.0	26.7	22,151.6	22.7
Technical, sales and admin.	2,495.1	35.5	29,593.5	30.3
Service	1,031.9	13.9	12,629.4	12.9
Farming, forestry and fishing	95.1	1.8	2,811.3	2.9
Production, craft and repair	777.6	10.4	12,594.2	12.9
Operators and laborers	1,131.1	15.2	17,859.3	18.3
Total	7,440.7	100.0	97,639.3	100.0

Source: U.S. Department of Commerce, Bureau of the Census, *1980 Census of Population,* vol. 1, ch. C, part 34, p. 155.

Both in 1972 and 1977, the state's unemployment rate was higher than that of the nation. But despite the job losses New York suffered between 1972 and 1982, its unemployment rate in 1982 was lower than the national average: 8.6 percent and 9.7 percent, respectively—a circumstance partly due to outmigration and partly to the economic recovery (Table 6-8). The fact that the state's unemployment rate in 1982 was lower than in 1977 confirms the findings about the impact of the recession on New York State: the situation in 1982 was worse than in 1972, but better than in 1977.

The decline in total employment also resulted in an increased number of people living in poverty: in 1980, at a time when the national average was decreasing, 13.4 percent of the population in the state was living below the poverty level—50.5 percent more than in 1970 (Table 6-9).

Despite this huge increase, per capita income in the state between 1970 and 1980 more than doubled. By 1984, it was over three times the amount it had been in 1970, and 11.8 percent higher than the national average. In 1984, then, income in the state was less evenly distributed than in 1970 (Table 6-10).

HIGH-TECHNOLOGY SECTOR

A high level of research and development (R&D) activity exists in both New York universities and industries. New York ranks second in R&D expenditures among the states included in this report. In receiving federal R&D obligations in 1983, New York ranked third among the states; on a per capita basis, however, New York ranked only sixteenth. Only a small portion (2.3 percent)

TABLE 6-8

Unemployment Rate in New York State
and in the United States, 1972, 1977, and 1982
(%)

Year	New York	United States
1972	6.9	5.6
1977	9.4	7.1
1982	8.6	9.7

Source: U.S. Department of Labor, Bureau of Labor
Statistics, *Handbook of Labor Statistics*, 1985, p. 96;
U.S. Department of Commerce, Bureau of the Census,
Statistical Abstract of the United States 1978, p. 408.

TABLE 6-9

Individuals below the Poverty Level in New York State
Compared to the United States, 1970 and 1980
(%)

	New York	United States
1970	8.9	13.0
1980	13.4	12.1

Source: U.S. Department of Commerce, Bureau of the
Census, *1980 Census of Population*, vol. 1, ch. C, part
34, p. 29; idem, *1970 Census of Population*, vol. 1,
part 34, p. 1371.

TABLE 6-10

Per Capita Income and Percentage Change in New York
Compared to the United States, 1970, 1980, and 1984
(income in $, change in %)

	New York	Change	United States	Change
1970	4,695	—	3,945	—
1980	10,242	118.1	9,494	140.7
1984	14,318	39.7	12,789	34.7

Source: U.S. Department of Commerce, Bureau of Economic Analysis, *1984
Survey of Current Business*, p. 18; idem, Bureau of the Census, *Statistical
Analysis of the United States 1984*, p. 457.

of these funds went to federal performers such as federal laboratories, whereas the shares received by industry and universities (65.3 and 27.1 percent, respectively) were considerably higher than the national average (49.1 percent and 18.8 percent, respectively, see Table 6-11). The relatively small proportion of federal obligations from NASA (only 1.0 percent) reflects the nominal presence of aerospace industry in the state (Table 6-12).

In 1982, the employment share of high-technology industries in New York was substantially higher than that of the nation—23.8 percent and 16.5 percent, respectively. The growth rate of those industries in the state, however, was significantly slower than the national average (Table 6-13).

A comparison of the employment growth rates of all manufacturing industries yields an interesting result: whereas the whole manufacturing sector showed steep declines in growth (10.2 percent between 1972 and 1977 and 5.7 percent between 1977 and 1982), the industries characterized as high-technology exhibited remarkable growth rates.

TABLE 6-11
Federal Obligations for R&D by Performer in New York
and Share Compared to the United States, 1983
($ million and %)

Performer	Funds	Share	U.S. Share
Federal facilities	57.7	2.3	27.1
Industry	1,649.0	65.3	49.1
Universities	685.2	27.1	18.8
State & local government	33.2	1.3	4.5
Other	98.1	3.9	0.5
Total	2,523.2	100.0	100.0

Source: National Science Foundation, *Federal Funds for Research and Development*, vol. 33 , 1984, p. 142.

TABLE 6-12

Share of Federal Obligations for R&D in New York
by Agency Source Compared to the United States, 1983

(%)

Agency	New York Share	U.S. Share
Agriculture	0.9	2.2
Commerce	0.2	0.9
Defense	62.3	61.0
Energy	12.2	12.0
Health & Human Services	18.2	11.5
Interior	0.2	1.0
Transportation	0.5	0.9
EPA	0.1	0.6
NASA	1.0	7.0
NSF	4.3	2.8

Source: National Science Foundation, *Federal Funds for
Research and Development,* vol. 33, 1984, p. 150.

TABLE 6-13

High-Technology Manufacturing Employment in New York State
and Percentage Change, 1972, 1977, and 1982

(employees in 1,000s, change in %)

	1972 Emp.	Change	1977 Emp.	Change	1982 Emp.
Drugs	16.4	10.3	18.1	- 7.7	16.7
Industrial organic chemicals	8.8	-19.3	7.1	-22.5	5.5
Office/computing machines	—	27.3	33.9	31.2	—
Communication equipment	46.5	-10.9	41.4	23.4	51.1
Electronic components	45.1	- 7.2	44.6	28.0	57.1
Aircraft & parts	27.2	13.6	30.9	- 5.5	29.2
Missiles/space vehicles	0.4	—	—	—	—
Instruments	96.4	4.3	100.6	11.3	112.0
Total high-tech employment	243.8	9.1	266.0	13.8	302.8
All manufacturing	1,513.4	- 0.2	1,509.9	-18.7	1,271.6
Percentage of high-tech	16.1	17.6	23.8		

Note: Statistics for some industry groups are withheld to avoid disclosing
figures for individual companies.
Source: U.S. Department of Commerce, Bureau of the Census, *1982 Census of
Manufacturing, Geographic Area Series: New York,* pp. 10-18; idem, *1977
Census of Manufactures, Geographic Area Statistics,* pp. 33-12.

138

Science and Technology Policy

New York, like its New England neighbors, has always been home to a combination of agriculture and industry. The state's system of colleges and universities, both public and private, has a long and distinguished record of educating the state's youth. And, last but very important, the cooperative-competitive relationship between New York City and the rest of the state affects nearly all politics and policy developments in Albany, the state capital. These points have influenced the development of science and technology policy in New York State.

HISTORICAL ACCOUNT

Prior to the formulation of an explicit state science and technology policy, New York financially supported basic research in higher education institutions and had in place a solid agricultural extension service. As explained below, the first steps the state took in the 1960s were to expand and focus state aid to university research. Yet neither existing policy for agriculture or university support was used as a model for New York State's current science and technology policy.[7] Rather, the state's efforts seemed to develop out of economic, political, and national concerns.

In 1959, as part of the widespread change in the attitude of American citizens and public officials toward the importance of science, the recently elected New York governor, Nelson A. Rockefeller, established the State Advisory Council for the Advancement of Industrial Research and Development. This council brought together forty-four scientists, educators, and industrial researchers "to promote industrial research, the seedbed of modern growth industry."[8]

But the council did not assume the strong leadership role that Rockefeller had intended for it. In his 1963 State of the State address, he proposed a "greater emphasis on improving the quality and quantity of research and development activities and an all-out dedication to assure economic growth."[9] Rockefeller's early gubernatorial years were a time of affluence, and he was determined to "point the way to industrial expansion and increased job opportunities," not only for New Yorkers but for all Americans.[10]

When Rockefeller signed the New York State Science and Technology Foundation (NYSSTF) into existence on April 20, 1963, the original purpose of the foundation was twofold: to stimulate R&D and to promote scientific and engineering education.[11] In 1964, the state legislature appropriated $500,000 to the foundation and confined its purpose to "attracting leading scientific and technological educators to join the faculties of the state universities and to foster and support the already impressive state scientific education structure."[12]

In the early years, the foundation's board of directors was very active. Executives from Corning, IBM, AT&T, and GE served on the board along with the state's commerce and education commissioners. The foundation sponsored symposiums on topics ranging from air pollution to human biology, and grants in the $50,000 range were made to institutions, even though the foundation lacked any organized programs to disburse funds. In the early 1970s, the economy of both the country and the state began to falter, and the interest of people and politicians in science and technology to wane.

By the time Governor Rockefeller had made his curious way to the vice presidency under Gerald Ford in 1973, his "indulgent" policies had placed New York's economy at serious risk.[13] Rockefeller's lieutenant governor Malcolm Wilson lost the election in November of 1974 to the Democratic challenger, Hugh Carey.

One of the new governor's first actions to "cut bureaucracy" was to remove Rockefeller supporters from patronage positions; funding for the board of the Science and Technology Foundation was terminated.[14] Six months later, in August 1975, Carey established the Economic Development Board to encourage economic growth and attract jobs to the state.[15] The sparks that generated this move were the bankruptcy and default crisis of New York City, the state's failed attempt at assistance, and the eventual federal bailout. By that time, "the business climate had become so poisoned that a . . . survey gave the Empire State undisputed last place for 'attractiveness of business climate.'"[16] The recession hit New York harder in 1975 than elsewhere in the nation, and Carey spent the next five years trying to get New York's "public and private economies in order."[17] When massive economic growth plans were defeated by both the legislature and the public, Carey began to focus his efforts on expanding the private sector.

Not until 1979 was the tactic of encouraging the creation and expansion of high-technology industries used to try to enact a more comprehensive state approach to economic development. The innovative suggestion grew from the failure of the governor's director of economic affairs' High Technology Opportunities Council. Created in 1978, it met only once in early 1979.[18] The Assembly leader, Democrat Stanley Fink, and the Senate Leader, Republican Kenneth LaValle, picked up the high-technology opportunities idea and, with the assistance of the Assembly's Program Development Group (PDG), developed and floated in the legislature a series of five bills "to aid companies by providing scientific and management services, referring investors, and securing federal and state grants."[19] In 1980, the Speaker and the PDG held a conference entitled Growth Industries for New York's Future for the members of the legislature, and the Legislative Commission on Science and Technology was created.[20]

The commission, however, was ineffective in pushing Fink and LaValle's agenda. In his 1981 State of the State address, Carey called for state efforts to expand dynamic industries in New York State; to have the state "lead the second industrial revolution as it lead the first."[21] The assembly established the Task Force on University-Industry Cooperation and the Promotion of High

Technology Industries. With the state on its soundest economic footing in over a decade, the task force, with assistance from the governor's office, convinced the legislature to finally pass a comprehensive high-technology policy for the state.

It was intended that the new New York State Science and Technology Foundation, reconstituted as a public authority by the legislature in April 1981, would spur the development of high-technology industry in the state.[22] Therefore, the newly appointed foundation's board of directors' first action in late 1981 was to contract with Batelle Columbus Laboratories for a major study to "assist the foundation in assessing the job creation potential for expanding industries and activities linked to new and evolving technologies, and to provide a strategy for the attraction and expansion of these activities."[23] The study was completed in 1982.

The study reviewed over a hundred high-technology industries according to growth potential, market and supply relationships, market and utility size, and overall feasibility.[24] Twenty manufacturing industries and one service industry were identified as the most desirable high-technology activities. For the identification of new technology industries, over 250 industries were reviewed, using criteria of likelihood of commercialization within five years, economic feasibility, employment impacts, technical impacts, and overall societal benefits.[25] Most of the thirteen new technologies identified fell into two general groups: electronics-information and medical-biological.

Specifically, the study suggested the foundation establish programs that would focus on three goals: (a) retention of existing strengths; (b) expansion of high-technology sectors, and (c) attraction of new industry to New York State. Many of the programs recommended by the study are now in place.

MAJOR POLICY COMPONENTS AND STRATEGIES

The New York State Science and Technology Foundation's efforts focus on improving and enhancing relationships between business, academia, and government. A primary strategy is to encourage technology transfer, that is, turning laboratory innovations into profitable commercial goods and services. The foundation, a government entity, functions as a conduit between business and academia, pursuing mutually beneficial relationships and advocating linkages between research and entrepreneurial efforts, thereby promoting successful technology transfer. The ultimate goal of the foundation is economic development and growth.

Another strategy employed by the foundation is to provide business incentives. Through various programs, the state supplies or helps to locate the funds and/or facilities for research projects that have potential but are not being actively explored. The programs promote and assist entrepreneurs in areas like marketing, grantsmanship, production, and worker training.

The foundation's six major programs are intended to fill gaps and break barriers. The Corporation for Innovative Development (CID) fills the funding gap that exists for early-stage and startup technology-based industries by leveraging private investment capital. By providing this business incentive, CID helps attract newcomers to the technology-based sector of New York's economy.

The Centers for Advanced Technology (CAT) overcome the barriers that normally exist between basic and applied research. By improving the relations between industries and university researchers, the CATS have contributed to the growth of technology-based industry in the state.

The Research and Development Grants (R&D Grants) fill the gap between applied research and commercialization by providing financial support. The R&D Grants program brings together and improves the relations between industry and academia while directly aiding technology transfer.

The regional technology development organizations (TDO) build upon the existing strengths of regional economies by bringing together researchers and businesses to share information. TDOs break the communications barrier that normally results from the competitive nature of high-technology industries.

The Small Business Innovation Research (SBIR) program fills two gaps: the information gap of how best to write proposals for funding under the federal SBIR program and the funding gap that occurs between the completion of federal SBIR Phase I and the awarding of Phase II contracts. This program provides an incentive for participation in federal SBIR, which helps attract and retain new technology-based industries in the state. (See the appendix for further description of this program.)

The Productivity Development Program (PDP) brings together non-technology-oriented businesses with technology-oriented problem-solvers to improve the production of goods and services. The program makes previously inaccessible technological advances more available with help the state's overall economy. (See the appendix for further description of this program.)

Since its reconstitution, the New York State Science and Technology Foundation's responsibilities have grown to meet the needs of the state. The legislature and the governor have developed additional programs for the foundation to implement. Consequently, the foundation's overall budget and number of professional staff have increased (Table 6-14).

The NYSSTF's dozen staff members administer and coordinate the six programs mentioned above. The staff also prepares for the meetings of the board, studies policy options for the board and the governor, and provides incidental technical assistance, But most important, the staff enhances the foundation's linkage with other economic development units in New York's public and private sectors.

TABLE 6-14
Development of the NYSSTF between 1981 and
1985: Funding, Programs, and Staff

Fiscal Year	Funding in $	Number of Programs	Staff Level
1980-81	270,000	1	5
1981-82	650,000	1	7
1982-83	1,300,000	5	7
1983-84	3,200,000	6	10
1984-85	9,800,000	8	11
1985-86	13,300,000	12	14

Source: In-house information of the New York Science and Technology Foundation, used for presentations.

Program Assessments

Of the programs implemented by the NYSSTF as part of the New York State science and technology policy, four programs are assessed here:
• the Centers for Advanced Technology,
• the Regional Technology Development Organizations,
• the Research and Development Grants Program, and
• the Corporation for Innovation Development Program.

The criteria used in the selection process concerned the programs' age, size, and uniqueness. The programs selected have been in existence for more than three years. The size of the budgets and number of participants and staff for the selected programs are relatively large. Finally, some of the chosen programs are examples of nontraditional policy approaches.

As far as is known, none of the four programs has yet been evaluated by an independent body. The CAT program underwent a semiformal evaluation by the foundation in September 1985. The TDO program's staff members did an informal evaluation of the TDOs in the summer of 1985. Both the CID and R&D Grants programs are constantly being evaluated.

The assessments that follow are based on a review of the foundation's literature on the programs and on interviews conducted in Albany and New York City in January 1986 with individuals from the private sector, the legislature, agencies of the state, program participants, and the foundation staff.[26]

CENTERS FOR ADVANCED TECHNOLOGY

Under the Centers for Advanced Technology (CAT) program, the foundation provides funds for technology-focused R&D centers at the public and private institutions of higher education in New York State. When enacted in 1982, the CAT program's stated purpose was "to foster active collaboration between industry and academia in the areas of basic and applied research . . . to realize the potential growth that new technologies represent in shaping New York's economy in the years ahead."[27]

The legislative history of the CAT program is intertwined with the establishment of the Center for Industrial Innovation (CII) at Rensselaer Polytechnic Institute (RPI) and the growing understanding of the legislature of the potential of state-sponsored economic development programs. The late president of RPI, George Low, had a vision of what his school could do. After gaining extraordinary commitments from technology industry leaders in the Troy, New York, area to support the equipping and operation of a center for innovation, Low convinced the legislature to provide the additional financial support necessary from the public coffers. With a $30-million construction loan from the New York State Urban Development Corporation, CII was established in April 1982.

At the same time Low was gathering support for his vision, a number of conferences were being held for members of the legislature on the future of high technology in New York State. Bipartisan task forces to study this issue were also being established. Members of the legislature were beginning to believe that the state's universities, especially if linked up with industry, could make a significant contribution to R&D in areas in which the state had significant potential for economic growth.[28]

The legislators knew that they could not provide similar funds to other institutions. Therefore they developed the CAT program, allowed for limited technology-targeted funding, and precluded any additional state funding for construction purposes. The program had widespread bipartisan support when it was established in April 1982; the support continued through the selection process and is still enjoyed today.

The CAT legislation directed the NYSSTF to determine possible technological focuses for the centers. The Batelle report identified eight such areas. In response to the request for proposals, the foundation received nineteen which were reviewed by panels of nationally recognized experts. Ultimately seven CATs were designated (Table 6-15).[29]

Since the CATs have been established, the role of the foundation in the program has diminished. The small staff of the CAT program, a director and an assistant, keep the legislature informed of CAT activities. The staff also helps CAT directors and sponsors by sharing information about other CATs and by bringing the CAT directors together. In addition, they monitor the funding of the CATs, especially matching funds from non-state sources. Each CAT is eligible for up to $1 million from the foundation for each dollar received in corporate contributions. In FY 1984-1985, state funding of the program was $7 million and more than $9 million was contributed by the private sector.

The state and private-sector funds the CATs receive is used to endow professorial chairs, to provide scholarships, to upgrade facilities, and to purchase equipment, all of which, in theory, improve the quality of CAT

144

TABLE 6-15
New York State Centers for Advanced Technology

Institution	Technology Focus	Corporate Sponsor
Columbia University	Computer Hardware	Texas Instruments
Cornell University	Agricultural Biotechnology	General Foods
Polytechnic	Telecommunications	IBM & GTE
SUNY: Buffalo	Health Care Instruments	A.O.-Reichert
SUNY: Stony Brook	Medical Biotechnology	Eli-Lilly, Pfizer
Syracuse University	Computer Software	General Electric
University of Rochester	Advanced Optical Technology	Bausch & Lomb

Source: New York State Science and Technology Foundation, *Centers for Advanced Technology*, 1983, pp. 8-21.

research. The bulk of CAT activities are research projects, the selection and scheduling of which are influenced by the CAT structure. Basic and applied research projects with potential for technology transfer are preferred, and projects with great potential can be "accelerated."[30] In some CATs, representatives from both academia and industry map out the research agenda.[31] Also, formal presentations of research findings are made for CAT sponsors.

Other CAT activities are more informal—corporate researchers are loaned by sponsors to work temporarily with CAT faculty and students; ideas are discussed in forums; students find employment with sponsoring firms; sponsors provide "incidental" assistance to their CAT colleagues. An example of such "incidental" assistance was cited by the Columbia CAT's acting director, Bob Dunne. When a microchip designed by a Columbia CAT project and manufactured in California had a short circuit when tested at Columbia for the first time, a corporate sponsor who happened to be visiting took it back to his company's facilities, fixed it, and had it back functioning in the CAT lab in two days. Without this "incidental assistance," the chip would have been sent back to California for repairs that could have taken weeks.

This combination of formal and informal activities is achieving the state's expressed goal of fostering collaboration. CATs provide a concrete setting for cooperation between the two institutions of academia and industry. Opinions were sought on how well this collaboration is working. According to foundation board member Juliette Moran, before the creation of CATs, relationships with universities were not attractive to most of the private sector and most universities did not want their research agendas influenced by the private sector; CATs have revealed how mutually beneficial friendly relations between businesses and universities can be.[32] The relationship was described as "synergistic" by Columbia CAT sponsor and president of the Fifth Generation Computer Corporation, Jacob Sternberg. "The universities engage in idea-generating activities of interest to industry, and the real world of industry can feed into the university community its needs; each gives to and takes from the other," says Sternberg.[33]

All possible measurements for CAT assessment seem to be flawed. The amount of private funds contributed, often suggested as an indicator of involvement, does not take into account the value of time donated by corporate staff or of use of corporate equipment. Instances of technology transfer might also be thought an indicator of CAT success, yet clear examples of technology transfer or job creation attributable to CAT research are hard to find, although their number is expected to increase in the future. Two often-cited examples of technology transfer are: (a) Columbia CAT's developed DADO technology, a computer architecture of high speed and capacity, being transferred from Columbia to the newly established Fifth Generation Corporation, which will manufacture computers that use DADO; and (b) Syracuse CAT's developed software, which uses NMR, a chemical analysis with applications in chemistry and physics research, being transferred to a firm established to market it.[34]

Another indicator difficult to judge is the impact CATs have had on the state's educational programs in science and engineering by increasing faculty hirings and allowing for new equipment purchases. Quantification is possible, but interpretation is inherently subjective. According to Frank Mauro, secretary to the New York State Assembly, creating CATs is the most significant action taken by the legislature to build New York's "foundation for the future."[35] And Ed Reinfurt of the Business Council of New York State believes that the CAT program has done more than any other initiative to improve the status of the state universities of New York.[36]

Issues

This assessment of New York's CAT program raises a number of issues:

• Public vs. private — In New York State, the oldest and most respected universities are private. The public university system is young and in need of ways to compete with the private, "independent," schools. In New York, both public and private schools receive state aid, but the private schools are better able to gain legislative support for special projects. An acceptable balance between public and private institution involvement and funding in a center's program should be struck. A center's program might also showcase those institutions, public and private, that do not have top-notch reputations in the public arena.[37]

• Geography — Even though it was not a statutory requirement, the seven centers are geographically dispersed throughout the state. This geographic spread has allowed for an increase in public support for the CATs.

• Funding time frame — In the legislation, there is a provision that state funding of CATs is limited to four years. It is widely assumed in Albany that this provision will be changed in the 1986 reauthorization of the program, because all the CATs need and want funding continued. It seems that once such centers are established, they will forever be a part of the state budget. The reasons are political; members want to financially support recognized effective programs.

• Funding by merit — Regardless of the success of a particular CAT's activities, or the relative expense of its technology, all seven are funded at the same level. At the time of the legislation's passage, to have done otherwise would have been politically impossible and practically infeasible. But now there is a move being made to allow variation while still retaining the match. This would allow those with the greatest private-sector support to receive more in state funding.[38]

• Technology focus — The decision to focus the centers on specific technology areas has proved valuable in attracting industry into collaborative activities with academia. But it is widely believed that this was only possible because of the quality and diversity of the higher-education institutions already present in New York.[39] In states where no such base exists, more general technology centers may be a better choice.

• The role of community colleges — The most often-cited criticism of the CATs is the lack of an organized role for the state's many community colleges. The potential to involve them in training students in the skills technology-based industries seek in employees is being ignored.[40] In a few instances, consortiums of New York community colleges are joining CATs to develop such training programs. A clear role for community colleges should be included from the start of a center's program.

REGIONAL TECHNOLOGY DEVELOPMENT ORGANIZATIONS

Under the Regional Technology Development Organizations (TDO) program, the foundation provides funds to establish and fund organizations comprised of a region's business, labor, academic, and government leaders whose activities stimulate, develop, and expand technology-based industry. According to the literature of the foundation, the main reason for establishing this program was to spark economic development by exploiting distinct regional strengths of the state.

The TDO program was enacted as part of Chapter 197 of the Laws of 1981, which reconstituted the foundation as a public authority. The legislators' goal was to focus, improve, and expand existing relationships among regional businesses. Technology seemed to be the right vehicle. Frank Mauro, secretary to the New York State Assembly, explained: "The legislators wanted a retailing concept for the state, because it is so large and diverse; with just a little seed money, the state could create regional promotional tools. . . TDOs."

Grants of $25,000, with a required match by the private sector, were authorized under the program. Continuation grants of $20,000, also requiring a match, are available annually to established TDOs. Since the request for

TABLE 6-16

New York State Technology Development Organizations

TDO	Location
Capital Region Technology Development Council	Albany
Central New York High Technology Council	Syracuse
High Technology of Rochester, Inc.	Rochester
Mid-Hudson High Technology Council	Poughkeepsie
Mohawk Valley Applied Technology Commission	Utica
Northern Technology Council	Potsdam
Western New York Technology Development Center	Buffalo
Regional Industrial Technical Education Council of Long Island, Inc.	Commack

Source: New York State Science and Technology Foundation, *Technology Development Organizations* , March 1985, p. 23.

proposals was first issued in 1982, eight TDOs have been created by the foundation (Table 6-16). Almost all of the New York State Department of Commerce's ten regions have active TDOs. Size and structure of the TDOs vary, but all have representatives from business, academia, government, and labor from their region.

Once a TDO is established, the role of the foundation diminishes. Plans for the year are reviewed, negotiated, revised, and approved by foundation staff. In no way does the state dictate activities to be carried out by TDOs. No state-labeled experts are dispatched to the regions.[41] The program is managed by one person on the foundation's staff.

The formal activities of TDOs vary greatly. They include marketing a region; matching university and industry resources; brokering or finding venture capital funds; establishing incubator facilities; assisting emerging small high-technology businesses; publishing directories; and establishing databases. Choosing and implementing chosen activities is not easy for the TDOs. There are many established groups in the regions, such as chambers of commerce and county economic development agencies, which are already doing various things for industry. The TDOs must overcome parochialism and be careful "to supplement and not in any way supplant these groups' efforts."[42]

The formal activities of TDOs are enhanced by their informal activities. TDO members and staff are matchmakers and favor-askers. For example, an Albany attorney spent many afternoons advising, for free, a new, small firm's owner in Glen Falls, which is more than an hour's drive from Albany, because a member of the TDO asked him to do so.[43] This TDO role is considered important to facilitating regional economic development.

Since the activities and efforts of TDOs are so diverse and no central or comparable records are maintained, no measurements were identified for determining the impact of TDOs; instead, subjective opinions were sought.

According to the program's manager, Lawrence Barker, the state can justify TDO funding as worthwhile "negative leveraging," for the funds prevent freelancing and promote cooperative efforts.[44] And, he added, since regional economic development benefits the entire state, the funding is simply seen as the state paying its fair share of each region's cost of sparking economic development.

Instead of having a statewide structure too large to manage, the TDOs are small and use the close linkages they establish and the regional pride they tap to have positive impact on the regions. According to David Harvey, director of the Capital Region Technology Development Council, "TDOs harness the region's resources for the benefit of the region, and what benefits the region benefits the state."

Issues

This assessment of New York's TDO program raises a number of issues:

• Membership of TDOs — To avoid having the state support business councils, representative regions' higher-education institutions, labor organizations, and government must be included in TDOs. The dynamic of harnessing the regional resources of all four sectors makes the TDOs effective and worthy. One successful New York TDO does this by employing the political skills, tactics, and abilities of a former lobbyist as its executive director.

• Selecting TDOs from RFP submissions — Free from political pressure, the foundation's board is able to select candidates on their merits. But board members must take into serious consideration the question of whether or not a proposed TDO has the support of all the key players in a region. If this requirement is not met, the likelihood for success is diminished.

• "Ingredients" — In some regions, the right "ingredients" for a successful TDO were there; a balanced combination of talent, facilities, capital, and personal enthusiasm. In other regions, they were not. The state decided it was also valuable to establish TDOs in those regions lacking "ingredients," because whatever services the TDOs would offer would be better than none.[45]

• Geography — Even though it was not a statutory requirement, a TDO has been established in nearly every region of the state. Not only does this make the unique services of TDOs available throughout the state, it yields tremendous constituency support for the foundation and encourages industries to locate in all parts of the state.

• Funding on merit — Even though the regions of New York differ in size and needs, the funding for TDOs was designed to be equal for all. There is at present no intention of changing this procedure. This is because those TDOs that desire increased funding for a particular project have so far been successful in obtaining special appropriations from the legislature.

• Funding time frame — Although a TDO in one region was replaced by another, practically all established TDOs have received continuation grants each year. State TDO funding was originally planned to be phased out; for a variety of political and economic reasons, this has not happened. The leveraging of cooperation of the sectors, it is believed, continues best if government remains a financial participant.

• Role of the state — The key to the success of New York's TDO program is the absence of a list of activities developed in the state capital that all TDOs must carry out. This allows the TDOs to be regional, to meet their region's unique needs, and to be pragmatic.[46]

• Staffing of TDOs — The size of staffs and the ratio of professionals to volunteers should be decided by the TDOs, not the state. The willingness of members to devote their time and the scope of the activities will influence and indicate staffing needs.

Involvement of new and small businesses and entrepreneurs. Because the TDO activities go beyond the weekly breakfasts of chambers of commerce, entrepreneurs and small business owners find involvement in TDOs to be valuable. The program makes the groups aware of other state programs and services available to them.

RESEARCH AND DEVELOPMENT GRANTS

The Research and Development Grants (R&D Grants) program was established in 1963 to counteract the "brain drain" of scientists and engineers from New York State and to assist the development of university-based centers of excellence. According to the foundation, this program was highly successful in attracting scientists to the state's research institutions and in leveraging other funds in a six-to-one ratio.[47]

In 1980, with the revitalization of the Science and Technology Foundation, the R&D Grants program was resumed with a new orientation: the new goals of the program are to encourage university-industry collaboration and to stimulate the process of technology transfer by focusing on the applied-research phase of the innovation process. The program is concentrating its support on those university and nonprofit laboratory-based research projects which show a distinct potential for industrial application and commercialization and which are likely to be carried out in cooperation with private firms. The R&D Grants program complements the CAT program: whereas the CAT program is more geared toward fostering basic research, concentrated on a particular field of technology, the R&D Grants program supports applied research primarily with a strong emphasis on fast industrial application and commercialization and addresses a wide variety of technological fields.

150

Operation of the Program

Each year, the foundation solicits proposals for the R&D Grants program to approximately 160 universities and not-for-profit industrial laboratories across the state. The proposals are selected according to the following criteria:

- the project should demonstrate a distinct potential for industrial application and commercialization;
- the project should be carried out in cooperation with a New York State firm, preferably a small business (according to the U.S. Small Business Administration);
- the technological area of the proposal should cover the following areas, although exceptions may be made in cases of unusually strong proposals in other areas:

  - automation & robotics
  - biotechnology (agriculture)
  - computers & information systems
  - computer application & software
  - medical diagnosis & therapy

  - medical instruments & devices
  - optics
  - semiconductors & integrated circuits
  - telecommunications.[48]

Whether a project is based at an "independent" (private) state or city university does not influence the selection process; this is reflected in the awards granted to the different university systems. Although private universities received 45.7 percent more funds than the public universities, the awards in the different years do alternate between the different university systems: whereas the ratio of awards granted to independent and public universities in 1981 was three-to-one, it was the opposite in 1982. The higher quality of the independent institutions due to a longer history, more experience in research as well as higher graduate enrollments may explain these ratios (Table 6-17).

TABLE 6-17
New York State R&D Grants Awards by Recipient

	Independent Universities		Public Universities		Nonprofit Laboratories		Total per Year	
Year	No.	Amount	No.	Amount	No.	Amount	No.	Amount
1981	6	$186,118	2	$55,000	—	—	8	$241,118
1982	1	21,595	3	65,000	—	—	4	86,595
1983	6	153,193	1	25,000	1	$25,000	8	203,193
1984	3	75,000	3	75,000	2	50,000	8	200,000
1985	11	341,000	10	313,000	3	96,000	24	750,000
Total	27	$776,906	19	$533,000	6	$171,000	52	$1,480,906

Source: New York Science and Technology Foundation, *Research and Development Grants Program. Projects for Applied Technology*, January 1985, pp. 9-16, and in-house information of the NYSSTF.

Performance of the Program

Between 1981 and 1985 the foundation received and screened 728 preliminary proposals. Out of these, 147 were selected to be evaluated by the foundation's Research and Review Committee, which recommended a total of 52 grant awards totaling $1,480,906.

Of the twenty-one projects that received awards between 1981 and 1983, eleven succeeded in leveraging industrial support, so the ratio of foundation support to industry support was two-to-one.[49] In addition, one dollar spent by the foundation leveraged $1.2 spent by industry and universities. This is a rather poor result, but progress has been made. In the first year of the program, only 25 percent of the projects receiving R&D Grants awards succeeded in leveraging other funds; in 1983, eight out of nine projects leveraged other funds; in 1985, all of the funded projects succeeded in raising other funds (Table 6-18).

Staff members of the foundation explain that these weak leverage rates are due to the completely different "cultures" that this program tries to bring together, the university and the private sector. Dr. Ozarow, the program manager, points out that the very fact that in 1985 all projects succeeded in finding a cooperating private company is a great success for the program.

Unfortunately, there are only very limited data available on the commercial success or the number of industrial applications of the projects. In early 1985, the foundation published the following evaluation of the programs funded between 1981 and 1983.[50] At the time of the evaluation, twelve projects, supported between 1981 and 1982, had been completed;

TABLE 6-18
Leveraged Funds of the New York State R&D Grants Program

Year	No. of Projects	Foundation Support	No. of Projects Funded	Total Industry Support	University Support	Leverage Rate
1981	8	241,118	2	47,000	142,885	.78
1982	4	86,595	1	15,000	50,874	.75
1983	9	203,193	8	197,581	186,404	1.88
1984	8	200,000	—	—	—	—
1985	24	750,000+	24	564,198	467,976	1.37

+ The dramatic increase of the program's budget from 1984 to 1985 (250 percent) is, according to the program manager, due to additional appropriations from the legislature and the foundation itself. The original budget of the program was only $150,000.
Source: New York Science and Technology Foundation, Research and Development Grants Program, *Projects for Applied Technology* , 1985, p. 9; NYSSTF, *1984-85 Annual Report*, 1984, p. 11, and in-house information of the NYSSTF.

• three had found commercial application;
• six showed promise for eventual commercialization;
• one contributed vital information pertaining to hazardous-waste legislation;
• two projects were not mentioned.
Of the nine projects funded in 1983:
• two resulted in commercial application;
• one had good prospects for being applied;
• two had reasonable prospects; and
• four were ongoing at the time of the evaluation.

These carefully worded data do not allow valid conclusions on the results of the projects. It remains to be seen whether the program is able to overcome the big differences between the private sector and universities. The legislature, however, must be confident in the performance of the program; it appropriated $1 million for the Research and Development Grants program for 1986.

Issues and Questions
The following issues should be considered before establishing a program like the Research and Development Grants program:
• Cooperation with private sector — It can be very difficult for universities to find private coinvestors. A large amount of private leverage funds in a short period of time cannot be expected. Much effort and dedication will be needed to overcome the differences between the universities and the private sector.
• Funding — A state should not fund the projects completely. The project director should look for additional support from the university, the private sector, and other sources in order to improve the leverage rate.
• Private vs. public — In New York State, both public and "independent" universities receive aid from the state government, but the "independent" institutions, due to higher quality, are better able to compete for state funds. An acceptable funding balance should be struck.

CORPORATION FOR INNOVATION DEVELOPMENT

The Corporation for Innovation Development (CID) program is a venture capital program that provides direct financial assistance to technology-based new business ventures or new product-process developments in existing businesses. It received an appropriation of $1 million to match a $1-million grant from the U.S. Economic Development Agency as part of the 1981-1982 State Purpose Budget Bill. These funds were the foundation for a revolving fund that was intended to be self-sustaining in several years.

The program is based on the premises that only a small portion of venture capital is directed toward startup financing, and that the state should help fill this "funding gap."[51] The goals of the program are the formation and development of innovative, technology-based new business ventures that have a significant potential for creating jobs and leveraging private investment capital.

Operation of the Program
The four staff members of the foundation who are managing the program are responsible for public relations, analysis and selection of applications, and after-funding assistance.

In a three-step selection process, the foundation selects applications according to the following criteria.[52]

• The application must have an innovative technology orientation; based on the results of the Batelle Study the foundation prefers to make its investments in the technological areas of electronics/information sciences and medical/biological sciences.

• The product or service must show good potential for market acceptance.

• The applicant must have, or be prepared to have, collaborative relationships with other sources of capital, generally a minimum of 1:3, foundation to other investments.

• The application must show job creation potential.[53]

Every applicant must provide the foundation with a full business plan or complete a preliminary application. Based on this information, the program staff prepares a staff investment report which is presented to the Investment Review Committee. This committee, established by the board of directors, makes the final recommendations to the board of directors, which makes the final investment decision. The Investment Review Committee is composed of bankers, venture capitalists, and leading administrators who are very familiar and experienced with the venture capital business and enjoy a high level of respect throughout the business community and the state government. All interviewees emphasized that the composition of the Investment Review Committee is one of the most critical aspects of the program: its composition determines whether the business community is going to support the program or not.[54]

The investments of the CID program range between $50,000 and $250,000 and may be in the form of debt financing, equity financing, or a combination of both. The federal share of the investment fund is governed by EDA guidelines, whereas the state share is invested as flexibly as possible.

The management of the program also provides the funded companies with business and management assistance as well as help in finding later-stage funding. One entrepreneur complained, however, that these efforts could be improved, especially the support in finding later-stage funding. In order to overcome this problem, the CID management began to arrange outside management assistance for CID-funded companies.

Justification of the Program
As explained before, the purpose of this program is to overcome the shortage of early-stage venture capital investments. But does this shortage really exist? This seems to be a legitimate question, especially since New York City, the

financial center of the world, is located in the state. But research indicates that in 1984 only 5 percent of all venture capital investments in the nation were made in New York State.[55] The same study also indicates that only 2 percent of all venture capital in the United States is placed in seed investments and 12 percent in startup investments, whereas the portion of venture capital invested in second-stage and later-stage investments amounts to 52 percent. These figures indicate that the "funding gap" may exist. But as they only cover the supply side of venture capital, and as no data exist on demand, it seems impossible to determine an actual figure for the size of such a gap.

All persons interviewed about the program agreed that the gap does exist and that it is a result of conservative investment habits. Bankers, as well as venture capitalists, consider early-stage investments to be too risky—there is no previous performance record; too small—while venture capital investments usually range from $500,000 to $1 million, most early-stage investments range from $25,000 to $250,000; and not profitable enough—conventional venture capitalists expect profit rates of over 50 percent for early-stage investments, which most new companies cannot promise.[56]

Performance of the Program

Following almost one year of initial public relations and screening, the CID management closed its first investment in December 1982. Table 6-19 shows the increasing interest in the program in terms of inquiries as well as the increased activity of the program management in terms of processed applications. By March 1986, the portfolio of the CID program contained sixteen companies, with investments totaling $2.2 million (Table 6-20).

TABLE 6-19
Activity Level Indicators for the New York State CID Program

FY	Received Inquiries	Received Pre-Applications	Received Full Applications	Investments
1981-1982	125	15	3	0
1982-1983	225	35	8	4
1983-1984	275	50	15	4
1984-1985	320	50	7	6
1985-1986	500	100	20	10

Note: The figures for FY 1985-1986 are estimated.
Source: In-house information of the New York State Science and Technology Foundation, used for presentations.

TABLE 6-20
CID-Investment Portfolio, March 1986

Company	Location	Industry	CID Investment	Closing Dates
Applied Robotics, Inc.	Latham	Robotics	$ 150,000 34,193	3/16/84 8/23/85
BSI Industries, Inc.	Watertown	Factory automation	60,000 40,000	8/22/84 6/28/85
Clean Room Technology, Inc.	Syracuse	Modular clean rooms	150,000	3/21/86
Dataspan, Inc.	Orchard Park	Tele- communications	150,000 50,000	7/27/84 4/30/85
Fifth Generation Computer Corp.	Manhattan	Artificial intelligence	50,000	7/25/85
Gremar Industries, Inc.	Sand Lake	Factory automation	50,000 30,000	3/31/83 1/24/84
Infocenter Software, Inc.	New Paltz	Computer software	125,000 43,400	8/13/84 8/21/85
Ironics, Inc.	Ithaca	Computer hardware and factory automation	140,000 60,000	3/27/84 11/30/84
Knowledge Systems Concepts, Inc.	Rome	Artificial intelligence	80,000	12/15/82
Laboratory Microsystems, Inc.	Troy	Laboratory automation	50,000 50,000	1/17/83 3/25/83
Micropen, Inc.	Pittsford	CAD/CAM circuit manufacturing	50,000	8/16/84
Optal Bar Code Systems, Inc.	Rochester	Bar code scanners	150,000	11/22/85
Playnet, Inc.	North Greenbush	Tele- communications	50,000 150,000	8/15/84 12/20/84
Precision Materials, Inc.	Rochester	Laser technology	50,000 25,000 25,000	3/25/83 7/20/83 3/13/84
Sono-Tek Corporation	Poughkeepsie	Ultrasonic technology	150,000	8/01/83
Xertronix, Inc.	Rochester	Semiconductor fabrication automation	250,000	11/16/83

Source: In-house information of the New York Science and Technology Foundation.

According to the foundation, these companies maintained or created over 200 direct jobs by 1985, with estimates of over 2,000 jobs by the end of 1989.[57]

The CID program also achieved good leverage rates. Whereas in FY 1982-1983, one dollar invested by the foundation was matched by $3.32 from other funds, in FY 1984-1985, one dollar invested by the foundation was matched by $4.70. Therefore, the foundation is well beyond its original one-to-three match requirement.

TABLE 6-21

Investments Of the CID Program

FY	No. of Funded Companies	CID Investment	Leveraged Funds	Leverage Rate
1982-1983	4	280,000	920,000	3.32
1983-1984	4	870,000	2,920,000	3.35
1984-1985	6	645,000	3,040,000	4.71

Source: New York State Science and Technology Foundation, *1984-85 Annual Report*, 1985, p. 10, and in-house information of the NYSSTF.

Issues and Questions

During the interviews with program participants a number of issues arose. The interviewees in the Department of Commerce argued that the program administration should be expanded on a regional level. Deputy Commissioner Dennis Rapp proposed to multiply the CID program all over the state in order to decentralize the loan criteria and to adapt them to the specific structures of the regional economies. This would result in a decentralized process of information collection and therefore a better information exchange. His proposals, however, met resistance from the program managers and program participants who claimed that it would be difficult to find enough qualified individuals to make up review committees and program staff for each region. Also, they argued, the review committees and the program staff would be too close to program participants and therefore in danger of personal and political pressure.

The second issue that was raised in several interviews was the expansion of the program toward first- and second-stage investments. The program participants pointed out that they especially had difficulties in finding first- and second-stage funds and that additional support from the foundation would be very helpful.

The third issue was again raised by Deputy Commissioner Dennis Rapp: he proposed not to confine the investments to high-technology industries. The decisive selection criteria should be the growth opportunity of a company, the replacement of old jobs, and the development of growth products. However, the program staff did not think that this kind of expansion would help improve the program.

A state considering a similar program should pay attention to the following.

• Organization — The management team should be composed of individuals with both venture capital investment and real management experience. This team should be given enough time for preparation and for the initial screening process. The CID program managers estimated that a period of at least nine months of preparation time is necessary before the first investment can be made. The amount of paperwork for the applicants should be kept as low as possible. The program management should be capable of offering true management assistance for the program's portfolio companies.

• Selection — The investment review committee is the key for the success of this kind of program; it should be composed of experienced individuals who enjoy a high level of respect throughout the business community and the state government. Only a few, but solid, rules are sufficient.

• Funding — The initial funding of the program should be adequate to the venture capital demand in the state. It should also be considered carefully whether to limit the funding on early-stage investments or make it also available for later-stage investments.[58]

Although both program participants interviewed for this study think that they would have been able to launch their projects without the support of the foundation, they agreed that the CID investments accelerated the growth of their companies and helped introduce their business plans to venture capitalists and therefore helped attract additional venture capital funds.

Asked how they would assess the impact of the program on overall economic development, all interviewees pointed out that it would have only marginal effects on the economy. But the program does help to initiate and accelerate venture capital investment in the state.[59] They also pointed out that the program helps link entrepreneurs with venture capitalists and therefore improves the business climate. Due to a recapitalization in 1985 of $2.2 million of the CID program fund, the program will be able to increase its investment activity in the coming years.[60] According to the program management, the revolving fund of the program will be self-sustaining in a few years.

Conclusions

The programs of the NYSSTF directly address the needs and potential of New York State's science and technology-based industries. Taken together, they form a comprehensive approach that helps New York State develop businesses in this sector of its economy. The programs are very complementary; no program stands alone, each is reinforced by the other programs, and all the acclaim goes to the foundation itself.

The foundation has enjoyed bipartisan support, freedom from bureaucratic constraints, and has seen growth in its budget, staff, and the number of programs it operates despite gubernatorial changes and shifts in the leadership and structure of the state's economic development efforts.

After years of change in the management of the state's economic development efforts, the state's economic development director issued a comprehensive report in September 1985.[61] This strategic plan, *Rebuilding New York—The Next Phase from Recovery to Resurgence,* has the full support of the governor and has been embraced by a large number of the state's leaders. It codifies a systematic plan for economic development and cites the science and technology policy as an integral part of the plan.

In assessing the programs of New York's science and technology policy, three issues of concern and caution surfaced repeatedly.

• Funding — There are various funding issues beyond the question of "how much." Matching requirements must be determined reasonably to achieve the desired leveraging results. In addition, immediate results should not be expected and funding time frames must be tailored to the program.

• Selection process — Great care should be taken in selecting program participants and grant recipients on the basis of merit, potential for success, and clear knowledge of risk of failure. Selection processes must be free of any political or personal bias.

• Geography — Although there is a natural political desire to have program efforts geographically cover the state, the reality is that programs will flourish only where the right "ingredients" and enough personal enthusiasm exist.

Overall, the use of a quasi-public authority as the major implementing structure for New York State's science and technology policy has worked very well in the political context of the state. The expertise of the business leaders on the NYSSTF's board of directors is utilized to the fullest in the selection process. This is insured by having the nominations of private-sector officials to the board made by the governor and approved by the legislature, and by these positions being volunteer, not salaried.

The programs are developed jointly by the legislature, the agencies, and the governor's office. The foundation's staff and board are then able to do their jobs of implementing that policy relatively free from political pressures. The strategies and methods of the programs are achieving the goals of retaining, expanding, and attracting technology-based industries and jobs in New York State.

Appendix

PRODUCTIVITY DEVELOPMENT PROGRAM (PDP)

To complement the foundation's efforts to create new technology-based industries in New York, PDP tries to increase the competitiveness of all industries. This program is focused on bringing technological advances to existing industries that would otherwise not look to technology to improve their productivity. The program works by teaming selected industries with productivity problems with consultants who work on the problems and help implement proposed solutions. The foundation selects industries whose problems have potential solutions of wide application that can aid job retention and economic expansion. The program is designed to provide easy access to experts. In this way, the program encourages and establishes relations between a large range of businesses and public and private specialists.

NEW YORK STATE
SMALL BUSINESS INNOVATION RESEARCH PROGRAM (SBIR)

Since the creation of the SBIR program in 1982, New York State has been actively encouraging the participation of its small business community in the federal program. Its goal is to encourage the startup and growth of small R&D businesses in the state. An SBIR Phase I training program was designed to improve the quality of the proposals: by January 1985, 5,000 firms had been contacted and ten training sessions had been held across the state.

In July 1984 the SBIR program was established within the New York State Science and Technology Foundation. This program authorized the foundation to award matching research grants of up to $50,000 to small businesses (those with 200 employees or fewer) that had already received Federal Phase I SBIR grants. The program bridges the "funding gap" that often occurs between the completion of Phase I work and the awarding of Phase II contracts.

During the program's first year, the foundation awarded $400,000 to ten small New York businesses that had already received Federal Phase I SBIR support and applied for Phase II awards.[62]

NOTES

1. New York State Science and Technology Foundation (hereafter NYSSTF), *1981-1982 Annual Report*, Albany, 1982, 17.
2. Batelle Columbus Division, *Final Report: A Strategy for the Development of High-Technology Activities in New York State*, Columbus, OH, April 1982, VI. 7.
3. According to a research project at the University at Albany, "the net loss for the state . . . between 1975 and 1980 . . . among college graduates was nearly 100,000, or 23 percent of its total population loss among persons 25 years of age and older. The loss was almost exactly the same size among individuals who had completed between one and three years of college. . . . The state's loss of college-educated individuals due to the migration of the 1970's is worrisome because of its bearing on one of New York's chief appeals to new industry—namely, the presence of a highly trained workforce." See Richard D. Alba and Michael J. Batutis, *The Impact of Migration on New York State*, The University at Albany, 1984, 30 and 32.

160

During the same period, New York State also lost more than 100,000 individuals in managerial and professional occupations—one third of the state's total loss in labor force. See ibid., 38-43.

4. Batelle, *Final Report*, VI. 7.
5. Ibid., VI. 5. — VI. 9.
6. Ibid., VI. 4.
7. Interview with Frank Mauro, secretary of the assembly, Albany, January 7, 1986.
8. *New York Times,* text of governor's annual message to the legislature as 1961 session opens, January 5, 1963, 23.
9. *New York Times,* text of Governor Rockefeller's address at inaugural in Albany, January 2, 1963, 7.
10. *New York Times,* "Rockefeller Says U.S. Growth Lags," April 21, 1963, 4.
11. Ibid., 1.
12. *New York Times,* "Directors Named for Science Body," December 15, 1964, 53.
13. *New York Times,* "A New Common Sense," May 5, 1981, 27.
14. *New York Times,* "Carey Budget Would Affect Twenty State Panels," January 31, 1975, 39.
15. *New York Times,* "Carey Named Economic Board in Effort to Attract New Jobs," August 26, 1975, 49.
16. Peter D. McClelland and Alan L. Magdovitz, *Crisis in the Making: The Political Economy of New York State since 1945* (New York: Cambridge University Press, 1981), 7.
17. *New York Times,* text of governor's address to the legislature, January 6, 1976, 8.
18. Interview with Mauro.
19. *New York Times,* "Four Bills in Albany Seek to Attract Plants with High Technologies," February 8, 1981, 42.
20. Task Force on University-Industry Cooperation and the Promotion of High Technology Industries, *A Report to the Legislature,* Albany, December 1984, 1.
21. *New York Times,* text of governor's state of the state address, January 8, 1981, 6.
22. NYSSTF, *1983 Annual Report,* 3.
23. Batelle, *Final Report,* 15.
24. The Batelle study defines high-technology industries as those "with a significant amount of the work force associated with professional and technical positions, and that pay above average wage rates. They are characterized by above average investments in research and development, are often capital intensive, tend to be rapidly growing and have unique ties to academic and vocational training programs." See ibid., 5.
25. The Batelle study defines those industries as "being formed in response to major technological breakthroughs in technology and manufacturing processes; to the manufacturers of products, or provision of services which have relatively new markets and new applications—often where the types of resources and attributes required are still evolving, and the true market significance for the industry might not yet have been defined." See ibid.

26. Additional interviews were held with NYSSTF executive director, Graham Jones; NYSSTF deputy director, John Deffigos; NY Commerce Department deputy Commissioner for policy and research, Dennis Rapp; NY Urban Development Corporation vice president, Lee Webb; Governor Cuomo's associate for economic development, Kevin O'Conner; associate with the NYS Assembly Program Development Group, Laurel Wienegar; and NY Department of Education associate for higher education, Cecilia Diamond.
27. Governor Hugh Carey, statement on approving L. 1982, c. 562, July 22, 1982.
28. Interview with Mauro.
29. NYSSTF *1983 Annual Report*, 6.
30. Interview with Bob Dunne, acting director of Columbia CAT, New York City, January 6, 1986.
31. Interview with Bill Horne, CATs program manager, Albany, January 7, 1986.
32. Interview with Juliette Moran, NYSSTF director of the board, New York City, January 13, 1986.
33. Interview with Jacob Sternberg, president of Fifth Generation Computer Corporation, New York City, January 6, 1986.
34. *1984-85 Annual Report*, 7.
35. Interview with Mauro.
36. Interview with Ed Reinfurt, lobbyist for the Business Council of New York State, Albany, January 9, 1986.
37. Interview with John Chrisanti, assistant to Senator LaValle, Albany, January 9, 1986.
38. Interview with Horne.
39. Interview with Gordon Ambach, commissioner of education, Albany, January 9, 1986.
40. Interview with Reinfurt.
41. Interview with Moran.
42. Interview with Stanley Landgraf, president of the Capital Region Technology Development Council, Albany, January 9, 1986.
43. Interview with David Harvey, director of the Capital Region Technology Development Council, Albany, January 9, 1986.
44. Interview with Lawrence Barker, TDO program manager, Albany, January 7, 1986.
45. Interviews with Rapp and Harvey.
46. Interview with Moran.
47. NYSSTF, *Research and Development Grants Program: Projects for Applied Technology*, Albany, January 1985, 5. From 1964 to 1977, the foundation awarded $ 5.7 million in grants, peaking at $973,581 in FY 1967-1968.
48. See "Solicitation for Proposals, May 1984," in ibid., 18 — 9. According to the program manager, the program range will be expanded to include advanced-materials and hazardous-waste businesses, technological areas which are of great significance for the economic development in the state.
49. There is no data available on the amount of leveraged funds in 1984 and 1985. The foundation, due to limited staff, is not able to reassess this program.

162

50. NYSSTF, *Research and Development Grants Program*, 9.
51. NYSSTF, *1983 Annual Report*, 4.
52. NYSSTF, *1981-82 Annual Report*, 14.
53. According to experienced observers, these criteria are comparable to those of any private venture capital firm. Entrepreneurs who have received funding through the program, however, complain that the selection process is not well explained and that the foundation's staff lacks insight in particular technological areas.
54. Deputy Commissioner Dennis Rapp, member of the Investment Review Committee, pointed out that the banking community places such confidence in the program that if a company has once received funds from this program, the banking community will invest in the company itself.
55. "Venture Capital Investments Set New Record: $3 billion Invested in 1984," in *Venture Capital Journal* (May 1985): 12.
56. See the results of a study prepared for the Joint Economic Committee, in U.S. Congress, Joint Economic Committee, *Venture Capital and Innovation: A Study*, Washington, D.C., 1985, 25-26.
57. NYSSTF, *1984-85 Annual Report*, 10.
58. The program manager estimated that the initial funding should amount to at least $2 million. Deputy Commissioner Dennis Rapp proposed that the program be expanded to a regional structure and that it also provide funding for first- and second-stage investments.
59. One entrepreneur explained that a few years ago there were almost no deals made in the Hudson Valley, whereas there is an increasing amount of venture capital investment going on today.
60. The recapitalization is composed of $800,000 via an unrestricted appropriation by New York State and $600,000 from the U.S. EDA matched by $800,000 of New York State matching funds.
61. Vincent Tese, *Rebuilding New York—The Next Phase from Recovery to Resurgence: A Strategic Plan for Expanding Economic and Job Development in New York State*, Albany, September 1985.
62. NYSSTF, *1984-85 Annual Report*, 9.

7

NORTH CAROLINA

North Carolina's economy has historically been dominated by manufacturing (especially textiles) and agriculture. One form, then, of science and technology policy for economic development would have been to apply technological innovations to those existing industries. Instead, the state under Governor James Hunt tried to expand its economic base beyond traditional manufacturing and agriculture. State policies encouraged new advanced-technology industries, such as microelectronics, to either start in or move to North Carolina. Only under a new governor, James Martin, did the state begin to study science and technology policies to aid the state's traditional industries as well as to continue expanding its economic base.

Demographic and Economic Profile

POPULATION CHARACTERISTICS

North Carolina's population of about six million people is growing more rapidly than that of the United States as a whole (Table 7-1) but the state's age distribution remains the same as the rest of the country (Table 7-2). While just over a quarter of the United States population lives in rural areas, over half of North Carolina's population does so (Table 7-3). The state also has a much higher concentration of minorities, especially blacks (Table 7-4). North Carolinians are generally less educated than other Americans: 54 percent, as opposed to 66 percent nationally, hold high school degrees (Table 7-5).

TABLE 7-1

Population of North Carolina and Percentage Change
Compared to the United States, 1970, 1980, and 1984
(in 1,000s and %)

	North Carolina	North Carolina Change	U.S. Change
1970	5,084	—	—
1980	5,882	15.6	11.4
1984	6,165	4.8	4.1

Source: U.S. Department of Commerce, Bureau of the Census, *1980 Census of Population,* vol. 1, part 1, p. 1-43; idem, *State Population by Age and Components of Change: 1980 to 1984, Current Population Reports,* p. 7.

— *This chapter was written by Mark Howard and Mary Kragie.*

TABLE 7-2

Age Distribution in North Carolina

Compared to the United States, 1970 and 1980

(%)

Age Group	1970		1980	
	North Carolina	United States	North Carolina	United States
0-19	38.8	37.8	32.3	32.0
20-44	33.4	31.7	37.8	37.2
45-64	19.7	20.6	19.6	19.7
65+	8.1	9.8	10.3	11.3

Source: U.S. Department of Commerce, Bureau of the Census, *1980 Census of Population*, vol. 1, part 1, pp. 42, 174; idem, *1970 Census of Population*, vol. 1, part 1, p. 305.

TABLE 7-3

Urban and Rural Composition of North Carolina

Compared to the United States, 1970 and 1980

(%)

Age Group	1970		1980	
	North Carolina	United States	North Carolina	United States
Urban	45.5	73.6	48.0	73.7
Rural	54.5	26.4	52.0	26.3

Source: U.S. Department of Commerce, Bureau of the Census, *1980 Census of Population*, vol. 1, part 1, *Characteristics of the Population*, pp. 1-37.

TABLE 7-4

Racial Distribution in North Carolina

Compared to the United States, 1970 and 1980

(%)

Age Group	1970		1980	
	North Carolina	United States	North Carolina	United States
White	76.8	87.5	76.4	83.1
Black	22.2	11.1	22.6	11.7
Other	1.1	1.4	1.0	5.1

Source: U.S. Department of Commerce, Bureau of the Census, *Statistical Almanac of the United States*, 1985; idem., *1980 Census of Population* , vol. 1, part 1, p. 74; idem., *1970 Census of Population*, vol. 1, part 1, p. 293.

TABLE 7-5
Educational Levels in North Carolina
Compared to the United States, 1980
(%)

	North Carolina	United States
Elementary school (less than 5 years)	0.4	3.6
High school	54.2	66.5
College (4 or more years)	10.9	16.2

Source: U.S. Department of Commerce, Bureau of the Census, *Statistical Almanac of the United States, 1985,* idem, *1980 Census of Population,* vol. 1, part 35, pp. 44-45.

In general, North Carolinians are poorer than other Americans. In 1984 North Carolinians' incomes were, on average, about 15 percent lower than other Americans (Table 7-6). Consequently, more residents of North Carolina lived below the poverty line—14.8 versus 12.1 percent nationally (Table 7-7).

TABLE 7-6
Per Capita Income and Percentage Change
in North Carolina Compared to the United States, 1970, 1980, and 1984
(in dollars and %)

	North Carolina	Change	United States	Change
1970	3,220	—	3,945	—
1980	7,753	140.8	9,494	140.7
1984	10,850	39.9	12,789	34.7

Source: U.S. Department of Commerce, Bureau of Economic Analysis, *Survey of Current Business,* August, 1985, p. 18; idem, Bureau of the Census, *Statistical Abstract of the United States 1984,* p. 457.

TABLE 7-7
Individuals Below the Poverty Level
in North Carolina Compared to the United States, 1970 and 1980
(%)

	North Carolina	United States
1970	20.3	13.0
1980	14.8	12.1

Source: U.S. Department of Commerce, Bureau of the Census, *1980 Census of Population,* vol. 1, part 35, pp. 230-251, 885; idem, *1970 Census of Population,* vol. 1, part 35, p. 45.

ECONOMIC PROFILES

Despite the state's high rural population distribution, only 3.4 percent of the labor force works in the agricultural sector. Manufacturing and wholesale and retail trade make up 54 percent of North Carolina's nonagricultural employment (Table 7-8), as opposed to 43 percent in those sectors nationwide. Nearly all of that difference lies in the manufacturing sector, on which the North Carolina economy is quite dependent. Manufacturing employment is not concentrated in any particular part of the state, but is widely dispersed among all regions.[1]

Within the manufacturing sector, the textile industry employs by far the greatest number of North Carolinians—28.7 percent in 1982, down from 38.2 percent in 1972 (Table 7-9). In fact, of the 875,700 people employed in the U.S. textile industry in 1977 (the most recent year from which data is available), 245,300, or 28 percent, worked in North Carolina. The textile industry has recently provided far fewer jobs as the growth of unions in North Carolina and cheaper labor in other areas have encouraged some companies to move overseas.

North Carolina cannot continue to be so dependent upon manufacturing to provide jobs. From 1972 to 1982, the wholesale and retail trade, government, and service sectors of the economy grew much faster than did the manufacturing sector (Table 7-8). Also, in 1982, 259 plants either closed or announced permanent layoffs, putting 25,496 people out of work.[2]

TABLE 7-8
Nonagricultural Employment and Share in North Carolina by Sector, 1972, 1977 and 1982 and Percentage Change between 1972 and 1982
(employees in 1,000s, shares and changes in %)

	1972 Emp.	Share	1977 Emp.	Share	1982 Emp.	Share	1972-1982 Change
Mining	4.1	0.2	4.7	0.2	4.7	0.2	+14.6
Construction	120.0	6.3	106.8	4.9	104.0	4.4	-13.3
Manufacturing	756.8	39.6	780.9	36.0	781.3	33.4	+3.2
Transportation	99.1	5.2	103.4	4.8	115.6	4.9	+16.6
Wholesale & retail	347.6	18.2	421.9	19.4	477.4	20.4	+37.3
Finance & insurance	75.6	4.0	84.5	3.9	97.7	4.2	+29.2
Services	233.4	12.2	300.6	13.8	359.2	15.4	+53.9
Total	1,911.9	100.1	2,170.4	99.9	2,338.4	99.9	+22.3

Source: U.S. Department of Labor, Bureau of Labor Statistics, *Employment, Hours, and Earnings, States and Areas, 1939-1982*, vol. 2, pp. 618-628.

TABLE 7-9

Manufacturing Employment and Share in North Carolina by Industry,
1972, 1977 and 1982 and Percentage Change between 1972 and 1982
(employees in 1,000s, shares and changes in %)

	1972		1977		1982		1972-1982
	Emp.	Share	Emp.	Share	Emp.	Share	Change
Nondurable							
Food/kindred	37.4	5.2	39.1	5.3	43.9	5.7	17.4
Tobacco	23.1	3.2	23.4	3.2	23.1	3.0	0.0
Textile	275.6	38.2	245.3	33.2	219.4	28.7	-20.4
Apparel	79.1	10.9	77.1	10.4	77.5	10.1	-2.0
Paper products	16.5	2.3	9.4	2.6	20.3	2.7	23.0
Printing/publishing	13.8	1.9	15.7	2.1	20.7	2.7	50.0
Chemicals	27.0	3.7	33.0	4.5	35.4	4.6	31.1
Petroleum refining	0.2	0.03	0.3	0.04	0.4	0.05	100.0
Rubber & plastic	16.0	2.2	21.9	3.0	26.8	3.5	67.5
Leather	3.6	0.5	4.3	0.6	5.1	0.7	41.7
Total nondurable	492.3	68.1	479.5	64.8	472.6	61.8	4.0
Durable							
Lumber & wood	31.0	4.4	32.6	4.4	32.0	4.2	0.6
Furniture & fixtures	70.3	9.7	78.9	10.7	76.3	10.0	8.5
Stone, clay, glass	15.0	2.1	15.8	2.1	15.9	2.1	6.0
Primary metal	6.4	0.9	5.9	0.8	7.9	1.0	23.4
Fabricated metal	17.0	2.4	26.3	3.6	27.7	3.6	62.9
Nonelec. machinery	30.7	4.2	33.0	4.5	43.9	5.7	43.0
Electrical equip.	35.4	4.9	40.1	5.4	55.9	7.3	57.6
Trans. equip.	8.7	1.2	11.3	1.5	15.0	2.0	72.4
Instruments	8.5	1.2	8.4	1.1	9.6	1.3	12.9
Miscellaneous	6.3	0.9	7.6	1.0	7.2	0.9	14.3
Total durable	230.1	31.9	259.9	35.2	291.4	38.2	26.2
Total mfg.	722.4	100.0	739.4	100.0	764.0	100.0	5.5

Source: U.S. Department of Commerce, Bureau of the Census, *1982 Census of Manufactures, Geographic Area Series, North Carolina*, pp. 9-15; idem, *1977 Census of Manufactures, Geographic Area Series*, pp. 34.11-34.18.

Those job losses were partially offset by new jobs in high-technology companies. But those companies are concentrated in the Piedmont area, especially around Research Triangle Park. The problem of regional benefits thus arises as most of the state suffers high unemployment while one region enjoys economic growth and prosperity.[3]

Data on North Carolina's economy and employment patterns point to factors that may influence the state's science and technology policies. For example, programs that address manufacturing in general and textiles and apparel in particular will affect the largest segment of the population and will provide benefits to several different regions in the state; such programs could be classified as technology transfer policies designed to increase the technological capabilities of existing industries. Also, in an effort to attract new businesses, especially advanced technology companies, the state might target educational levels for improvement: company owners must be sure that the state's labor pool can perform at the level they require.

HIGH-TECHNOLOGY SECTOR

One way to evaluate the advanced-technology sector in a state is to look at the funds it has available for research and development activities. That funding comes from federal, state, and industrial sources. North Carolina's sources and distribution of R&D funds differ greatly from the other states considered in this study.

Traditionally, the greatest supporter of advanced-technology R&D in the country is the federal government. North Carolina does not receive as much federal R&D funding as do many other states: in 1983 its absolute national ranking was twenty-fourth. On a per capita basis, this translated to a ranking of thirtieth. (Of the seven states treated in this study, it had the lowest rankings.) North Carolina also differs from the rest of the country in its apportionment of federal R&D funding. In the other states, most of the federal funds go to industry (49 percent nationally versus 16 percent in North Carolina). In North Carolina, 45 percent of federal funds go to universities and to federal agencies operating within the state, as opposed to 19 percent nationally (Table 7-10).

Distribution of federal R&D funds from federal agencies is also different in North Carolina (Table 7-10). In the rest of the country, the Department of Defense comprises 61 percent of federal R&D funds; in North Carolina, it constitutes only 20.2 percent of federal funds. The Department of Health and Human Services contributes 50 percent of federal R&D funds in North Carolina, compared to 11.5 percent nationally. Finally, the Environmental

TABLE 7-10
Federal Obligations for R&D by Performer
in North Carolina and Share Compared to the United States, 1983
($ million and %)

Performer	Funds	Share	U.S. Share
Federal facilities	108.5	34.7	27.1
Industry	50.5	16.2	49.1
Universities	140.5	45.0	18.8
State & local government	1.3	0.4	0.5
Other	16.5	3.7	4.5
Total	312.5	100.0	100.0

Source: National Science Foundation, *Federal Funds for Research and Development,* vol. 33, 1984, p. 142.

TABLE 7-11

Share of Federal Obligations for R&D in North Carolina
by Agency Source Compared to the United States, 1983

(%)

Agency	North Carolina	United States
Agriculture	6.0	2.2
Commerce	1.2	0.9
Defense	20.2	61.0
Energy	1.7	12.0
Health & Human Services	50.0	11.5
Interior	0.9	1.0
Transportation	0.3	0.9
EPA	13.2	0.6
NASA	1.6	7.0
NSF	4.8	2.8

Source: National Science Foundation, *Federal Funds for Research and Development*, vol. 33, 1984, p. 150.

Protection Agency spends a larger part of North Carolina's federal R&D funds than the national average. The higher spending by HHS and EPA is probably attributable to the fact that both agencies have large laboratories and research facilities in the state.

Although most R&D funds spent in a state's institutions of higher education come from the federal government, North Carolina's state government provides a higher percentage of funds to its universities and colleges than do any of the other states in our study; state government provides 18.1 percent of R&D expenditures in North Carolina, compared to 11.9 percent or less in all of the other states studied.[4] Of the funds spent on academic R&D within the state, a higher proportion is spent on life sciences than in most of the other states.[5]

Research and development in a state is also financed by industry. North Carolina's industries spend far less money on R&D than any other state in our study. In 1979, Florida industries, the next smallest spenders, spent $620 million compared to $327 million spent by North Carolina industries. California companies spent $7.4 billion on R&D, followed by New York at $2.9 billion.[6]

Another way to assess a state's high-technology sector is to look at the number of people it employs in this sector. In North Carolina, relatively few people are employed in the high-technology sector (Table 7-12). In 1982 in the United States, the eight industries the CBO highlights employed 16.6 percent of the populace—the comparable figure in North Carolina is only 5.6 percent. North Carolina has no missile and space industry and no instruments industry, two areas the CBO study designated as high-technology.

170

TABLE 7-12

High-Technology Manufacturing Employment in North Carolina
and Percentage Change, 1972, 1977, and 1982
(employees in 1,000s, change in %)

	1972 Emp.	1972 Change	1977 Emp.	1977 Change	1982 Emp.
Drugs	—	—	6.7	23.9	8.3
Industrial organic chemicals	.4	42.9	2.0	15.0	2.3
Office/computing machine	—	—	—	—	—
Communication equipment	—	—	9.2	77.2	16.3
Electronic components	—	—	5.1	135.3	12.0
Aircraft & parts	—	—	—	—	1.0
Missiles/space vehicles	—	—	—	—	—
Instruments	—	—	—	—	—

Note: Statistics for some industry groups are withheld to avoid disclosing figures for individual companies.
Source: U.S. Department of Commerce, Bureau of the Census, *1982 Census of Manufactures, Geographic Area Series, North Carolina*, pp. 9-15; idem, *1977 Census of Manufactures, Geographic Area Statistics* pp. 34.11-34.18.

Science and Technology Policy

HISTORICAL ACCOUNT

Early evidence of North Carolina's standing support of science and technology can be found in the state's long-standing commitment to higher education. In the 1950s, North Carolina State University was one of the largest engineering schools in the country and the University of North Carolina at Chapel Hill and Duke University led the nation in the number of chemistry degrees conferred.

Because the state economy was and is based on industries like textiles, tobacco, tourism, and furniture, most science graduates had to leave the state to find work. Recognizing this problem, industrial and educational leaders came together in the late 1950s to form the Research Triangle Foundation, a nonprofit corporation whose purpose was to promote the resources of the area and encourage the establishment of scientific and research-oriented organizations in the state. In 1958 the foundation raised $1.5 million to create the Research Triangle Park, a 6,200-acre, university-affiliated research campus contained within the boundaries connecting Duke University, the University of North Carolina at Chapel Hill, and North Carolina State University. The Research Triangle Park was seen as a means to attract to the state industrial and government research groups which would benefit from relationships with the universities. By the 1970s, more than half of the state's science and engineering graduates were staying in North Carolina.[7]

Governor Luther Hodges described the concept of the park as an answer to the industrial development needs of the South: "Scientific research, both academic and industrial, is a type of activity from which other activities proceed—the development of new products, new uses of material resources, new processes, and new living standards."[8] As of 1985, more than thirty-five organizations representing government, industry, and universities had established facilities in the park.

While no public money was used to establish the Research Triangle Park, the state did help develop the area—building access roads to the park, for example. Support of the park marked the state government's first formal science and technology initiative.

Other programs soon followed. In 1962, Governor Terry Sanford appointed a Scientific Advisory Committee which proposed the creation of the North Carolina Board of Science and Technology. The board was established in 1963 with an appropriation from the General Assembly of $2 million. Its charge was to "encourage, promote, and support scientific, engineering, and industrial research applications in North Carolina to the end that the State will benefit from, and contribute to, the economic and technical development resulting from advances in the space and related sciences."[9] The governor was to serve as chairman. In 1979, the General Assembly reorganized the board, granting it an annual budget and increasing its power. The board does not make policy decisions for the North Carolina government; rather, it advises elected officials in their decisions about the use of scientific, engineering, and technological resources in the interest of the state.

CURRENT STRATEGIES

North Carolina is following a two-track approach in its science and technology development policy. One track is to attract established out-of-state companies to North Carolina. The Research Triangle Park, the Microelectronics Center, the Biotechnology Center, the School of Science and Mathematics, the Customized Job Training Program, and the overall strength of the University of North Carolina system are considered crucial components of this strategy. The other track is to develop new small businesses within the state. In 1983 the General Assembly passed the New Technology Jobs Act, which provides for "startup" funds and incubator facilities for small businesses and funds for programs to foster joint industry-university research in biotechnology.

Overall science and technology policy in North Carolina is guided by the Board of Science and Technology. The board effectively acts as the coordinating body and spokesman for the state's programs.

MAJOR SCIENCE AND TECHNOLOGY POLICY COMPONENTS

Policymaking and Coordinating Bodies

North Carolina science and technology policy involves activities in four categories: policymaking and coordination; education, training, and employment; linking university and industry research; and business incentives for technological innovations. This section presents an overview of North Carolina science and technology initiatives.

• North Carolina Board of Science and Technology — Functioning as a focal point for state science and technology efforts, this group links state government with public and private research institutions, firms, and agencies. Its fifteen members are drawn from public and private universities, state and local government, and private industry. The governor serves as chairman.

The board developed plans that led to the creation of the North Carolina Microelectronics Center, the Biotechnology Center of North Carolina, and the North Carolina School of Science and Mathematics. In addition, it has organized programs designed to improve public understanding of science, to assist state agencies and local governments, to improve the quality of science and mathematics education in the state's elementary and secondary schools, and to assist private industries and institutions.[10] Appropriations to the board have increased from $200,000 in 1979 to $1,667,395 in 1984.

The board's mandate is to identify important research needs of both public and private agencies, institutions, and organizations in North Carolina. The board also makes recommendations concerning policies, organizational structures, and financial plans that will promote effective use of scientific, engineering, and technological resources in fulfilling identified research needs. The funding the board receives is allocated to support the board's Small Research Grants Program and also to employ consultants who conduct research projects the board requests.

• Governor's Task Force on Science and Technology — In 1982 Governor James Hunt appointed the Task Force on Science and Technology to "examine the means by which North Carolina can strengthen and more fully utilize its scientific and technological resources to promote economic and social development." The underlying assumption behind its creation was that plans for the future should be developed during periods of recession and limited financial resources so that as conditions improved, planned courses of action could be vigorously pursued.

The Board of Science and Technology functioned as the core of this larger group. Task force membership consisted of 15 persons appointed by the governor and representing such categories as financial institutions, public and private colleges and universities, state and local governments, industrial labor and management, and the North Carolina General Assembly. The majority of the task force members were not board members. The task force was subdivided into three program committees: elementary and secondary education, research and higher education, and technological innovation. The committees drew their initial membership from the task force, but additional resource persons were drawn from state governments, academia, and the business community.

During its tenure the task force undertook several activities:

• It created four special working committees — Long Term Program Support, North Carolina and the World Community, Agriculture and Forestry, and Science, Technology, and Human Values — to supplement the work of the major committees.

• It sponsored five regional forums on science and technology. The forums enabled task force members to exchange ideas about local issues with citizens at the local level.

• It worked with other state government and education agencies to sponsor programs on small-business innovation, mathematics and science education, and the role of the humanities in public policy issues.

• It worked for passage of legislation creating the North Carolina Technological Development Authority, establishing new initiatives to strengthen science and mathematics education, and establishing expanded research programs in biotechnology and environmental management.

In 1984 the task force issued several volumes detailing their findings and recommendations.

Education, Training, and Employment

• Secondary public education — The North Carolina state government has recently attempted to improve technical education in schools at the secondary level. To its 1983-1985 public school budget, North Carolina added $1 million to employ 350 high school science and math teachers for six weeks in the summer and nearly $8 million for microcomputers and other technical equipment.

• North Carolina School of Science and Mathematics — Located in Durham, this selective residential facility is the most visible secondary-school program in the state. Established in 1980, the school has led the United States in its proportion of National Merit Scholarship finalists for the past two years. A more detailed discussion of the school will be presented.

• Customized Job Training Program — This program, administered through the Department of Community Colleges, is a cooperative effort to bring new and expanding private businesses together with the fifty-eight North Carolina community college facilities. It is one of the largest programs of its kind in the country; in 1981 - 1982 it served eighty companies and 5,819 trainees. In 1983, training in advanced technologies was added to the program at a cost of more than $15 million. The program will be closely examined later in this report.

Linking University and Industry Research

• Research Triangle Park — The Research Triangle Park was founded in 1959 by North Carolina government, industry and educational leaders. The 6,200 acre park is contained within the boundaries of a triangle connecting Duke University, North Carolina State University, and the University of North Carolina at Chapel Hill. The park houses more than thirty-five research organizations, including the United States Environmental Protection Agency, Monsanto, and the Semiconductor Research Corporation. The Research Triangle Foundation promotes and manages the park.

• Research Triangle Institutes — The Research Triangle Institute is a not-for-profit organization, established in 1959, that conducts research under contract to federal government, state government, and industry. It is located on a 147-acre campus in the Research Triangle Park and has received state grants totaling more than $1 million. Several research centers exist within the institute, including the Mass Spectrometry Center, one of the largest centers for material analysis in the country. The institute will be discussed in greater detail later in this chapter.

• The Microelectronics Center of North Carolina (MCNC) — This nonprofit research consortium is composed of five universities and the Research Triangle Institute and is located at the Research Triangle Park. Its aim is to accelerate the transfer to industry of research in semiconductor materials, computer sciences, and integrated -circuit design.

In 1981 the North Carolina General Assembly appropriated $24 million for the creation of MCNC. An additional $17 million was appropriated for fiscal years 1983-1985. These appropriations are the largest financial commitment ever made by a state in support of microelectronics research.

• North Carolina Biotechnology Center (NCBC) — NCBC was established in 1981 at the Research Triangle Park. It serves as the focal point for the state's biotechnology efforts. The center works with universities, industry, financial institutions, and the federal government to strengthen research and education programs and industrial development in biotechnology.

From 1981 to 1984 the center operated under the North Carolina Board of Science and Technology and was funded under the board's appropriations. The center is now organized as a nonprofit corporation with its own governing board. The governor appropriated $1 million for the center.

• North Carolina Technology Research Center — The center, which is now a unit of the Department of Commerce Business Assistance Division, was founded in 1963 as one of six regional dissemination centers funded by NASA. The center's primary purpose is technology transfer.

• North Carolina Alternative Energy Corporation — This nonprofit corporation, created by order of the State Public Utility Corporation, seeks to reduce the need to build new electricity-generating facilities through use of renewable energy sources, load management techniques, and energy conservation. The corporation is located in the Reseach Triangle Park and is funded by all major regulated and nonregulated electric utilities in North Carolina. Funding is approximately $2.2 million per year.

• The North Carolina Agricultural Extension Service — With offices in all 100 counties and on the Cherokee reservation, the state extension service's simple goal is to disseminate useful information. Most of its information comes from research findings in North Carolina's land grant and home economics universities. Helping the service distribute information are 1,524 Extension Homemakers Clubs, 2,200 4-H Clubs, 600 Community Development Clubs, and numerous other farm organizations.

Business Incentives for Technological Innovation
• The North Carolina Technological Development Authority — An outgrowth of the Governor's Task Force on Science and Technology, the authority was established in 1983 by the General Assembly through enactment of the New Technology Jobs Act. The authority is under the jurisdiction of the North Carolina Department of Commerce.

The authority has a twelve-member board of directors. Its purpose is to increase the rate at which new jobs are created throughout the state by stimulating the development of new and existing small businesses. The authority is responsible for the administration of two new small-business development programs: the Incubator Facilities Program and the Innovation Research Fund. During 1984-1985 it invested over $1.4 million in small businesses and incubators. The authority will be discussed later in the chapter.

• Debt and equity capital — North Carolina allows counties to issue industrial revenue bonds in denominations of more than $500,000. In 1982, ninety-five industrial revenue bonds worth $331.3 million were issued in North Carolina. The state also has an equity financing program, the North Carolina Innovation Research Fund, that provides a pool of money to be invested in new and existing small businesses engaging in innovative research. The program's 1983-1985 budget is $425,000.

Program Assessments

This section of the study presents more detailed reviews of five North Carolina programs. In addition, issues of science and technology policy surrounding these programs are presented.

Several criteria were considered in selecting programs for further study. These guidelines included focusing on:
• programs whose implementation and benefits are statewide, not just regional;
• programs that display involvement and commitment by governmental, industrial, and academic institutions in the program;

- programs that place emphasis on supporting and applying emerging technologies to the present industrial sectors of North Carolina;
- programs that work toward long-term as well as short-term goals and economic development; and
- programs or bodies that provide coordination, oversight, and integration of state efforts to aid economic development through science and technology programs.

In light of these guidelines, the following North Carolina science and technology programs were selected for study:
- the North Carolina Board of Science and Technology;
- the North Carolina Community Colleges Customized Job Training;
- the North Carolina School of Science and Mathematics;
- the North Carolina Technological Development Authority; and
- the Research Triangle Institute.

The Microelectronics Center and the Biotechnology Center were not included largely because they appear to benefit directly only a small region of the state. The Research Triangle Park was not included because a large body of literature about the park already exists.[11]

As mentioned earlier, North Carolina has followed a dual-track policy toward science and technology as an aid to economic development. On the one hand, North Carolina works to attract outside businesses to the state. On the other hand, the state seeks to develop its own small businesses. These programs represent both parts of this policy. The following sections present descriptions of each program and assessments of how each one fits into North Carolina's strategy.

NORTH CAROLINA BOARD OF SCIENCE AND TECHNOLOGY

Legislative Goals and History

The North Carolina Board of Science and Technology was established in 1963 by the General Assembly. In 1979 the board was reorganized and in 1985 it was moved from the Department of Commerce to the Department of Administration. Its primary duties include identifying important research needs of the state and administering the Small Research Grants Program.

The activities and focus of the board have varied over the years. It has studied issues involving scientific research and technological innovation and has recommended state policies to address them. These issues have ranged from pollution prevention research to math and science education in the public schools to biotechnology. In addition, the board has annually administered a research grants program for young North Carolina scientists.

The board was most active during the last six years of the Hunt administration (1979-1985) under the executive directorship of the science advisor to the governor, Quentin Lindsey. Governor Hunt became heavily involved in planning North Carolina's economic development through science and technology, and he used the board as an advisory body to help structure his policies. Under Mr. Lindsey, the board proposed and supported several very substantial science programs in the state, including the Microelectronics Center of North Carolina, the Biotechnology Center, and the North Carolina School of Science and Mathematics.

Administration and Implementation

The governor's science and public-policy advisor serves as executive director of the board. The only other full-time staff member in 1986 was an administrative assistant. A portion of the board's members serve on the executive committee. The board is further divided into program or project committees designed to guide particular activities.

Support for the board's project activities comes from internships, consulting arrangements, grants, and contracts. An example of a project directly funded by the board is a survey of scientific equipment in the state's universities.

Recent policy proposals for the board under the administration of Governor Martin suggest a shift away from developing costly, one-of-a-kind projects (like the Microelectronics Center) and toward other functions that the board is in a unique position to carry out. These include emphasis on the advisory efforts of the board as well as on issue identification and integration of its activities into the strategic planning process of the North Carolina government.

In addition, the board also administers a Small Grants Research Program. The program supports research the board has identified as important to the needs of the state and which carries significant potential for advancing the state's economic and social development. Research grants are also awarded for the purchase of scientific equipment and the construction of facilities which will contribute to the state's scientific capabilities.

Awards are granted on a competitive basis to researchers in public and private academic institutions and established research organizations in North Carolina. An annual request for proposals is published in colleges and universities. In recent years the board has assigned priority to investigators not having previously received substantial independent research support and to established researchers who are moving into a new scientific field. Since 1964 the board has received over 1,302 requests for funding, of which 384 have received awards totaling more that $23 million. Examples of Small Research Grant Awards include:

- $35,000 in 1980 awarded to the Solid State Electronics Groups at North Carolina State University to help support the purchase of an Extrion 400kv Ion Implanter.
- $6,000 in 1980 awarded to a North Carolina State University geneticist to explore the potential for genetic engineering in corn.

The board's budget is a line item in the state budget. Funding for the board decreased from $1.4 million in FY 1984 to $665,000 in FY 1985.

Assessment of Goal Attainment

The North Carolina Board of Science and Technology was created to provide scientific and technical support for economic development in the state. In addition to studies the board has commissioned, it has also administered a small research grants program since 1964. These grants are awarded to scientists in the state involved in research the board believes will benefit the state. The board claims that the state gets a return of $23.94 for every $1.00 it spends due to additional federal and private research monies these state funds leverage.[12] Although the board admits it would be an overstatement of the value of the Small Research Grants Program to suggest that the additional funds attracted by the researchers would have been impossible to get without the board award, they do contend that without board money, the research may not have been conducted or at least would have been conducted in a less timely manner.

The fund-leveraging effects of the Small Research Grants Program provide the only means of directly measuring the board's activities. In general, the board acts as a focal point and nerve center for the state's science and technology programs, and with Governor Hunt's active support has been successful in publicizing and promoting science and technology in the state. It is difficult to devise a meaningful performance measure for this type of activity.

Issues and Questions

During the past decade, the board has operated very much as an autonomous entity, unconnected to any department in the state. This position has advantages and disadvantages. Independence allows the board to maintain a broad perspective on complex issues that involve government, industry, and universities. Its administrative independence also makes the board better able to launch large projects like the Microelectronics Center and the School of Science and Mathematics in a relatively short period of time. The board is able to marshal political and financial support without working through the obstacles that an entrenched bureaucracy can present.

The main disadvantage of this autonomous position is that the board is often removed from the ongoing operation of the state government and even from interdepartmental strategic planning. Thus, when the board does have to work with older, more established state agencies, it can meet resistance to change and have very little power.

In short, as state science and technology advisory bodies go, the North Carolina Board of Science and Technology has been successful: it has been actively involved in most of the science and technology programs initiated by the state since 1979. However, that success has depended strongly on the fact that it has been headed by a dynamic, respected scientist. Now that Quentin Lindsey has left the position of executive director, the future of the board is in question. Whether it maintains its influential role seems to depend on the actions of its new leader.

CUSTOMIZED JOB TRAINING PROGRAM

Legislative History and Goals

The Customized Job Training Program is administered by the Industry Services Division of the North Carolina Department of Community Colleges. The division was created in 1960 specifically to administer the Customized Job Training Program after the state suffered a drop in agricultural employment. The state's legislature recognized a need to broaden North Carolina's economic base in order to foster new types of activity and to provide more jobs. The Industry Services Division was intended to attract new, nonagricultural businesses to the state.

The Customized Job Training Program works to achieve two goals. First, it trains unemployed or dislocated workers for jobs in new and expanding industries. Second, it tries to create new jobs for the citizens of North Carolina by attracting new businesses to the state.

The program works with new and growing companies to meet these goals. Program personnel claim to be able to meet virtually any training need a company may have. State lawmakers justify funding the program with the rationale that a trained work force at no cost to a relocating company is a strong incentive for that company to move to North Carolina.

Administration and Implementation

The Industry Services Division that administers the program has a staff of a director, an assistant director, and five project managers (PMs). Each PM is responsible for one area in the state containing eight to twelve community colleges.

Most initial contacts between the Industry Services Division and companies considering relocation or expansion in North Carolina are through referrals from the North Carolina Department of Commerce. After the Industry Services Division becomes aware of a potential client, its representatives meet with representatives of the company to assess the company's training needs. The PM who oversees the area of the state in which the new company is locating then contacts the local community college and plans the training program.

Each training program is unique. A program can last for two weeks or for several years, and it can provide training in manual skills or in clerical tasks. The company may guarantee that it will hire all of the graduates, or it may reserve the right to reject some of them. The same program may be conducted once or offered many times. The instructors may be from the local community college, from the company, or from some other source.

The relationship between the company and the division is governed by an "agreement of understanding" which acts in lieu of a contract. Neither the state nor the company assumes any firm obligations under the agreement. Instead, the parties merely state that they will work together to establish a new training program in a specified area of the state. A spokesman from the division says that, despite the absence of firm commitments, using the agreement rather than a contract has caused very few problems over the years. The only difficulties have arisen from "misunderstandings," and they have been minimal.

The relationship between the division and the local community college is governed by the budget. The college provides all the administrative services, from recruiting to record-keeping, but the division pays all the bills. All training done under the Customized Job Training Program is kept separate from the college's other activities for budgeting purposes.

In FY 1985, the Customized Job Training Program had a budget of $5.5 million. The division funded 120 training programs in thirty-nine of North Carolina's fifty-eight community colleges. There were 7,355 graduates of the programs; unfortunately, there are no records of how many were employed by the companies who requested their training. The programs were spread all over the state—52 percent in the Piedmont area, 26 percent in the coastal area, and 22 percent in the mountain area. The programs were conducted for many different industries, including electronics, textiles, chemicals, manufacturing, and services. The program is one of the largest of its kind in the country.

Assessment of Goal Attainment

The Industry Services Division does not keep any data that could be used to measure how well it achieves its goal of creating more jobs for North Carolinians. That the work it does is successful seems to be an article of faith among persons interviewed. The program enjoys widespread political support: according to the assistant director of the Industry Services Division, the legislature has never denied a request for an appropriations increase from the division.[13] Governor Hunt frequently referred to the program as a way to attract new businesses to relocate in North Carolina.

There is also ample anecdotal evidence of the program's success. Numerous businessmen have stated how impressed they are with the program's flexibility and ability to meet their needs. Others have said the program was the major reason that their companies located in North Carolina. Such stories figure prominently in the Industry Services Division's official literature on the program.[14]

Thus, while it is difficult to measure the program's success in meeting the goal of creating more jobs, North Carolina businessmen and lawmakers seem to believe that such a measurement is unnecessary. A large number of people are satisfied that the program is meeting their business and public-policy needs, and the belief is widespread that it has been successful.

Issues and Questions

A major issue concerning the Customized Job Training Program is the question of whether the state should be paying for training that the companies might finance themselves. North Carolina policymakers justify the expense by stating that the state offers no tax moratoriums, credits, land deals, or other favors to new companies moving to the state; instead, the state relies on the drawing power of a trained work force.

Another issue revolves around the current heightened interest in advanced-technology industries. The program has historically focused on manufacturing and textile companies, and has only recently begun to target its efforts toward high-technology companies. The division will have to change and adapt to the demands of the newer, very different industries. The state may also have to bear increased expenses in incorporating the advanced-technology industries into the program. In addition, short, intense training programs may not prove to be adequate—the new industries may need employees with skills gained over a longer period of time.

Does the program serve as a good model for other states? Its success is based largely on the state's community college system, which is one of the largest and most extensive systems in the country, and which allows great flexibility in meeting different business needs. Without such a framework, a similar program might be much more expensive than North Carolina's.

Finally, is the program responsible for creating new jobs in the state? The weight of opinion is firmly in the program's favor. But it is difficult to judge whether, and to what degree, the program has met its stated goals, or merely been credited for events that might have occurred anyway.

NORTH CAROLINA SCHOOL OF SCIENCE AND MATHEMATICS

Legislative History and Goals

The North Carolina School of Science and Mathematics was proposed and championed in the late 1970s by both Governor Hunt and Quentin Lindsey of the Board of Science and Technology. The General Assembly passed the legislation establishing the school in 1980. The school was established in Durham and opened its doors to its first class of students in the fall of 1982.

The purpose of the school is to create excellence in science and math education in the North Carolina public school system. The educational benefits are to be realized not only by those who attend the school, but also by the rest of the public school system who will have the school as a model to follow.

Administration and Implementation

The school is a residential high school for eleventh- and twelfth-grade students. It is open to applicants from anywhere in the state on a competitive basis. There is no tuition or board—all costs are paid by the state and by private sources. In FY 1985, the state paid $4.4 million to fund the school, and private donations totaled $500,000. Four hundred students were enrolled in the school in 1985-1986.

The school teaches a normal high school curriculum and meets all state educational requirements, but it places special emphasis on the sciences and mathematics. The curriculum requirements include six semesters of science, four of English, four of foreign languages, and two of history. In addition to the rigorous curriculum, students must demonstrate computer proficiency and complete one year of community service and two years of a work service program called the Mentor Program.

The school enjoys a unique relationship with the universities and businesses in the Research Triangle Park. Through the Mentor Program, students go to work in scientific laboratories at such places as Burroughs-Wellcome and Duke University. The principal of the school, William Youngblood, describes these jobs as not just "test-tube-cleaning exercises." The students participate in actual research and scientific exploration in order to give them "real-world experience."

The composition of the school's faculty is also unusual. Fifty percent of the school's instructors hold doctorates, and nearly all the others have master's degrees. In the words of the school's principal, "the level of instruction is very high."

Assessment of Goal Attainment

It is, again, not possible to quantify the school's success in meeting its goal. The school is only three years old, so its graduates have not yet begun to contribute to the state's economy. Also, the only evidence of the school's effectiveness as a model to the rest of the public school system is anecdotal. It is likewise difficult to identify changes that can be attributed to the School of Science and Mathematics.

The school measures its success by scholastic measures. In 1984-1985, it had the highest percentage of National Merit Scholarship finalists of any school in the country—about one out of every three graduating seniors are semifinalists. A very high percentage of graduates go on to "first-tier" scientific colleges such as MIT and Cal Tech. The school also considers its ability to attract and sustain outside support through the Mentor Program a sign of success.

The school does not, however, enjoy the support of the rest of the public school system in North Carolina. Critics claim that the school deprives other schools of the leadership and example of the best students in the state. Public educators also argue that a disproportionate amount of money goes to the school. In FY 1985, the school received $9,000 per student from the state, while the rest of the public school system received only $2,000 per student.

Governor Hunt vigorously supported the school: now that he is out of office, the school is having to broaden its political base. According to the principal, building that political support has been difficult. The school has gained a reputation for elitism, which has further alienated it from potential supporters.

But the school does enjoy the support of the business community. It continues to receive large cash donations, advanced equipment, and support for the Mentor Program from companies in the Research Triangle Park. Universities both in and out of North Carolina also express support for the school. Its graduates are gaining a reputation for being excellent, motivated students at the college level. The local universities also participate actively in the Mentor Program.

Issues and Questions

The school is facing several difficult issues. One of them is its position in the school system in North Carolina. The school is treated as somewhat of an outcast by public school educators. It must cultivate support in the schools in order to be accepted as a model for the rest of the state. The school is moving in this direction. A seminar in computer utilization designed for 30 teachers drew about 150.

Another question concerns the school's political base. Now that its strongest supporter is no longer in power, it may lose the political support it enjoyed previously. That loss may be translated into less funding, which may threaten the quality of education in the school.

Finally, the school must demonstrate that it aids North Carolina's economic development. Will the school's graduates stay in the state to contribute to the local economy? The school's principal, William Youngblood, says that he does not want to send his graduates to the "degree factories" of the University of North Carolina and North Carolina State University. He would prefer that his students go to MIT or Cal Tech, "where they won't have to waste their time being dragged down by less well educated students." This issue will obviously have a bearing on the political and public support that it will be able to gather.

NORTH CAROLINA TECHNOLOGICAL DEVELOPMENT AUTHORITY

Legislative History and Goals

The North Carolina Technological Development Authority (NCTDA) was first proposed by Quentin Lindsey, former chairman of the Board of Science and Technology, in the late 1970s. When the North Carolina General Assembly passed the New Jobs Technology Act in 1983, the bill included initial funding for NCTDA.

The authority's objective is simple: to create more jobs for the citizens of North Carolina. The NCTDA's attempts to accomplish this objective by (a) providing seed capital to small companies with growth potential, (b) aiding companies working with technological innovation, and (c) fostering a productive business climate in local communities.

Administration and Implementation

The NCTDA is governed by an executive board of twelve members. The governor appoints eight members of the board, the lieutenant governor appoints two members, and the Speaker of the House names the other two members. The executive board oversees all NCTDA activities, makes final decisions on awards, and sets general policy for the authority's actions.

The NCTDA administers two official programs: the Innovation Research Fund (IRF) and the Incubator Facilities Program (IFP). The full-time three-person staff keeps the executive board informed of all activities concerning these programs. The staff also acts as the contact between applicants to the programs and the board. Finally, the staff conducts an outreach program for small businessmen.

The Innovation Research Fund provides one-time loans of up to $50,000 to small businessmen who are engaged in producing and marketing new, advanced-technology products. The authority considers this fund a lender of last resort; applicants must show that they are unable to obtain funds from other sources.

Applicants are subject to rigorous review. At least four volunteer academicians with knowledge of the field in which the applicant is working evaluate the proposal for scientific and technical merit. If the reviewers find the applicant's idea feasible and worthwhile, a volunteer panel of businessmen, including bankers, venture capitalists, and accountants, then studies the proposal for its business merit. An application cannot be eliminated at the business review, but the review can inform the NCTDA which businessmen may need special help or advice.

The authority's executive board then evaluates the proposals on the basis of the NCTDA's investment portfolio (the other companies in which they have invested) and the state's policy goals, especially job creation. The board decides which applicants will receive loans and in what amounts. In FY 1985, the NCTDA awarded $375,000 to eleven businesses.

The relationship between the authority and award recipients is governed by a contract. The document specifies that the businessmen must make periodic reports to the board on their companies' progress. The contract also specifies when and in what amount loans are repaid to the IRF. The terms depend on how long it takes the companies to commercialize their products. The maximum repayment is 500 percent of the original loan if marketing takes five to fifteen years. If marketing never occurs, no repayment is required.

The NCTDA hopes that the IRF will become largely self-sustaining. Repayments of loans will be used for awards to other applicants. Hypothetically, the only money needed from the state will be for administrative expenses.

The Incubator Facilities Program gives one-time grants of $200,000 to nonprofit organizations and to local governments that wish to establish incubator facilities that will provide low-rent space and administrative support to new small businesses. In FY 1985, the IFP awarded $600,000 to three nonprofit organizations.

Applicants must prove that they have financial support that at least matches the $200,000 grant from the state. The NCTDA wants to ensure that these organizations have other community support and are not relying exclusively on the state to fund their proposed facilities.

Winners of an IFP award must also sign a contract governing their relationship with the NCTDA. The organization building the facility must report periodically on its progress. The NCTDA will not become involved in the daily operations of the facility unless it appears that the investment may be lost. Repayment is not required. The state hopes that the aid given new businesses will result in new jobs and economic prosperity, and that repayment will occur through increased tax receipts.

Assessment of Goal Attainment

In its two years of operation, the NCTDA has awarded sixteen loans through the Innovation Research Fund and four grants through the Incubator Facilities Program. Only one of the companies receiving an IRF award has begun repaying the loan, and none of the incubators has begun operation. It is too soon to tell how successful the authority will be in meeting its goal of creating new jobs for North Carolina. In addition, one cannot predict which companies may have been successful without the NCTDA award.

The authority does seem to have good political support, but it is conditional support. The IFP has already had trouble getting help from some legislators who want an incubator in their own districts. A spokesman for the NCTDA said the IFP has become a very "political" program. In addition, the authority is often viewed as Quentin Lindsey's "baby"; and now that he is no longer on the Board of Science and Technology, the authority's most vocal support is gone.

Some of NCTDA's features are appealing. The IRF's potential to become self-sustaining makes it very attractive to state lawmakers who are facing tight budget constraints. The IFP can be a valuable and visible source of state support to communities that may not otherwise be able to build incubator facilities, thus making it easier for small businesses to start in their towns.

Issues and Questions

One main question arises about NCTDA's role in economic development. To what extent is the state providing loans and incubator facilities for businesses that may have become established without state help? The state may be paying for job creation that would have happened anyway.

There are also questions of politics. Can the IFP avoid becoming prey to "pork-barrel politics," with each legislator demanding an incubator in his or her district? Can the NCTDA continue to receive legislative support now that its strongest supporters, Governor Hunt and Quentin Lindsey, are no longer in power?

Finally, the NCTDA faces the issue of how it will spread its benefits statewide without refusing some well-qualified businessmen. While the agency emphasizes giving loans to all parts of the state, most of its applicants will naturally come from the Research Triangle area. The NCTDA may find itself accepting less qualified or less promising applicants simply to maintain its goals of statewide benefits.

RESEARCH TRIANGLE INSTITUTE

Legislative History and Goals

Unlike most other science and technology programs in North Carolina, the Research Triangle Institute is supported only indirectly by the state government. The Research Triangle Institute was established in 1958 as a focal point for research within the Research Triangle Park on 147 acres of land donated by the state government. The goal of the institute was to stimulate and attract research organizations to the park by providing high-quality research services. The institute is legally controlled by three universities of which two, the University of North Carolina at Chapel Hill and North Carolina State University, are public institutions, and one, Duke University, is private.

The Research Triangle Institute had broad-based support from industrial, educational, and governmental leaders when it was established in the late 1950s. This remains true today. The success of this venture is reflected in consistently increasing research contract revenues for the institute from federal and private groups and in continued cooperative ventures among the triangle universities.

Administration and Implementation

The Research Triangle Institute is governed by a twenty-seven-member board that includes thirteen members who represent the founding universities, thirteen elected from the business and professional communities, and the institute president. The institute operates under a highly decentralized organizational structure headed by the president. Fourteen vice presidents oversee the administrative and finance sections and each of ten primary research groups.[15]

Throughout the 1970s a distinguishing mark of the institute's operations was the degree of involvement in programs aimed at improvements in the quality of life. By the end of the decade, three quarters of the institute's research effort was directly concerned with (a) medical-care costs, health systems, and health resources; (b) educational evaluation and assessment of educational outcomes; (c) crime, delinquency, and justice; (d) alcohol and drug abuse; (e) biochemistry and the synthesis of new drugs; (f) environmental monitoring and measurement; (g) pollution-control strategies; (h) air navigation; and (i) biomedical engineering.[16] With a shift in national priorities, reflected in the federal budget since 1980, the institute is devoting increased attention to industrial innovation and productivity, process engineering and advanced-technology application for defense and the private sector, new materials, management services, energy conservation, and microelectronics.

The institute is a not-for-profit organization whose only source of revenue is the research contracts it secures. Since 1959, the Research Triangle Institute has earned over $300 million in research revenues from a total of 2,200 research assignments. The institute's cumulative net revenues of $8.2 million have been reinvested in institute facilities and equipment.[17] The institute's 1985 budget was about $50 million, approximately 85 percent of which came from the federal government, 10-12 percent from private industry, and the rest from state and foreign contracts.

Assessment of Goal Attainment

The Research Triangle Institute's most important performance measure is the amount of research contract funding it can attract. The institute does not coordinate its research efforts directly with the state government, but it does take advantage of the strengths of the associated state universities. Some observers note that what is good for the institute is good for the universities—is good for the state.

The institute fulfills its goal of providing a focal point for research by steadily increasing its funding, its clientele, and its staff. The Research Triangle Institute has, under the leadership of its one and only president, George Herbert, continued to integrate itself into the state universities associated with it. The institute's working ties with its three founding universities have been very important to the institute's success. Relationships encompass board governance, consulting agreements with several hundred faculty members, teaching appointments for institute staff, patent management, and access to computation and library facilities.

In addition, the institute serves as a model to both public and private universities wishing to develop similar university-affiliated research ventures. However, despite the reputation and success of the Research Triangle Institute, no state benefit performance measure has been developed.

Issues and Questions

The Research Triangle Institute, existing on state-donated land and legally controlled by North Carolina public universities, is an example of indirect state support of science and technology. As an independent, self-sufficient entity, the institute enjoys a freedom that state-controlled ventures cannot. It is not subject to policy changes originating from changes in state government administration. This insulation has allowed the institute to coordinate its activities with the state, but has not required it to justify its efforts to state legislators.

188

Issues for groups considering a venture similar to the institute concern both the state government and the state research community. First, the state government must allow such ventures to exist. In some states this is not a legal problem, but in others enabling legislation must be passed. For example, Utah passed such legislation and in doing so created a supportive state environment for such an institute.[18] Second, and probably most important, the impetus for this kind of venture must originate from the state research community. It cannot be imposed by legislators or administrators. The institute is in the business of securing research contracts, and without aggressive support of researchers such a venture is doomed to fail.

Conclusions

The programs discussed in this chapter represent both parts of North Carolina's dual-track policy toward science and technology as an aid to economic development. The Research Triangle Institute and the Customized Job Training Program are examples of North Carolina's attempt to attract new companies to the state that can benefit from relationships with the state's universities and state-affiliated research organizations. The North Carolina Technological Development Authority and the North Carolina School of Science and Mathematics focus their efforts on internal economic and educational development. The Board of Science and Technology developed this policy and suggested many of the programs that comprise it.

But North Carolina's programs do not share a coordinating body to help them accomplish different parts of an overarching goal. The Board of Science and Technology would be the logical choice to coordinate and direct the state's science and technology policy; at present, though, the board's role is strictly advisory.

North Carolina's dual-track policy works against a system of complementary programs. Agencies working to attract out-of-state businesses will pursue different strategies, different clients, and will try to meet different needs than will organizations developing in-state business and education. In addition, the programs operating in North Carolina today do not themselves coordinate their efforts. For example, on the in-state development track, the School of Science and Mathematics does not encourage its graduates to consider starting small businesses with loans from NCTDA. On the out-of-state track, RTI does not refer clients to the Customized Job Training Program.

It is too early to tell if the programs begun at the board's suggestion are adaptable to changes in state policy. There are several reasons for this. First, the programs themselves represent changes in state policy. Many of them, like the NCTDA and the school, have not had time to show any attunement to changes in state policy. Second, several of these programs are working to become largely self-sustaining with minimal state funding. If they should succeed, they would have little need to be attuned to changes in state policy.

The programs that are fully institutionalized in North Carolina's state government, such as the Research Triangle Institute and the Customized Job Training Program, are very well attuned to changes in state policy. When Governor Hunt began a new policy of actively recruiting new companies into North Carolina, the RTI acted as a symbol of the state's commitment to science and technology. As jobs have decreased in the traditional manufacturing sectors, the Customized Job Training Program has begun to offer more training programs in skills needed for advanced technologies. These two organizations have certainly adapted their work to meet new state policy goals and to fit into North Carolina's dual-track policy.

Common Problems and Issues

Many of these programs are considered successful because they have had powerful and influential advocates, especially Governor Hunt and Quentin Lindsey. But this close identification may be a mixed blessing. The programs must in the future broaden their political base and justify their existence more convincingly than they have done so far.

Another problem is that many of the new programs receive little or no institutional support from the rest of the state government. Their autonomy may at first look attractive and efficient, but their missions are broad and entail working with many state agencies and local governments. With better integration and greater involvement and support from other governmental units, these new programs will be more likely to reach the state leaders' ambitions.

There is also the basic question of whether the state should be involved in some of these activities at all. Is the state responsible for actively creating new jobs and for lending money to new businesses, or should the private sector bear more of the burden? The benefits gained may not make up for the costs incurred.

Another issue North Carolina faces is the state's lack of public-private cooperation. For the most part the programs studied represent substantial state investment.[19] Required private-sector investments, in the form of matching funds, are noticeably absent in most of North Carolina's science and technology programs. In some cases, such as the School of Science and Mathematics, the fact that the state has accepted almost total responsibility for funding puts the programs' future in jeopardy. Economic development is impossible without coordination of effort between public and private sectors. In an age of scarce state resources, North Carolina may have to either change the current programs or create new programs to take greater advantage of the support available from the state's private sector.

190

Finally, all of these programs must address the issue of performance measures. At present, there is no way to quantify information about goal attainment. None of the programs has had to produce convincing reasons for continued state funding because each has enjoyed strong political support. But with that support noticeably weakening and the state facing times of economic stress, these programs will have to work harder to show they deserve the funding they request.

NOTES

1. North Carolina Board of Science and Technology, *New Challenges for a New Era*, vol. 2, *Economic Revitalization through Technological Innovation*, 58-66.
2. Ibid. 67.
3. Ibid. 67-68.
4. National Science Foundation, *Academic Science/Engineering R&D Funds, FY 1983* (Washington, D.C., 1985).
5. Ibid.
6. National Science Foundation, *Research and Development in Industry, 1983*, Washington, D.C., 1985.
7. North Carolina Board of Science and Technology, *North Carolina Commitment to Research: Excellence through Science and Technology*, May 1985, 48.
8. Southern Regional Education Board, *Research and the Future of the South* (paper presented at the Eighth Annual Legislative Work Conference of the Southern Regional Education Board, October 15-17, 1959).
9. North Carolina General Assembly, bill number 143B-440.
10. Governor's Task Force on Science and Technology, *New Challenges for a New Era*, vol. 3, Raleigh, NC, May 1985, 19.
11. See, for example, Michael Franco, "Key Success Factors in University-Affiliated Research Parks: A Comparative Analysis," Dissertation, University of Rochester, 1985.
12. North Carolina Board of Science and Technology, *North Carolina Commitment to Research: Excellence through Science and Technology*, May 1985, 4.
13. Interview with John Wiles, assistant director of Industry Services Division, North Carolina Department of Community Colleges, January 6, 1986.
14. North Carolina Department of Community Colleges, *Training Is Working in North Carolina*.
15. These research groups are: Chemistry and Life Sciences; Analytical and Chemical Sciences; Environmental Sciences and Engineering; Chemical Engineering; Statistical Methodology and Analysis; Survey and Computing Sciences; Economics and Social Systems; Public Policy and International Development; Biomedical Engineering; and Electronics and Systems.
16. "Research Triangle Institute: The Bellwether of the Park," *North Carolina* (June 1981): 4.
17. Ibid., 3.
18. In Utah this was the Utah Non-Profit Corporation Association Act of 1972.
19. The exception is RTI, which is largely supported by federal and private funds.

8

PENNSYLVANIA

Pennsylvania exemplifies the popular conception of the declining manufacturing state. At the turn of the century Pennsylvania was, as Texas is today, the nation's energy capital. In addition, the state used its natural resources to become a leading manufacturer. A combination of this early success, national economic cycles, and business competition have resulted in the state's present condition. Its traditional industries are becoming outmoded and disinvested. Unemployment has risen tremendously in some industries, with little expectation of recovery.

The state government has recognized the need for action. Four program areas are receiving attention: economic development, scientific and technological development, job training, and income maintenance. The goals of these programs are to provide employment, improve work force skills, help the industrial mix adapt to the changing national economy, and assist those unable to maintain an acceptable standard of living. Like many other states, Pennsylvania believes that promoting high technology will help achieve these positive structural changes and has designed a variety of policies and programs to foster the development of scientific and technologically advanced industries and to apply new technology to existing industries.

A two-step methodology was used in conducting the research for this report. The first stage consisted of completing detailed background research on Pennsylvania's demographics, economy, policies, and programs. From this general information, certain programs were selected for extensive field study. The second stage consisted of field interviews with program administrators, program personnel, board members, other government personnel, and representatives of groups involved in the state's efforts. Additional written material was also collected at this time. The following report is the result of this effort. It begins with a demographic and economic profile, followed by a discussion of the state's current advanced technology programs and institutions. The chapter concludes with a closer assessment of three such programs.

Demographic and Economic Profile

Employment patterns show that the Pennsylvania economy is undergoing significant changes. The population is also being altered by demographic changes partially caused by the economic restructuring.

— This chapter was written by Andre Brunel and Michael Burke.

POPULATION CHARACTERISTICS

Pennsylvania is currently ranked as the fourth most populous state in the Union (Table 8-1). It lost the third position to Texas in the 1980 census, the result of both an increase in Texas' growth rate and a decrease in Pennsylvania's. Pennsylvania is in fact approaching zero population growth. It is predicted that the total population will actually begin to decline in the 1980s and will continue to decline until the end of the century. The growth rate is expected to be -1 percent between 1980 and 1990 and to reach -4 percent by the year 2000, the result of a lower birth rate, an aging population, and additional emigration.[1]

Between 1980 and 1984, 1 percent of the population moved out of the state; this rate is expected to increase.[2] Most people leaving Pennsylvania are leaving from urban areas; Pennsylvania experienced a 2.5 percent decline in its urban population between 1970 and 1980. In contrast, the rural population grew by 8.3 percent during the same time period (Table 8-2). It should be noted that while the Pennsylvania economy is heavily dependent on its manufacturing sector, the population is less urbanized than the national average.

As a result of natural processes and emigration, the state's population is gradually becoming older than the national average. The greatest difference is in the 45-64 and 65-and over age groups (Table 8-3). A predicted effect of the population aging is that by 1990 those workers currently in the work force will comprise 90 percent of the labor supply.[3]

In addition to being older than the national average, many workers will be less educated (Table 8-4). Pennsylvanians rank below the national average in numbers graduating both from high school and from four-year colleges. If, as Gordon de Jong has suggested, many of those leaving Pennsylvania are the youngest, brightest, and most skilled workers, a decline in the median number of years of school completed can be expected.[4]

TABLE 8-1

Population of Pennsylvania and Percentage Change
Compared to the United States, 1970, 1980, and 1984
(in 1,000s and %)

	Pennsylvania	Pennsylvania Change	U.S. Change
1970	11,809	—	—
1980	11,880	0.5	11.4
1984	11,901	0.3	4.1

Source: U.S. Dept. of Commerce, Bureau of the Census, Statistical Abstract of the United States, 1985, pp. 11-13; idem, State Population Estimates, by Age and Components of Change: 1980-1984, p. 7.; idem, Estimates of the Population of the United States and Components of Change: 1970-1984, p. 9; idem, 1980 Census of Population, vol. 1, part 1, p. 1.

TABLE 8-2

Urban and Rural Composition of Pennsylvania

Compared to the United States, 1970 and 1980

(%)

	1970		1980	
	Pennsylvania	United States	Pennsylvania	United States
Urban	71.5	73.6	69.0	73.7
Rural	28.5	26.4	31.0	26.3

Source: 1. U.S. Department of Commerce, Bureau of the Census, *1980 Census of Population* , ch. B, part 40, p. 8.; ibid., part 1, p.1; idem, *1970 Census of Population* , vol. 1, part 40, p. 8.

TABLE 8-3

Age Distribution in Pennsylvania

Compared to the United States, 1970 and 1980

(%)

	1970		1980	
Age Group	Pennsylvania	United States	Pennnsylvania	United States
0-19	36.1	37.8	30.1	32.0
20-44	30.0	31.7	34.8	37.2
45-64	23.2	20.6	22.3	19.7
65+	10.8	9.8	15.9	11.3

Source: U.S. Department of Commerce, Bureau of the Census, *1980 Census of Population,* vol. 1, ch. B, part 40, p. 91; ibid., ch. B, part 1, p. 1.

TABLE 8-4

Educational Levels in Pennsylvania

Compared to the United States, 1980

(%)

	Pennsylvania	United States
Elementary school (less than 5 years)	1.8	3.6
High school	65.8	66.5
College (4 or more years)	14.0	16.2
Median years of school completed	12.4	12.5

Source: U.S. Department of Commerce, Bureau of the Census, *Statistical Abstract of the United States, 1985,* p. 134; idem, *1980 Census of Population,* vol. 1, ch. C, part 40, p. 172.

Pennsylvania's demographic trends, then, are that young, educated, and trained workers are migrating, leaving behind an older, skilled work force. A future labor shortage may ensue which could adversely affect the state's advanced technology policy goals.

ECONOMIC PROFILE

The Pennsylvania economy, like the national economy, is undergoing dramatic structural changes. Significant losses have been registered by all sectors of the traditional industrial sector (Table 8-5). Only the mining industry experienced employment growth between 1972 and 1982 and it too suffered losses in the 1977-1982 period. Because the decline in employment within the construction, manufacturing, and transportation industries was offset by increases in various service and sales industries, total employment rose slightly between 1972 and 1982, but Pennsylvania's employment increase of approximately 4 percent compares poorly to the national increase of 22 percent over the same time period. Unemployment was also above the national average, increasing from 5 percent in 1972 to 11 percent in 1982.[5] Total manufacturing employment, including 155,000 workers in the durable goods sector and 103,100 workers in the nondurable goods industries fell 17 percent from 1972 to 1982 (Table 8-6). In comparison, national employment in durable and nondurable goods rose 7 percent during this period.

TABLE 8-5

Nonagricultural Employment and Share in Pennsylvania by Sector, 1972, 1977, and 1982 and Percentage Change between 1972 and 1982 (employees in 1,000s, shares and changes in %)

| | 1972 | | 1977 | | 1982 | | 1972-1982 |
	Emp.	Share	Emp.	Share	Emp.	Share	Change
Mining	40.2	.9	48.0	1.1	45.6	1.0	13.4
Construction	203.1	4.6	183.9	4.0	166.8	3.7	-19.6
Manufacturing	1,444.0	32.8	1,341.9	29.4	1,167.1	25.6	-22.0
Transportation	266.0	6.0	261.6	5.7	248.0	5.4	-10.0
Wholesale & retail	855.3	19.4	938.9	20.6	970.0	21.3	9.8
Finance & insurance	200.5	4.6	217.5	4.8	238.5	5.2	13.0
Government	651.9	14.8	710.9	15.6	680.4	14.9	0.7
Services	739.0	16.8	862.5	18.9	1,044.8	22.9	36.3
Total	4,400.0	100.0	4,565.2	100.0	4,561.3	100.0	3.7

Source: U.S. Department of Labor, Bureau of Labor Statistics, Employment, Hours, and Earnings, States and Areas, 1939-1982, vol. 2, pp. 709-723.

TABLE 8-6

Manufacturing Employment and Share in Pennsylvania by Industry,
1972, 1977, and 1982 and Percentage Change between 1972 and 1982
(employees in 1,000s, shares and changes in %)

	1972 Emp.	Share	1977 Emp.	Share	1982 Emp.	Share	1972-1982 Change
Nondurable							
Food/kindred	99.1	7.0	92.3	6.9	85.1	7.2	-14.1
Tobacco	6.9	0.5	3.3	0.3	2.4	0.2	-65.2
Textile	61.0	4.3	46.8	3.5	40.0	3.4	-34.4
Apparel	155.7	11.0	132.6	10.0	116.1	9.8	-25.4
Paper products	42.4	3.0	39.9	3.0	37.6	3.2	-11.3
Printing/publishing	69.1	4.9	68.6	5.2	73.9	6.3	7.0
Chemicals	47.9	3.4	44.0	3.3	38.7	3.3	-19.2
Petroleum refining	12.1	0.9	11.0	0.8	9.9	0.8	-18.2
Rubber & plastic	35.3	2.5	37.9	2.9	34.7	2.9	-1.7
Leather	23.8	1.7	18.3	1.4	14.4	1.2	-39.5
Total nondurable	553.3	39.2	494.7	37.3	452.8	38.3	-18.2
Durable							
Lumber & wood	22.2	1.6	20.4	1.5	17.0	1.4	-23.4
Furn. & fixtures	23.7	1.7	20.1	1.5	18.9	1.6	-29.3
Stone, clay, glass	56.7	4.0	54.0	4.1	44.4	3.8	-21.7
Primary metal	194.5	13.7	181.2	13.6	118.6	10.5	-39.0
Fabricated metal	108.4	7.7	104.5	7.9	95.3	8.1	-12.1
Nonelec. machinery	122.7	8.7	129.7	9.8	123.8	10.5	0.9
Electrical equip.	116.5	8.2	103.9	7.8	94.5	8.0	-18.9
Trans. equip.	68.2	4.8	70.2	5.3	60.3	5.1	-11.6
Instruments	33.1	2.3	38.0	2.9	37.8	3.2	14.2
Miscellaneous	14.3	1.0	25.3	1.9	19.6	1.7	37.1
Total durable	760.3	53.6	747.3	56.2	630.2	53.4	-17.1
Total mfg.	1,417.5		1,329.2		1,180.6		-16.7

Source: U.S. Department of Commerce, Bureau of the Census, *1982 Census of Manufactures; Geographic Area Series, Pennsylvania,* p. 13-20; idem, *1977 Census of Manufactures, Geographic Area Series,* part 2, pp. 39.15-39.24; idem, *1972 Census of Manufactures, Geographic Area Statistics,* part 2, pp. 39.12-39.18.

In addition to this absolute loss of jobs, structural changes occurred in Pennsylvania that resulted in a rearrangement of the industrial rankings. From 1972 to 1977 the top four industries were primary metals, apparel and other textiles, nonelectric machinery, and electric and electronic equipment; these four industries accounted for 41 percent of all manufacturing employment in 1977 (Table 8-6). Of them only nonelectrical machinery grew during the 1972-1982 time period. Thus, in 1982, nonelectrical machinery became the top employer, followed by primary metal, apparel and other textiles, and fabricated metals. These industries claimed 38 percent of all manufacturing employment.

Pennsylvania, with 35 percent of its labor force belonging to unions in 1980, has the reputation of being a high-wage state. Despite this, per capita income has lagged behind the national average (Table 8-7). This is the result of lower average hourly earnings in all sectors except manufacturing.[6]

Even though Pennsylvania's economy experienced employment losses between 1970 and 1980, the number of individuals below the poverty line did not change significantly (Table 8-8). A number of factors could account for this, including the migration of workers, the smaller number of youths between the ages of 0-19, the greater number of citizens over 65 years of age, and the state's unemployment and worker compensation programs.[7]

TABLE 8-7

Per Capita Income and Percentage Change
in Pennsylvania Compared to the United States, 1970, 1980, and 1984
(in dollars and change in %)

	Pennsylvania	Change	United States	Change
1970	3,928	—	3,945	—
1980	9,384	138.9	9,494	140.7
1984	12,314	31.2	12,789	34.7

Source: U.S. Department of Commerce, Bureau of Economic Analysis, *1984 Survey of Current Business*, p. 18; idem, *Statistical Abstract of the United States, 1984*, p. 457.

TABLE 8-8

Individuals below the Poverty Level in Pennsylvania
Compared to the United States, 1970 and 1980
(%)

	Pennsylvania	United States
1970	10.6	13.0
1980	10.5	12.1

Sources: U.S. Department of Commerce, Bureau of the Census, *Statistical Abstract of the United States, 1985*, p. 457; idem, *1980 Census of Population*, vol. 1, part 40, p. 397.

HIGH-TECHNOLOGY SECTOR

Within high-technology manufacturing industries in Pennsylvania, employment patterns between 1972 and 1982 varied (Table 8-9). High-technology industries in 1982 employed 10 percent of all manufacturing workers, an increase of 9 percent from 1972, but also a decrease of 3 percent from 1977. Nationally, high-technology employment represented 17 percent of all manufacturing employment in 1982.

While Pennsylvania's high-technology industries did achieve modest growth in employment, the rate of growth was significantly smaller than the national figure of 37 percent. Interestingly, three industries that nationally experienced an average growth rate of 38 percent—communication equipment, electronic components, and aircraft and parts—suffered an absolute decline in Pennsylvania. Likewise, employment growth of the office and computing industry in the state, while increasing 24 percent from 1977 to 1982, was also well behind the national average of 94 percent. These differences, and the decline in several of Pennsylvania's high-technology sectors, illustrate the problems faced by the state in fostering high-technology growth.

TABLE 8-9
High-Technology Manufacturing Employment
in Pennsylvania and Percentage Change, 1972, 1977, and 1982
(employees in 1,000s, change in %)

	1972	Change	1977	Change	1982
Drugs	13.0	13.8	14.8	-7.4	13.7
Industrial organic chemicals	3.9	53.8	6.0	-20.0	4.8
Office/computing machines	—	—	8.0	23.7	9.9
Communication equipment	15.1	-50.3	7.5	41.3	10.6
Electronic components	31.5	12.1	35.3	-14.7	30.1
Aircraft & parts	11.3	3.5	11.7	-8.5	10.7
Missiles/space vehicles	—	—	—	—	—
Instruments	32.7	16.2	38.0	-0.5	37.8
Total high-tech employment	107.5	12.8	121.3	-3.0	117.6
All manufacturing	1,417.0	-6.2	1,329.2	-11.2	1,180.6
Percentage of high-tech	7.6	9.1	10.0		

Note: Statistics for some industry groups are withheld to avoid disclosing figures for individual companies.
Source: U.S. Department of Commerce, Bureau of the Census, *1982 Census of Manufactures, Geographic Area Series, Pennsylvania,* p. 13; idem, *1977 Census of Manufactures, Geographic Area Statistics,* p. 39-1; idem, *1972 Census of Manufactures, Geographic Area Statistics,* part 2, p. 40-1.

Between 1981 and 1983, federal obligations for research and development increased 8 percent in Pennsylvania.[8] In the ranking for federal obligations, the state was tenth in 1981, eighth in 1982, and eleventh in 1983. The major increase was in funds directed toward industry and universities; funding in these sectors exceeded national increases. This increase was offset by the decrease in funding for federal facilities within the state. Obligations to the federal sector fell 11 percent in comparison to a national increase of 22 percent.[9] Table 8-10 shows how Pennsylvania compares to the nation for 1983 federal obligations.

In federal government obligations for R&D Pennsylvania ranks sixth out of the eight states studied for this project. Table 8-11 shows how Pennsylvania compares to the nation for agency obligations. The most significant difference was in Department of Defense (DOD) obligations: Pennsylvania was 17 percentage points behind the national figure of 61 percent in DOD obligations, placing it ahead of only North Carolina. The Department of Energy obligation in the state, however, was 17 percentage points above its closest competitor in this study (New York) and the national figure.

Within Pennsylvania universities, total R&D expenditures increased from $187.1 million in 1976 to $369.5 million in 1983, a 98 percent increase. In relation to the states included in this study, Pennsylvania in 1983 ranked fourth in this category, the same as its position in 1976.

The major source of university funding in 1983 was the federal government. Federal funds accounted for $25 million (68 percent) of the universities' total expenditures for R&D. Other sources of university funds were institutions at $49 million (13 percent), industry at $33 million (13 percent), endowments and donations at $32 million (9 percent), and state and local government at $5 million (1 percent). The distribution of funds for R&D was concentrated in the life sciences (52 percent) and engineering (17 percent).

TABLE 8-10

Federal Obligations for R&D by Performer in Pennsylvania
and Share Compared to the United States, 1983
($ million and %)

Performer	Funds	Share	U.S. Share
Federal facilities	$262.2	22.3	27.1
Industry	586.6	50.0	49.1
Universities	259.5	22.1	18.8
State & local government	2.6	0.2	4.5
Other	62.4	5.3	0.5
Total	$1,173.3	99.9	100.0

Source: National Science Foundation, *Federal Funds for Research and Development*, vol. 33, 1984, p. 142.

TABLE 8-11

Share of Federal Obligations for R&D in Pennsylvania
by Agency Source Compared to the United States, 1983

(%)

Agency	Pennsylvania	United States
Agriculture	2.3	2.2
Commerce	0.1	0.9
Defense	43.7	61.0
Energy	29.0	12.0
Health & Human Services	17.0	11.5
Interior	1.9	1.0
Transportation	0.5	0.9
EPA	0.3	0.6
NASA	1.9	7.0
NSF	3.3	2.8

Source: National Science Foundation, *Federal Funds for Research and Development*, vol. 33, 1984, p. 150.

Research and development expenditures by industry increased 148 percent, from $1,537 million in 1974 to $3,814 million in 1983.[10] In this category of the study, Pennsylvania occupied the third of eight places, trailing California and New York. It also employed the fourth largest number of engineers and scientists: in 1982, 68,700 scientists and 96,700 engineers were at work in the state.

POLICY IMPLICATIONS

The Pennsylvania economy is undergoing significant sectoral shifts in employment. Though declining in terms of absolute level of employment, manufacturing remains strong. In addition, demographic changes, particularly the emigration of younger workers and the general aging of the population, are altering the state's population structure, resulting in an older and less well educated work force. This factor may limit the attractiveness of the state for certain types of industries and may compound its economic problems.

The need for effective action has been recognized, and government, business, and labor have formulated an advanced-technology policy. Specific programs have been created and some traditional ones redirected to achieve the new policy goals.

Science and Technology Policy

HISTORICAL ACCOUNT

The changes in Pennsylvania's economy between 1970 and 1980 demanded some response from the state government. Remaining inactive when the electrical machinery and the needle trades, which comprised 36 percent of Pennsylvania's manufacturing employment, lost 68 percent of the manufacturing jobs in the state was politically impossible. A discussion of some of the factors considered in choosing a response that included an activist, comprehensive science and technology policy follows.

Higher Education

One of Pennsylvania's strengths is technological innovation. Pennsylvania has a large base of capabilities and a history of being able to commercialize results. The state was associated with some of the early microelectronics developments—the first commercial transistor was produced by Western Electric in Allentown, and the world's first electric computer, ENIAC, was developed at the University of Pennsylvania.[11]

The higher-educational system that supports such technological innovation is extensive. Pennsylvania has the third-largest number of colleges and universities among the fifty states, including a number of world-class research universities. In 1980, Pennsylvania ranked sixth nationally in R&D expenditures in science and engineering. Three of the top ten undergraduate colleges in the country are in Pennsylvania.[12] Since access to colleges and universities is important to advanced-technology industries, the state attempted to make use of this strength when responding to the state's economic changes.[13]

State appropriations per student for public higher education increased between 1981 and 1983, a sign of the continued importance assigned to higher education in the state.[14] In 1984, the state university system came into existence, bringing fourteen institutions of higher learning together.[15] The state's vocational-technical education system is also extensive; however, there is concern that it is not sufficiently geared to the training needs of adult workers, since its eighty-six area vocational education schools have historically focused on training adolescents.[16]

As the demographic and employment trends detailed earlier indicated, the state serves as a significant net exporter to other states of trained graduates.[17] The need for the state to stimulate knowledge-intensive job growth to stem this loss is further justification for promoting emerging-technology industries.

Transportation

Transportation costs affect the price a firm must pay for its raw materials and charge for its product. A comprehensive transportation network in good condition is therefore important for a state's economic development.

Additionally, two of the five factors mentioned most frequently by advanced-technology executives as influencing their decision to locate their business are proximity to markets and commuting distance.[18] Pennsylvania is strategically located near the great markets of the Northeast, Midwest, and upper South. With the state's transportation network, these national and international markets are accessible in a variety of ways.

Pennsylvania has the fourth largest highway system in the country, and it spends considerable sums to maintain it. In addition, Pennsylvania has one of the most extensive rail systems in the country coupled with three terminals—Philadelphia, Pittsburgh, and Erie—that link it to national and international markets. The state also has an extensive mass transit system.

Unionization

As mentioned earlier, Pennsylvania is one of the most highly unionized states in the country. In 1978, 34.2 percent of the nonagricultural work force in Pennsylvania belonged to unions, as compared to 23.6 percent nationally. There is evidence that corporations, particularly those that are labor intensive, tend to locate new production facilities in states with right-to-work laws because the work force is less likely to unionize.[19] This factor was addressed by incorporating labor through the MILRITE Council (to be discussed later in this report) to support a state advanced-technology policy.

Finance

Pennsylvania has a well-developed financial market; nonetheless, it has a shortage of two types of capital, that is, venture capital for young firms with significant growth potential, and long-term, fixed-rate financing for more established and medium-sized companies.[20] Since businesses need access to different sources and types of financing at various times over their life cycle, foreclosing either the variety or source of these funds can hinder survival and growth. In addition, recent evidence suggests that the public equity market for initial public offerings in Pennsylvania is unable to meet the needs of the firms that are ready to go public.[21] Such imperfections hinder the startup of businesses with insufficient private resources and slow the expansion of existing operations short of retained earnings.

Pre-existing Policy Components

Existing economic programs have also helped shape the state's response to the economic changes of the past decade and a half. One of the first major programs to address serious economic problems of the state, the Pennsylvania Industrial Development Authority (PIDA), was created in 1956 by the Pennsylvania legislature. This program sought to increase employment by building or acquiring industrial buildings in critical economic areas of the state. PIDA offered low-interest loans to businesses for land and plant acquisition. Since 1956 the program has been amended almost every other year to revise lending practices and interest rates to meet the state's needs.

In 1965 Congress authorized a second program, the Appalachian Regional Commission (ARC), to address a thirteen-state, 195,000-square-mile region of chronic poverty, isolation, boom-and-bust economic cycles, inadequate public facilities, and unemployment. Seven of the region's fifty-two multicounty local development districts (LDDs) are in Pennsylvania. The commission has spent in the past twenty years over $500 million to relieve the problems of the region's inhabitants. Each ARC district provides grants and loans to various federal grant-in-aid programs. Most of these funds have been applied to highway construction; other uses included support for education, vocational training, housing, health, and industrial development projects. This program was the largest and most diversified effort of its kind ever undertaken in the United States.

A third program, the Pennsylvania Technical Assistance Program (PennTAP) was established in 1965 with state and federal funds to match small businesses and industries facing technical problems with a network of technical specialists. Clients, including businesses and industries, schools, government agencies, nonprofit associations, entrepreneurs, consultants, and municipalities, reported that by using PennTAP's services between 1979 and 1981 they saved a total of $29.5 million.[22]

Political Environment

In 1979, the newly elected governor of Pennsylvania, Dick Thornburgh, fulfilled a campaign promise and revitalized the State Planning Board in order to formulate a long-term strategic plan for economic development, community development, and resource management and conservation. The board, which had fallen into disuse in the 1970s, was given a more diverse membership that included cabinet officers, legislators, local government officials, businessmen, organized labor, and civic leaders. Working with the Governor's Office of Policy Development, the renewed board began a thirty-month effort that resulted in a September 1981 final report entitled *Choices for Pennsylvanians*. [23] Concurrently, the Pennsylvania MILRITE Council, a state-level organization of business, labor, and government leaders, began to analyze possible directions for state economic development policy.[24]

Broad consensus about the future direction of the state's economy emerged. First, these leaders recognized that Pennsylvania could not reverse the fundamental national and international economic forces affecting the state. A second point of agreement was that the traditional approaches of helping distressed areas with a variety of social welfare and public-works-oriented industrial development programs in order to attract new industries from other areas had had limited success. Coupled with increasing doubt about the efficacy of "smokestack chasing" was growing awareness of the importance of small businesses and entrepreneurial activity in job creation.[25]

Inescapably, private-sector decisions about investment, expansion, and relocation would dictate the future success or failure of the state's economic growth. Following President Reagan's new policy directions, the Republican Thornburgh administration saw the government's role as one that should enhance, not obstruct, private-sector decisions. The notion that government itself could directly create meaningful jobs was rejected as false. This administration believed that the solutions to the problems of a state economy in transition had less to do with spending money on these problems than with implementing policies and programs that would create an environment conducive to favorable private-sector investment decisions.[26]

MAJOR POLICY COMPONENTS AND STRATEGIES

While prior to 1982 there had been some state action recognizing the importance of science and technology, like the restructuring of the ARC toward the promotion of small entrepreneurial firms, the state had not yet developed a coherent policy toward emerging technologies. A policy shift in 1982 is quite clear. In this year a formal science and technology policy program emerged.

In early 1982, two legislative members of the MILRITE Council introduced the Advanced Technology Job Creation Act. This bill was designed to provide state funding for joint university-industry R&D that would lead to job creation in Pennsylvania. The MILRITE Council had helped develop the program, which was supported by the business community, organized labor, the administration, and both parties of the General Assembly. The act passed the House and the Senate unanimously and was signed into law by Governor Thornburgh in December 1982.[27] The legislation became Pennsylvania's Ben Franklin Partnership program (BFP).

During this activist period, the Thornburgh administration also issued the *Advanced Technology Policies for the Commonwealth of Pennsylvania*. This comprehensive and coordinated science and technology policy began to redirect old programs and create new ones.

Developing and applying new technologies to the state's economy is the overriding theme of Pennsylvania's current economic development strategy. First, state officials are attempting to help existing Pennsylvania businesses modernize and expand. Second, they are working to assist new, small firms start up and grow. Finally, the state is selectively recruiting investors from outside Pennsylvania.[28]

Overview

As the state's economic and population base began to decline during the 1970s and 1980s, it adopted an economic development strategy aimed in large part at promoting the growth of advanced technology.[29] The state government was to serve as a catalyst in promoting advanced technology by creating new or redirecting existing government programs to assist established and emerging industries and to help train workers.[30] This approach minimizes government involvement and uses resource pooling and private matching funds instead of solely relying on public appropriations. Primary responsibility for this policy lies with the Department of Commerce, which has established four policy objectives: (a) to increase the capital and financing available to advanced-technology industries; (b) to provide technical assistance and services; (c) to enhance the skills of Pennsylvania's work force; and (d) to promote the expansion of markets for advanced-technology products.[31]

The flagship program within this department is the Ben Franklin Partnership program. This program links private and educational research resources to make traditional industries more competitive in the international marketplace and to spin off new, small businesses on the leading edge of technological innovation.[32] The BFP Challenge Grants provided matching funds to establish four advanced-technology centers that represent consortiums of private-sector, labor, university, and economic development groups. During the 1985-1986 fiscal year the centers shared a state appropriation of $21.3 million, which was matched by more than $80.9 million from consortium members. The private sector contributed $53.8 million. On an annual basis this is the largest leveraged program of its type in the United States. Each $1 in state funds is matched by over $3 in private and other funds.

The four centers provide three services. First, they perform joint applied R&D efforts in specified areas such as robotics, biotechnology, and computer-aided design and manufacture (CAD-CAM). Second, they assist all higher-educational institutions in training and retraining workers in technical and other skill areas essential to firm expansion and startups. Finally, they help entrepreneurs connect with venture capitalists and other financial resources, assist them in the preparation of business plans and feasibility studies, and provide small businesses with incubator space and transfers of technology.

In addition to the BFP Advanced Technology Center (ATC) incubator facilities, $17 million was provided through the BFP during 1984-1986 for the creation and support of small business incubators, for building acquisition and renovation costs, and for equipment costs. In 1985 Pennsylvania had twenty incubator facilities in operation, more than any other state. Of these twenty incubator facilities, two were privately initiated; the rest were initiated by the public sector.[33]

The Ben Franklin Partnership program also addresses education and training needs. The 1984 Pennsylvania Economic Revitalization Fund provided $3 million in state funds for the Engineering School Equipment Grants, which generate a three-to-one match from the private-sector and help purchase equipment used in teaching graduate and undergraduate engineering students.

Moreover, the BFP addresses imperfections in the Pennsylvania economy. First, the Research Seed Grants for small businesses seeking to develop or introduce new products and production processes were increased to $550,000 for FY 1984-1985. To qualify, a business must employ 250 or fewer employees, with preference given to firms with 50 or fewer employees. Applications are evaluated on the basis of technical merit, potential for job creation, linkage with the Ben Franklin Partnership ATCs, and the firm's commitment to continue the project independent of aid. The maximum grant is $35,000.

Second, the Seed Venture Capital Fund is a challenge grant program through which the state's $3 million is matched by at least $9 million in private funds that provide equity financing to new Pennsylvania businesses in their earliest stages of growth. Individual investments are primarily in the $50,000-to-$250,000 range. The program is directed at filling a gap in capital markets currently not addressed by the private-sector venture capital market.

Third, the Pennsylvania Research Inventory Project (PRIP) has produced a cataloged inventory of private and university research capabilities available through depository libraries, regional economic development organizations, educational institutions, and the Department of Commerce. In addition, the Commerce Department provides computer profiles of research capabilities on the basis of equipment, geographic area, research focus, product, and other criteria, on specific request.

The Ben Franklin Partnership, in cooperation with the Department of Revenue, administers the Economic Revitalization Tax Credit Program, which provides a major incentive for business investment and expansion within Pennsylvania with particular emphasis on the retention and expansion of the industrial work force. The program permits corporations involved in any manufacturing, processing, and R&D activities to convert net operating losses that expired in 1981 and 1982 into 20 percent tax credits for new Pennsylvania plant and equipment investments.

Other major programs within the Department of Commerce complement the Ben Franklin Partnership program to promote long-term growth and economic diversification.[34] Some of these programs are briefly described below.

• The Pennsylvania Capital Loan Fund (PCLF) — This fund is a revolving loan program that pools funds from several state and federal sources for loans to small manufacturing and export service firms. For FY 1985-1986, PCLF has pooled $18.7 million.[35]

• Title III funding under the federal Job Training Partnership Act — This funding is used to establish programs to assist individuals who have lost their jobs and face little chance of returning to work as a result of plant closings, relocations, or lay-offs within the past two years. Some of these programs include on-the-job training, job search assistance, customized job training, remedial education, basic skills training, and institutional skill training.

• The Customized Job Training (CJT) Program — This program concentrates on short-term, entry-level training to meet the specific needs of employers who provide committed job opportunities. Training is provided for robotics technicians, mechanical design engineers, systems analysts, and electronics technicians. Funding was increased from $7 million in FY 1984-1985 to $12 million for FY 1985-1986.[36]

• The Small Business Development Centers (SBDCs) — These centers are located in nine colleges and universities across the state, and provide free planning, accounting, market research, financial analysis, and management assistance to small local businesses. State funding for the SBDCs for FY 1985-1986 is $100,000. Through the BFP, the ATCs provided an additional $508,000 in state funds during 1984-1985 to increase services to small advanced-technology companies.[37]

• The Small Business Action Center (SBAC) — The SBAC was created in 1980 to facilitate communication between small businesses and the government. Serving as a general expediter, the SBAC helps small firms meet license and permit requirements. It receives an average of 1,200 calls per month and is stocked with more than 1,000 official forms to save businesses the time and inconvenience of contacting individual state agencies.

• PennTAP — One of the nation's premier technology transfer agents, PennTap provides the means to transmit information generated through the BFP and other sources to new and existing industries in the state. Funding to PennTAP has been increased to $200,000 in FY 1985-1986.[38]

This program, like others, has been redirected to give special attention to emerging technologies. In 1980, the state procured an additional $178,877 in federal funds to allow PennTAP—sponsored jointly by the Department of Commerce and Pennsylvania State University—to expand its assistance to advanced-technology industries.

Finally, in response to both the development priorities of Governor Thornburgh and to cutbacks in federal funding, the ARC was redirected in 1981 away from traditional community assistance in the form of remedial social programs and out-of-state industrial recruiting and toward greater assistance to existing industries and communities in finding new markets, reducing the cost of doing business, stimulating new private-sector investment, and developing a better match between people and jobs. The regional agencies also provide integrated, tailored services to meet the critical needs of the new entrepreneurial firms whose products are capturing new domestic and international markets. Services available include financing assistance, help in bidding for federal procurement contracts, and foreign export assistance.

While the Ben Franklin Partnership program and its complements are the best known of Pennsylvania's science and technology policies, they are not the only substantial ones. At least three other programs not related to either the BFP program or the Department of Commerce address the same economic problems in different ways.

PIDA's lending policies have, as mentioned earlier, changed with the economic needs of the time. Since 1982, PIDA has helped smaller firms and nonmanufacturing clients. With over $50 million available for the 1985-1986 fiscal year, the PIDA board has adopted a policy directing 25 percent of its cash flow to advanced-technology industries.[39] In addition, advanced-technology companies are now eligible to receive the maximum participation rate from PIDA. PIDA also now considers computer software companies to be eligible industrial enterprises.

Legislation passed in July 1984 permitted up to 1 percent, or $100 million in venture capital of the state's pension funds to be invested. To date, $30 million from the State Employees Retirement Fund and $1 million from the Public School Employees Retirement Fund have been invested in venture capital firms based in Pennsylvania.

The Pennsylvania School for the Sciences offers science instruction to outstanding high school students planning to pursue careers in science and mathematics.

The authors selected for additional study the Pennsylvania Technology Assistance Program, the MILRITE Council, and the Advanced Technology Centers and the Seed Venture Capital Fund of the BFP program. These programs were selected for several reasons: they illustrate the diversity of Pennsylvania's technology development strategies, they target advanced technology specifically, they are innovative, they participate in policymaking, and they have sufficiently long histories to permit evaluation.

With one exception, a 1975 independent study of PennTAP, information currently available on these programs is limited to reports issued by the programs themselves.[40] These sources include PennTAP's annual report; a series of reports describing the Advanced Technology Centers issued at various times by the BFP and based on progress reports submitted by the centers; and a single three-year report published by the MILRITE Council.[41] The present study represents the first comparative appraisal of these programs.

THE PENNSYLVANIA TECHNOLOGY ASSISTANCE PROGRAM

The single purpose of PennTAP is to transfer existing technological knowledge from R&D facilities to organizations that can use it. PennTAP connects people who have questions and problems with people who have information.[42]

Political initiative for the creation of a technology transfer program was taken by Governor William Scranton in the early 1960s when he appointed an advisory committee from the industrial, academic, and political sectors to investigate ways in which state-supported research could economically benefit the private sector. The Science Advisory Committee concluded that industry would benefit more from an outreach program than it would from the direct state funding of research projects, and PennTAP was created in 1965.[43]

PennTAP claims that every dollar it spends saves the state economy $17.20 through the technical improvements made by its clients. This in turn increases the amount of tax paid and jobs created.[44] The source of data for this evaluation of the program is a one-page questionnaire sent by the PennTAP administration to all firms that have consulted PennTAP that year. Organizations are asked if they used the information gained through the aid of PennTAP, what the results were, whether they saved money, and if so, what dollar amount was saved. Only those firms that say they applied the information they gained are counted, and savings are credited to a single year, even though actual savings may be realized for several years. The response rate of the evaluation is 35 to 40 percent, and results are released only with client permission.[45]

Program Operations

PennTAP began with one secretary, one part-time administrator, a small, volunteer, part-time staff of academics, and the understanding that it must produce results in its first few years of operation or shut down. In its first three years, PennTAP funded many projects, including a mobile library and lectures, but found that mass distribution did not necessarily lead to technology transfer. In these years the program waxed and waned, but had enough success to continue.[46]

The most important issue of the early years was the difference between the large quantity of information supplied and the small quantity used by clients. Believing that personal contact with clients would help reduce the discrepancy, PennTAP hired its first technical specialist in 1971. The technical specialists often visited sites to clarify problems and provide appropriate information. This emphasis on personal contact has not changed since 1971 because experience has proved it works.[47]

PennTAP's first and present director, H. LeRoy Marlow, says the program's philosophy, its active advisory council, and dedicated technical specialists make the program successful. PennTAP's philosophy is expressed in the following maxims.

- Simply having information available does not guarantee that it will be located, used or understood by the client who needs it. Information should be relayed in the language of the users.
- The amount of information transferred and applied is directly proportional to the amount of face-to-face contact between the technical specialist and client.
- There is no need to reinvent the wheel. If a firm has a problem, another company has probably had a similar problem and may be able to help. Cost-benefit ratios should be properly evaluated.

PennTAP does not indiscriminately distribute materials, publish a costly newsletter, or consider the number of miles driven, the number of people that attend a meeting, the number of hours with clients, or the number of dollars spent on projects as measures of its work. Many agriculture extension programs and federal agencies do measure "results" this way. "They fund activities, not results," says Dr. Marlow.[48]

Another factor contributing to the program's success is PennTAP's advisory council, which is composed of fifteen executive volunteers from scientific, technical, and industrial organizations. It meets five times a year to set financial, manpower, and program priorities.[49] The members devote about eight days per year to PennTAP.[50] Staggered three-year terms ensure a continuous infusion of new ideas. In addition, there are five permanent resource members on the advisory council with specialized backgrounds.

The council concentrates on policy decisions and does not exercise any administrative control. Throughout the year, it works as a task force on special areas of interest.[51] Besides occasionally answering questions from the legislature about PennTAP, each council member is in weekly contact with the director about new clients and resources. The council also acts as a watchdog to ensure that PennTAP does not compete with consultants. This is done by always having a consultant on the council who represents Pennsylvania's consultants.[52]

In addition to the director, information coordinator, manager, and two secretaries, there are seven technical specialists. These specialists all have at least master's degrees and industrial experience; about half have PhDs. They work as the matchmakers, or transfer agents, between the researchers and users. Since inquiries are often expressed in terms of symptoms, technical specialists must often define the clients' problem before they can propose solutions. This they do willingly and with diplomacy. Dr. Marlow credits the success of PennTAP not to administration but to the day-to-day relationships between the technical specialists and the users.[53]

The line between consulting and information dissemination is at times a fine one. To prevent conflicts of interests, technical specialists are not permitted to be private consultants for firms in Pennsylvania. This removes any incentive to shape the clients' technical information to gain consulting work on the side.[54] Such measures help prevent PennTAP from competing with the private sector.

PennTAP is closely associated with Pennsylvania State University. While the director administers PennTAP, the formal responsibility for the program belongs to the vice president and dean of the university's Commonwealth Educational System and the assistant vice president and director of the Continuing Education Division.

Although the administrators and staff are located on PSU's campus, potential clients can call any of PSU's twenty-four Continuing Education offices throughout the state for information about PennTAP.[55] This administrative and referral relationship is reinforced by the state's land-grant university commitment to making practical knowledge available to the people.[56]

Until 1970, PennTAP was federally funded under the federal State Technical Services Act of 1965. In the early 1970s the Pennsylvania Legislature annually appropriated the organization at least $100,000.[57] Since then PennTAP's funding from the state has consistently grown but never exceeded $1,000,000. Currently, PSU and the Pennsylvania legislature through the Department of Commerce provide the bulk of PennTAP's funding.[58] PennTAP does accept additional funding if the constraints are consistent with the organization's mission.[59] Salaries, travel costs of the technical specialists, postage, and large telephone bills comprise most of the operating costs.

PennTAP does not charge for its services, and the issue of user fees has repeatedly surfaced. PennTAP has consistently argued against charging its clients for two reasons. First, collecting fees is an expensive process and fees would have to reflect these billing costs.

Second, PennTAP primarily serves small and medium-sized firms that have cash flow constraints and will not buy PennTAP's services unless guaranteed results. Many Pennsylvania citizens would not have benefited in the past twenty years if PennTAP had instituted user fees.[60]

PennTAP's major program activities are divided into response mechanisms and active mechanisms. Response mechanisms operate when a client knows enough about PennTAP to call and ask for help; the technical experts then give personal attention to the client until the case is closed. Each year the technical experts respond to 1,200-1,300 cases a year. Since PennTAP hired its first technical specialist in 1971 it has responded to 19,300 questions and problems.[61]

The active mechanism functions when PennTAP notifies some of its existing clients about new developments from federal labs and university research that might be of use to them. PennTAP then works with the clients in pilot programs to determine the usefulness of the information. If it shows economic potential, a series of workshops are organized for the users who might benefit.[62] With minor variations, the active mechanism accounts for 30 percent of PennTAP's work; the remaining 70 percent is response work.[63]

PennTAP does not restrict the type of technical problems that it will undertake because the demand for specialty questions is not great enough.[64] In addition, specialty technology transfer programs are often unable to answer questions outside their expertise. Since PennTAP has contacts with all of the national science labs, it can generalize.[65]

The known economic benefits of PennTAP's work from 1972 to 1984 total just under $80 million. During 1984 alone, the organization saved the Pennsylvania economy $10 million. From 1979 to 1984 the program created or saved over 500 jobs and from 1983 to 1984 it helped develop or improve fifty-five new products.[66]

PennTAP serves a variety of clients and answers a broad array of questions. Most often, the client is from business or industry and the question is about microelectronics or computers. During the 1970s the questions most often asked dealt with energy; in 1983, advanced-technology questions became the most frequently asked. This change reflects the needs of users.[67]

During its twenty years of existence, PennTAP has developed an extensive network of research resources that allows its staff members to be science and technology generalists. In addition to the obvious source of their own technical specialists, PennTAP draws on other specialists—the faculty and library at PSU and other universities; federal, state, and local technical information centers; information data bases; and national labs.[68]

Although PennTAP does not find newsletters to be cost effective, it must still make its services known to potential users. Most clients find out about PennTAP through referrals from other clients, the Department of Commerce, PSU branches, the advisory council, and the state-supported Small Business Development Centers. In addition, PennTAP shares visible success stories with legislators which they in turn can report to their constituencies. Finally, PennTAP representatives attend conferences throughout the year to generate visibility.[69]

Analysis of Goal Attainment

Overall, PennTAP is a very successful program. The cost-benefit ratios it reports are conservative—some clients simply do not report their results and they are not included in PennTAP's calculations—and, with one qualification, reasonable. The qualification is that certain operating services that PennTAP receives at no cost—free utilities from PSU; free legal, accounting, and public-relations services from other state supported institutions—are not figured into cost-benefit proportions.[70] If they were included—and they probably should be—the cost-benefit ratio would be lower. Even with this assessment note, the program remains a very effective and efficient one. The program's single-minded concern with results makes it effective. The ability of the program to generate such large returns for the state's economy with such low funding makes it very efficient.

Additional considerations support this assessment of PennTAP. In 1974 a review team concluded that "PennTAP is a program that other states should emulate."[71] Louis Rukeyser, host of *Wall Street Week in Review*, called PennTAP "the most sophisticated state program of its kind."[72]

PennTAP has received recognition in Pennsylvania for its work. The governor's Product of the Year award for 1985 went to a company that PennTAP had helped. In 1984 and 1985, PennTAP won the national competition of the National Association of Management Technical Assistance Centers in the area of technology transfer.[73]

Issues

The first issue has been mentioned earlier: PennTAP does not compete with the private sector, especially consultants. It identifies options for clients—when jobs go beyond information exchange, it refers clients to private-sector consultants. PennTAP does no research or design work. The advisory council protects both consultants and PennTAP since a consultant sits on the council to arbitrate any disputes.[74]

A second issue concerns concentration of services. Even though PSU's main campus is in a rural county, the number of cases handled there were higher than in Philadelphia, Pittsburgh, or Bethlehem. From 1972-1984, PennTAP handled 2,823 cases in its headquarters' county and from 136 to 459 cases in surrounding counties. In counties even farther away from PSU's main campus, PennTAP took from 1 to 1,122 cases; most caseloads were under 500. PennTAP might consider installing satellite stations for its technical specialists at PSU's branches in urban areas. Such satellites would increase awareness about the program and likely decrease the response time to clients farther from PSU's main campus—as is, the technical specialists "often have the problem of not getting the information to the firm fast enough."[75]

A third issue is that of expert staffing. Although PennTAP is part of a land grant university, association with it is not a significant factor in tenure decisions. Untenured faculty members, therefore, are not motivated to participate. This has become the biggest deterrent to having a university involved in a technology transfer program.[76] Since changes in the university tenure policies are not likely, only tenured faculty will be able to accept PennTAP technical specialist positions.

Finally, the PennTAP administration is required to seek funding every year. Given the program's record, the soft funding from PSU and the Department of Commerce could safely be converted into guaranteed minimum funding. This would likely increase the administration's efficiency. With any change in administration, guaranteed funding could be withdrawn until the competency of the new personnel was proven.

Given that the current Pennsylvania budget is running a surplus, future prospects for PennTAP look excellent. The current fashion of high-technology programs in government is also likely to lead to increased funding for PennTAP.

THE MILRITE COUNCIL

Program History
  The MILRITE Council was created by the Pennsylvania General Assembly
in 1978 at the instigation of the Pennsylvania AFL-CIO and the Pennsylvania
Chamber of Commerce. Established to be an agent for reforming the economy,
MILRITE is a tripartite council with representatives from labor, business, and
government.[77] The council is not high-technology specific; it was given a
broad mandate to (a) undertake research; (b) create plans for industrial
revitalization; (c) encourage coordination among federal, state, and local
programs; (d) recommend structural changes of the state government; and (e)
encourage business, labor, and government cooperative efforts in all these
areas.[78] In 1984 the council was also given administrative responsibilities for
the Area Labor-Management Committee grant program (ALMC).[79]

Program Operation
  The MILRITE Council is composed of representatives from business, labor,
and government. Members are appointed by the governor, with the AFL-CIO
and the Chamber of Commerce each nominating five members, the
Pennsylvania General Assembly, four members (from both the House and the
Senate), and the governor choosing his own representative.[80]
  The council operates with no set agenda; rather, it allows any topic, from the
investment of pension funds to high-speed rail passenger systems, to be
brought up at its monthly meetings. If further study of an issue is deemed
appropriate the staff is directed to undertake additional research. All public
pronouncements must reflect the views of the entire board membership; the
consensus decisionmaking process reinforces the council's image as a
nonpartisan body.[81] Due to its reputation for objectivity, the council can serve
as a forum for discussing controversial subjects.[82] Business, labor, and
government representatives can discuss legislative issues affecting the state's
economic growth in an arena outside the normal, and historically antagonistic,
channels.[83]
  The MILRITE Council's staff is small—an executive director and two
support personnel—and focuses on research efforts to substantiate the council's
positions. The addition of the Area Labor-Management Committee program
has greatly increased the staff's workload. The staff reports itself unable to do
more than fulfill its basic ALMC program responsibilities and finds its research
efforts severely hampered.[84] With hiring controlled by the governor's office, an
increase in staffing is unlikely. This illustrates the difficult position that the
council occupies in the government structure: while established as an

214

independent body, the council is dependent on the state for funding.[85] Consequently, a degree of political control exists over the council that can adversely affect its functioning as an independent advisory body.

Analysis of Goal Attainment and Evaluation

The MILRITE Council functions as a planning body and as an agent of business-labor cooperation; both functions are difficult to evaluate in terms of specific results. As a planning body the council develops ideas addressing the state's economic problems. Success as a planning body cannot be expressed as a ratio of the number of ideas implemented to ideas proposed—good ideas can be rejected, and ideas adopted can be rendered ineffective through the political process. Likewise, success as an agent of cooperation defies meaningful measurement. Assessing the effectiveness of the council as an advisory body and agent of cooperation is a matter of comparing and contrasting the opinions of the people involved. Some of those opinions follow.

The authorizing legislation for the council calls for it to formulate economic development plans and improve the functioning of government. Two impediments to the council's attainment of these goals have arisen. The first is the board's expertise. While business representatives are familiar with the economic issues, the labor members are not, being primarily concerned with job creation.[86] In addition, the governor's office is reluctant to let an independent group dictate state policy and in so doing gain political power. In recognition of these obstacles, the council members have elected to choose only specific issues of mutual interest where agreement can be reached.[87]

The council has limited its advisory role to three areas: labor-management relations, energy and transportation, and state development policies and programs.[88] All of the council's proposals have been passed by the General Assembly.[89] As a result, the council assumes partial responsibility for all of Pennsylvania's efforts in advanced technology.[90] Critics, however, attribute the council's success to its recommending only popular ideas that appeal to the lowest common denominator within the legislature.[91] They suggest that on difficult issues the council does not have the legislature's respect.[92]

In contrast to this debate, there is the general agreement that the council successfully fosters labor-management cooperation in areas outside of collective bargaining issues such as worker productivity, employee stock ownership programs, and area labor-management committees.[93] Interviewees agreed for the most part that the council should become involved in more programs like the ALMC and do more to engender labor-management cooperation.[94]

Issues

Three questions arise concerning MILRITE as a policy advisory body: (a) What is the council expected to accomplish? (b) What is the relationship of the council to the legislature and governor? (c) Who is to be represented on the council, and why should a particular group or sector be recognized? The third question is partially answered by looking at its members, the AFL-CIO and the Chamber of Commerce. By giving representation to these groups it was assured that their concerns would be addressed. However, some groups may be excluded from participation. There is a noticeable shortage of big-business and manufacturing-worker representatives on the council, apparently the result of internal politics and self-exclusion.[95]

Experience has shown that the objectives of the council should be limited and clearly defined. It appears that too broad an agenda was set for the council and the council has had to take time to find where it can be effective. This process can lead to wasted effort but is unavoidable unless the legislature narrows its expectations.

This raises the issue of the relationship between the advisory body and the rest of the government. Although the council is described as an independent body, its funding makes it subject to policymaking control by the governor's office. The council does have access to the General Assembly through its legislative board members, but its actual impact is difficult to determine. MILRITE has carved a niche for itself in labor-management issues outside the scope of collective bargaining and in smaller issues over which agreements can be reached, but the presence of government is at times seen as a hindrance.[96]

THE ADVANCED TECHNOLOGY CENTERS

The purpose of the Advanced Technology Centers, like the BFP, is to promote advanced technology throughout the state in order to create and retain jobs. The ATCs bear most of the burden in trying to meet the goal of creating 10,000 jobs within the first four years of the BFP's operations.[97] The BFP provides matching funds to the ATCs, which represent consortiums of private-sector firms, research universities, other higher educational institutions, and economic development groups.[98] By linking industry to research centers, the ATCs help create new firms, strengthen traditional industries for the international marketplace, and increase the level of investment in the state.[99] In short, the ATCs are catalysts[100] which focus on university-industry projects, not bricks and mortar.[101]

Program History

For reasons that became evident after the work of the Pennsylvania State Planning Board and the MILRITE Council, the state decided in 1982 that the ATCs should be the central program in the Ben Franklin Partnership Program. First, as mentioned earlier in this chapter, several excellent research institutions existed in the state. Second, more cooperation between the universities and industry was needed. Third, there was the recognition that most of the new jobs in the state would come from small businesses.[102] Last, and probably most important, there was political recognition that economic development was not

216

going to happen without state support.[103] By connecting universities with particular specialties of interest to industry, the ATCs could help achieve economies of scale in university research.

In 1982, only two Pennsylvania legislators sponsored the BFP bill. The 1983 appropriation of $1 million to be divided equally among the four ATCs passed with little debate—it was not considered to be an important program, and most legislators thought little would come of it. This attitude changed when in 1985-1986 the governor increased appropriations to the ATCs to $21.3 million. By 1988 the legislature will have spent over $100 million on the program.[104]

Most legislators in the state take a rather sophisticated approach to the ATCs. They recognize that the program is a long-term one that will not immediately produce jobs. In addition, most recognize that the program will work only if the level of political influence is kept to a minimum when the ATCs distribute funds.[105]

Program Operations

The ATCs are coordinated by BFP administrators who work for Pennsylvania's Department of Commerce under the direction of the governor. Each is unique in organization, but all four have close ties with at least one university. The Southeastern Pennsylvania ATC (SP/ATC) in Philadelphia is the most unusual because it is affiliated with the University City Science Center, a consortium of colleges, universities, and professional health institutions. The ATCs of Central and Northern Pennsylvania (C/N ATC) and the North East Tier (NET/ATC) are affiliated with Lehigh University and Pennsylvania State University, respectively. The Western Pennsylvania ATC (WP/ATC) is associated with a consortium led by the University of Pittsburgh and Carnegie-Mellon University.

Since the C/N ATC is responsible for the largest region in the state, it is permitted to have two satellites. Located in Erie and Harrisburg-York, the satellites help develop economic projects which are sensitive to the needs of the community. The SP/ATC and the NET/ATC also have quasi-satellites.[106] Although each ATC is expected to operate in its geographic region, projects from other regions may be undertaken by an ATC if they fall into its area of specialization.

The number of staff members in each ATC varies from seven to eleven, and staff members serve as project managers. To make sure that the industries and universities are doing their part to make the project successful, the project managers try to visit every project each year. The proximity of the staff to their projects makes these visits more or less difficult. Although the number of on-site visits depends upon the ATC, all four centers must obtain tri-annual reports from each project detailing its progress.

As mentioned earlier, funding for the ATCs has increased substantially since their establishment in 1983. After the initial allocation of $250,000 for each

ATC, the funding became competitive and is now based on a complex formula that uses matching funds as an indication of the private sector's commitment to the projects. The bottom-line goal of all four ATCs is jobs and the primary surrogate measure for job potential of the projects is matching funds—the ratio between outside funds and BFP funds to the ATCs must be at least one-to-one.

Funds for submitted project proposal are distributed to the four ATCs from three sources by the BFP. First, an equity fund of $1.5 million goes to each center. Second, matching funds based on the amount of funds from the private sector and other economic development organizations are distributed. Funds from smaller firms are given more weight than funds from larger corporations. The third and final source is based on eight past-performance measures—one, for example, assesses whether the projections made in the past concerning job creation have been accurate.[107]

The funding however, is not completely formulaic. The program has been in operation several years now, and the board is beginning to assess more accurately the reasonableness of each ATC's judgment about job-creation potential. In the past, the fifteen-member BFP board could not really determine which ATCs were submitting projects with the most job-creation potential. The board does not evaluate projects individually—they are presented as a package, and the board had to trust the ATCs' judgment.[108]

Initially, the four ATCs were able to match the $1 million state funding with over $3 million from the private sector and other organizations. In the 1983-1984 state budget, the legislature increased the ATCs' appropriation to $10 million, which leveraged $28 million (a 1:2.8 ratio), $16 million of which came from the private sector. The amounts disbursed by the state to the different ATCs ranged from $3.35 to $1.4 million for a total of 236 projects. In the 1984-1985 state budget, the funding increased to $18 million, which leveraged $55 million (a 1:3.08 ratio), $33 million of which was from the private sector. Finally, the state funds again increased in the fourth program year to a total of $21.3 million, which raised $80.9 million in matching funds, including $53.8 million from the private sector (a 1:3.80 ratio). The total ATC funds of $102.2 million funded 378 projects for FY 1985-1986. The grants to the different ATCs narrowed in range from previous years and were between $5.9 to $4.7 million.[109]

Growth in state appropriations, though dramatic, should be put into perspective. The legislature annually appropriates $23 million to the PSU Veterinary School. In 1983, the Democrats proposed a $1-billion economic development program, PennPride, which was a large tax-and-spend bill. This was rejected by the Republicans, who compromised on a $190-million economic development bond issue in early 1984.[110] Of that $190-million, $23 million was given to three programs under the BFP.[111] In absolute terms the funding for the ATCs is large; in relative terms it is not.

Proposals are submitted to the ATCs each spring from industries, universities, and entrepreneurs. The competition for funding at each ATC varies. For example, the NET/ATC received 250 proposals, 146 of which it found worth funding. Since its $9-million package was only funded at $5.9 million, the NET/ATC actually funded only 111 projects.[112] In contrast, the C/N ATC received 150 proposals and with $4.7 million funded 100 projects.[113]

The major program operations of the ATC are threefold. First, each ATC must fund joint university- and industry-applied R&D that focuses on new manufacturing processes and products. The private sector demonstrates dedication to a project through the use of matching funds; a company that is willing to invest $4 for every state dollar in a project must value the project highly and expect that it will show quick returns.[114] Those commercially feasible projects with the largest short-term job impact are given highest priority by the ATCs. Each has selected areas in which it specializes.

Second, each ATC must fund education and training programs in areas essential to firm expansions and startups that are not currently served by the region's educational institutions.[115] These programs help establish links among educational institutions in each region while initiating curriculum changes.[116]

Third, each ATC must promote entrepreneurship development by providing incubator space and entrepreneurial services. The incubators offer new small businesses a variety of services, including below-market rent for office and lab space; free secretarial, technical, management, marketing, financial, and legal services; below-market janitorial, security, utility, and computer services; and access to copying machines and conference rooms. Companies are admitted to an incubator center if they have a solid business plan and can reasonably project growth which will create employment. As recognition of the usefulness of incubators grows in the business world, some new companies are finding that participation in the programs gains them unexpected prestige and increases their fund-raising capabilities.[117] Some incubators permit their companies to remain for up to three years.[118]

While it was beyond the scope of this study to interview university officials and project managers, several important points concerning the relationship between the ATCs and the universities need to be mentioned. The ATCs have had different working experiences with their respective universities. The NET ATC at Lehigh University has consistently been awarded the greatest amount of competitive grant funds. Lehigh University has a tradition of working closely with industry—even prior to the NET/ATC, the Lehigh administration encouraged faculty to spend at least one day a week working with companies. These close ties shaped Lehigh's rise to excellence in fields of interest to industry such as CAD/CAM.[119]

The C/N ATC at Pennsylvania State University has consistently been awarded the least amount of competitive grant funds. In fact, its first proposal for funding as an ATC was rejected because of its academic approach. Representative Tom Murphy says the PSU administrators "have never really bought the idea that the university's role goes beyond teaching and research to include creating jobs."[120] C/N ATC has, however, steadily narrowed the difference in funding levels.

Being located in an urban area is an additional plus for an ATC. In contrast with the ATCs located in Philadelphia, Bethlehem, and Pittsburgh, the C/N ATC is located in the center of the state's rural area. The area is dotted with isolated communities that are used to solving their own problems. Events move quicker in an urban area, and there is also a greater supply of capital supporting a critical mass of industry and technology. The C/N ATC must develop what the urban ATCs can take for granted. In short, the C/N ATC must work harder to obtain a return similar to the other ATCs.[121] This rather stark difference between urban and rural areas is reinforced by Arthur Heim's suggestion that appropriate technology rather than advanced technology might be a better way to develop rural areas economically.[122]

The last important point concerns university rivalries. The SP/ATC in Philadelphia has been able to work through the University City Science Center (UCSC). Since the UCSC's creation in 1964, its neutrality has been an asset in its dealings with all the universities, especially the medical universities. This neutrality has permitted the universities to cooperate on research projects without feeling threatened. This cooperation can be contrasted with the WP/ATC, located in Pittsburgh. The rivalry and animosity between Carnegie-Mellon University and the University of Pittsburgh is so pronounced that an outside executive director has been hired to overcome this problem.[123] Potential hostilities between universities should be given careful consideration when the ATC-university relationship is structured.

Analysis of Goal Attainment

Since by August 1985 the ATCs had created or retained only 3,570 jobs, it is unlikely that the BFP will meet its ambitious and probably politically motivated goal of 10,000 jobs by 1987. This does not mean that the program is a failure. The long-term nature of the program makes it still too early to judge it on the basis of jobs creation—at least four more years are needed for a proper assessment. However, several comments about the program's strengths and weaknesses can be made.

On the positive side, the ATCs have played an important role within the BFP in creating a collective vision of job creation in the state.[124] The ATCs have caused industry and academia to work together on projects they both want to do.[125] In addition, competition among the ATCs for state funding simulates market competition and provides an incentive for each to be efficient; the success of the basically nonpolitical funding strengthens this point. Finally, the amount of money given the ATCs has increased with their experience—in the early stages, they would not have been able to spend large amounts as wisely.[126]

On the negative side, the manner of choosing and funding the C/N ATC was hardly businesslike. The C/N ATC was funded because it was affiliated with the state university, not because it had excellent projects backed with large amounts of private-sector matching funds that had strong job potential. Second, while the ATCs are supposed to be in partnership with labor, this sector is noticeable only by its absence. The ATCs have resorted to affirmative action plans to try to recruit labor's involvement. The siege mentality of the Pennsylvania labor unions, brought on by declining traditional industries and increasing lay-offs, has not changed over the years and is not expected to change at the hands of present union leadership.[127] Third, the ATCs were intended to become self-financing. Given that the funds for the ATCs continue to increase, the time when royalties and dividend checks begin to repay the state's direct investment is in the distant future.

The ATCs were a clear risk. Considering the potential payoff, the extreme economic situation the state was experiencing, and the relatively small amount of money the ATCs cost, it can be said that the program as of 1985 was worth the risk.

SEED CAPITAL VENTURE FUNDS

Legislative History

In 1982-1983 several studies were published that confirmed a general perception that there was a shortage of venture capital in Pennsylvania. The reasons for the shortage ranged from the simple unavailability of funds[128] to the state banks' conservative banking practices.[129] More specifically, early-stage funding for new firms was found to be a capital market not adequately addressed by the private sector.[130] The early stage includes the seed financing phase in which an inventor proves an idea, the startup phase of product development and initial marketing, and first-stage financing that begins commercial manufacturing and sales. New firms, by definition, do not have sales records or assets by which they can secure loans.[131]

The Seed Venture Capital Fund (SCVF) was created by the Pennsylvania legislature in 1984 in response to this perceived capital market gap.[132] The SCVF was not to compete with the private sector; rather, it was to increase early venture capital funding through matching state funds.

The legislation limited the ways in which the SCVFs could be invested in by the private venture capital funds (VCFs) in several respects. First, only firms in Pennsylvania (with less than fifty employees were eligible.[133] Second, the total amount invested by the VCF in a firm was not "ordinarily" to exceed $500,000 and the maximum in any one round of funding was not "ordinarily" to be above $250,000. Finally, other prior VCF funding in an individual firm was not "ordinarily" to have exceeded $250,000 over the life of the firm.[134]

The legislation did not specify any method by which the program should be evaluated. The normal business measure of success for VCFs is the rate of return (ROR) on investment; the single purpose of all VCFs is to make money for their investors. The state, in evaluating its investments, may assume that the most profitable can also create jobs. The state may also assume that the greater the ROR, the more successfully the VCF is choosing firms that will pay off. However, job creation will, from the VCF's point of view, be an unintended consequence of its work.

Program Operations
The 1984 authorization by the Pennsylvania legislature for the SCVF delegated disbursement of the funds through the Ben Franklin Partnership's four Advanced Technology Centers. Each ATC was permitted to invest $750,000 as a limited partner in a privately capitalized VCF. As a limited partner, the ATC has no control over individual investments. The level of matching funds from the private sector must be $3 for every $1 of the state's money.[135] By the end of 1985, the four funds were in various stages of closing. The C/N ATC at PSU was having an especially difficult time with the SCVF because no appropriate VCF existed in that rural area. In contrast, the Genesis Seed Fund, Ltd. had already decided to invest in small startup companies when the SP ATC decided to invest.[136]

Assessment of Goal Attainment
Because few investments had been made by the end of 1985, a program evaluation is impossible. However, one aspect of the SCVF program merits attention. If a state concludes that it has a venture capital shortage, and it assumes an active role filling that need, then the relationship between the government and the VCF should be strictly nonpolitical. VCFs are successful only if they can make purely business decisions about projects. The limited-partnership role of the ATCs should be the extent of state involvement. This relationship structurally prevents state government from exerting pressure on fund managers and does not force state reliance on a self-imposed separation of elected officials from fund managers.

Limitations of Study and Questions
There are two important issues concerning venture capital that are beyond the scope of this study. The first is whether a capital gap for startup firms really exists in Pennsylvania. Some argue that the lack of opportunities for venture capitalists and the small number of startups reduces the demand for private-sector VCFs in Pennsylvania. The real problem, they say, is the costs of production in the state.[137] Obviously, if a gap does not exist, the program is competing with and duplicating the private sector's role.

The second issue concerns the debate over uneven geographical distribution of venture capital projects. If, as some argue, venture capital for startups is limited to areas close to the venture capitalists for the sake of convenient consultation, then the existence of the "gap" can be confirmed. Others insist that venture capitalists will go anywhere to fund the best projects.

There are also two questions concerning the SCVF that should be raised. First, is it proper for banks to be venture capitalists? If not, the state may have to take a more active role in promoting private VCFs, especially if alternate private-sector investment companies do not already exist in the state. Second, do the state's guidelines permit enough, but not too much, discretion on the part of fund managers? Even if a gap in the capital market does not exist, the state may want, for whatever reasons, to invest in VCFs. In this case the limitations currently imposed on Pennsylvania VCF managers are unsound.

Conclusions

Pennsylvania's advanced-technology policy is intended to create an environment conducive to economic growth through programs designed to foster new ideas and apply newly acquired knowledge to existing and emerging industries. The ultimate policy objective is to reinvigorate the economy and produce jobs. Consequently, program success is measured by the number of jobs created or retained. To achieve this goal, the state attempts to promote cooperative endeavors among industry, labor, and public and private universities and to limit its own role to that of catalyst, with minimal control over operations after the programs are in place. In establishing the programs the state has attempted to build upon existing strengths, beginning with the higher-educational system. Once the programs are operating, additional responsibilities can be added, as in the case of the Advanced Technology Centers and the Seed Capital Venture Fund.

The programs included in this study were created over a span of twenty years. Each addresses a separate objective of the state's advanced-technology policy and interacts very little with the others.[138] Despite this, the programs reinforce each other. Taken together, they attempt to meet the needs of the economy through the application of advanced technology at all the stages of the business and product life cycle. In fact, one could arrange the programs in this study on a continuum covering the needs of businesses through their life span.

Pennsylvania's programs have been established under the philosophy that business can better achieve the state's objectives than the state can. As a result the programs operate independently from government supervision on a day-to-day basis. The primary means of control the state has is funding. The state can use the power of the purse to implement policy changes on the programs.

Certain programs, such as PennTAP, are entirely dependent on state funding. In this situation a program can be discontinued or allowed to languish if it falls from favor or expanded if it is a popular program. Other programs are based upon cooperation between sectors that have previously hesitated to cooperate. Should the government attempt to force changes not mutually agreed upon, it could alienate the participants and destroy the program. However, many of the cooperative programs are administratively independent and could become financially self-supporting, effectively eliminating any government control.

The state's ability to oversee its advanced-technology programs is also of concern. The BFP, the administrative body for most of the state's programs, seems ill equipped to accomplish this. It was acknowledged that the BFP does not have the expertise or the manpower to audit or verify many of the reports submitted to it.[139] This could require the General Assembly to either enlarge the BFP staff or assume a greater oversight role itself.

The basic question of whether or not advanced technology can meet the needs of Pennsylvania given its recent economic and demographic changes still remains. Advanced-technology policy is just one part of a general economic development program, but it is the showpiece of the state's activities. Expectations for the various programs are high. But there is concern that the state may be writing off a generation of workers.[140] These programs have been established with the understanding that results will appear five to ten years after becoming operational. Officials from all of the programs have admitted that if they were to be judged at this time on the basis of job creation, they would be considered failures. The state's advanced-technology policy doesn't seem to help the middle-aged workers who have been laid off, and they are a sizable population.

Pennsylvania's experience provides lessons that can be of benefit to any state interested in establishing a science and technology policy. The first is the importance of clearly defining policy objectives and designing programs specifically geared toward those goals. To accomplish this, a large number of groups with an interest in the policy area should be involved and accommodated. At the same time, the state must be aware of individual group motives, which may differ from the state's, and of any institutional rivalries that may exist between groups.[141]

Pennsylvania has also proven that an incremental approach to program creation can be effective if policy objectives are kept in mind. A state adopting a new policy does not have to create every conceivable program at one time. New organizations can be created and programs appended to existing structures as needed. This will give the state time to gain experience with the new policy and allow for a period of adjustment. The incremental approach can also be applied toward the funding of programs, with funding increasing as the program proves itself capable of achieving its objectives. At the same time, adequate financing at the start is important so that the program is not hampered by lack of funds.

While Pennsylvania's programs attempt to serve the economy in general, they can also assist the state in the performance of its own duties. The primary example of this is PennTAP, which helps state agencies and local governments with their technical problems just as it does for businesses.[142]

State economic policy should be attuned to the social philosophy and culture of the state. Pennsylvania is attempting to create a climate favorable to new businesses with the government trying to assist, not control development. Other states must examine their own prevailing attitudes towards government and determine for themselves what policies and programs are proper.

NOTES

1. U.S. Department of Commerce, *Statistical Abstract of the United States, 1985,* (Washington, D.C., 1984), t. 14, p.15.
2. U.S. Department of Commerce, *State Population Estimates, by Age and Components of Change: 1980-1984* (Washington, D.C.), 1985, 7.
3. The Pennsylvania MILRITE Council, *The Pennsylvania Economy: Past, Present, Future* (Harrisburg, Pennsylvania, 1984), 50.
4. Gordon F. De Jong, "Demographic Forces Reshaping Pennsylvania's Economy in the 1980s," Population Issues Research Center, Pennsylvania State University, 1983, unpublished manuscript.
5. U.S. Department of Labor, *Employment, Hours, and Earnings, States and Areas, 1939-1982,* vol. 2: *New Hampshire-Wyoming* (Washington, D.C., 1984), 709.
6. The Pennsylvania MILRITE Council, *Pennsylvania Economy,* 56.
7. At this time insufficient information exists to make a final determination on this topic.
8. National Science Foundation, *Federal Funds for Research and Development,* vol. 31, 141 (Washington, D.C., 1982); vol. 32, 142 (1983); vol. 33, 141 (1984).
9. Ibid.
10. National Science Foundation, *Research and Development in Industry, 1983,* tables B-50 and B-51 (Washington, D.C., 1985).
11. Greg E. Robertson and David N. Allen, "From Kites to Computers: Pennsylvania's Ben Franklin Partnership" (paper presented at the annual meeting of the American Society for Public Administration, Denver, Colorado, April 9, 1984), 4.
12. Coy, *Pennsylvania Economy,* 61.
13. Robertson and Allen, "From Kites to Computers," 20-24.

14. Barbara J. Frey, et al., *1985 Update: The Competitive Position of Pennsylvania Businesses* (Harrisburg, Pennsylvania: Business Council of Pennsylvania, 1985), 6.
15. Ibid., 7. The state's vocational-technical education system is also extensive; however, there is concern that it is not sufficiently geared to the training needs of adult workers, since its eighty-six area vocational education schools have historically focused on training adolescents.
16. Coy, *Pennsylvania Economy*, 62.
17. Frey, *1985 Update*, 7.
18. David N. Allen and Gregg E. Robertson, *Silicon, Sensors, and Software: Listening to Advanced Technology Enterprises in Pennsylvania*, (Harrisburg, Pennsylvania: Pennsylvania MILRITE Council, July 1983), 13.
19. Coy, *Pennsylvania Economy*, 57.
20. Michael Barker and Lawrence Litvak, *Pension Funds and Economic Development: How Public Funds Can Contribute to the Pennsylvania Economy* (Harrisburg, Pennsylvania: Pennsylvania MILRITE Council, 1983), 2.
21. Coy, *Pennsylvania Economy*, 60.
22. Governor Richard L. Thornburgh, *Advanced Technology Policies for the Commonwealth of Pennsylvania* (Harrisburg, Pennsylvania: Pennsylvania Department of Commerce, 1982), 6.
23. Governor Richard L. Thornburgh, "Economic Development in Pennsylvania: A Status Report and Blueprint for the Future" (paper presented to the Executive Committee of the National Governor's Association, Portland, Maine, 1983), 1.
24. Robertson and Allen, "From Kites to Computers," 2.
25. Ibid., 3.
26. Governor Richard L. Thornburgh, "State Strategies and Incentives for Economic Development," *Journal of Law and Commerce* 4, 1, (1984): 5.
27. The Pennsylvania MILRITE Council, *Partners in Progress: The Pennsylvania MILRITE Council Three Year Report* (Harrisburg, Pennsylvania, 1983), 28.
28. Pennsylvania Department of Commerce, James O. Pickard, Secretary, *Enterprise Development Update: July, 1985*, 1.
29. While the rest of this report does not differentiate between *advanced technology* and *high technology*, Pennsylvania believes that there is a difference. The phrase *advanced technology* as used in this chapter is the broader term and includes new technology used in existing industries' products or processes. This phrase includes high-technology firms.
30. Pennsylvania Department of Commerce, *Advanced Technology Policies for the Commonwealth of Pennsylvania* (Harrisburg, Pennsylvania, December 1985), 7, 16.
31. Department of Commerce, *Advanced Technology Policy*, 7-14.
32. *Pennsylvania Department of Commerce Update*, October 1985, 1-4. Circular.
33. Thornburgh, *Advanced Technology Policies*, 4-5.

226

34. *Enterprise Development Update, July 1985*, 1-7.
35. Thornburgh, *Advanced Technology Policies*, 3.
36. Ibid., 7.
37. Ibid., 6.
38. Ibid., 6.
39. Ibid., 2.
40. Stanley J. Drazek, et.al., *PennTAP: Report of Review Team*, University Park, Pennsylvania: Pennsylvania State University, 1975.
41. There is some discussion of eventually conducting an independent evaluation of the centers, but no definite plans have been made at this time. Interview with Roger Tellefson, director, Ben Franklin Partnership, Harrisburg, Pennsylvania, January 15, 1986.
42. PennTAP, *PennTAP: Technology Transfer and Dissemination* (University Park, Pennsylvania, 1985), 2.
43. Interview with H. LeRoy Marlow, EdD., director, PennTAP, Harrisburg, Pennsylvania, January 13, 1986.
44. Ibid.
45. Ibid.
46. Ibid.
47. Ibid.
48. Ibid.
49. Ibid.
50. Paul Houck, information coordinator, PennTAP, testimony before the Subcommittee on the Science, Technology and Space of the Committee on Commerce, Science and Transportation, U. S. Senate (Washington, D.C., April 17, 1985), 7.
51. For example, the current task forces include ones on advanced technologies, hazardous waste, and the future of technology transfer.
52. Since PennTAP is occasionally accused by private consultants to be offering consultant services, this council member determines the merits of the case.
53. Interview with Marlow.
54. Interview with Paul W. Houck, information coordinator, PennTAP, Harrisburg, Pennsylvania, January 13, 1986.
55. PennTAP, *PennTAP: Update 1983*, (University Park, Pennsylvania, 1984), 22,24.
56. Interview with Marlow.
57. Stanley J. Drazek, et al., *PennTAP: Report of Review Team* (University Park, Pennsylvania: Pennsylvania State University, 1975), p. 9.
58. Budget FY 1985-1986: $200,000 from Pennsylvania Department of Commerce, $440,000 from Pennsylvania State University for indirect costs, $100,000 from EDA University City Center Project (special project), $170,000 from Pennsylvania Department of Highways and Federal Highway Administration (special project), $305,000 from Pennsylvania State University's special project matching funds and regular cash share with Pennsylvania Department of Commerce. Total budget, $1.2 million.
59. For example, a technology transfer program for rural road maintenance funded by the Pennsylvania Department of Transportation and the Federal Highway Administration. Interview with Marlow.
60. Ibid.
61. Testimony of Houck, 3.

227

62. H. LeRoy Marlow, *Another Perspective on Technology Transfer: The PennTAP Experience* (College Park, Pennsylvania: Pennsylvania State University, 1984), 19-20.
63. Interview with Marlow.
64. For example, a technology transfer organization may specialize in one field only, such as polymers or solid waste.
65. Interview with Marlow.
66. Testimony of Houck, *External Environment*, 4.
67. Interview with Marlow.
68. Marlow, *Another Perspective on Technology Transfer*, 22.
69. Interview with Houck.
70. Interview with Marlow.
71. Drazek, *PennTAP: Report of Review Team*, Preface.
72. Louis Rukeyser, "PennTAP Advice Soothes Industrial Headaches," reprinted in *PennTAP: Technology Transfer and Dissemination*, with the permission of McNaught Syndicate, Inc., 1984.
73. Ibid.
74. Ibid.
75. Ibid.
76. Ibid.
77. Interview with Richard Reinhardt, MILRITE Council, Harrisburg, Pennsylvania, January 13, 1986.
78. MILRITE Council, *Partners In Progress, Three Year Report* (Harrisburg, Pennsylvania, 1983), 4.
79. MILRITE Council, *The Area Labor-Management Committee Grant Program, Annual Report for the Period July 1, 1984 to June 30, 1985* (Harrisburg, Pennsylvania), January 1986, 1.
80. MILRITE, *Partners In Progress*, 4.
81. Interview with Reinhardt.
82. Interview with Walter Plosila, Governor's Office of Science and Technology, Harrisburg, Pennsylvania, January 16, 1986.
83. Interview with Cliff Jones, Pennsylvania Chamber of Commerce, Harrisburg, Pennsylvania, January 17, 1986.
84. Interview with Bob Coy, executive director, the MILRITE Council, Harrisburg, Pennsylvania, January 17, 1986.
85. Funding for 1986-1987 is $211,000.
86. Interview with Jones.
87. Interview with Coy.
88. MILRITE, *Partners In Progress*, 14.
89. Interview with State Representative Tom Geist, Harrisburg, Pennsylvania, January 13, 1986.
90. Interview with Reinhardt.
91. Interview with Donald Mazziotti, executive director, the Business Council, Harrisburg, Pennsylvania, January 14, 1986.
92. Interview with Jones.
93. Similar comments praising the council's work in these and related areas were made by Robert Coy, MILRITE Council and Cliff Jones, Chamber of Commerce.
94. Interview with Jones.
95. Ibid.
96. Interview with Mazziotti.

97. Frederick Cusick, "A State Agency Takes Credit for Job-creating Relocations," *The Philadelphia Inquirer*, November 25, 1984, B7.
98. Department of Commerce, *The Ben Franklin Partnership Programs*, October 1985, 1.
99. National Council for Urban Economic Development, *Ben Franklin Partnership*, 2.
100. Interview with Arthur A. Heim, assistant director, C/N ATC, January 13, 1986.
101. Interview with Mary Frances Donley, public information coordinator, NET BFP, January 9, 1986.
102. National Council for Urban Economic Development, *The Ben Franklin Partnership: Linking Higher Education, Government and Business for Economic Growth* (Washington, D.C.: National Council for Urban Economic Development, November 1985), 4.
103. Interview with Representative Tom Murphy, co-author of BFP legislation, Harrisburg, Pennsylvania, January 15, 1986.
104. Ibid.
105. Ibid.
106. Interview with Heim.
107. Interview with Walter Plosila, director, Governor's Office of Policy and Planning, Deputy Secretary for Technology and Policy Development, Harrisburg, Pennsylvania, January 16, 1986.
108. Interview with Rep. Murphy.
109. Ben Franklin Partnership, *Ben Franklin Partnership Challenge Grant Program for Technical Innovation: 30 Month Progress Report* (Harrisburg, Pennsylvania: Department of Commerce, November 1985), 1-2.
110. Interview with Frederick Cusick, reporter, *Philadelphia Inquirer*, Philadelphia, Pennsylvania, January 15, 1986.
111. BFP, *30 Month Progress Report*, 17. One of these programs, the Seed Venture Capital Fund, will be analyzed later in this chapter.
112. Interview with Donley.
113. Interview with Heim.
114. Interview with Donley.
115. Pennsylvania Department of Commerce, *The Ben Franklin Partnership Programs: Advance Technology Initiatives*, (Harrisburg, Pennsylvania, October 1985), 1.
116. National Council for Urban Development, *Ben Franklin Partnership*, 8.
117. Interview with Louis Robinson, Jr., manager, NET ATC incubator center at Homer Labs, January 9, 1986. Most of the services mention are offered by the Homer Labs incubator center.
118. Ibid.
119. Interview with Bolton.
120. Interview with Rep. Murphy.
121. Interview with Heim.
122. Ibid.
123. Interview with Murphy.
124. Ibid.
125. Interview with Bolton.
126. Ibid.
127. Interview with Murphy.

128. Lawrence Litvak and Michael Barker, *Pension Funds and Economic Development: How Public and Private Pension Funds Can Contribute to the Pennsylvania Economy* (Harrisburg, Pennsylvania: Pennsylvania MILRITE Council, March 1983); Robert E. Mittelstaedt and Thomas Penn, *Venture Capital (Or Lack Thereof) in the Philadelphia Area* (Philadelphia: Wharton Innovative Center, University of Pennsylvania, August 1982).
129. Allen and Robertson, *Silicon, Sensors and Software.*
130. Pennsylvania Department of Commerce, *Pennsylvania Economic Revitalization Fund: Challenge Grants for Seed Capital Funds* (Harrisburg, Pennsylvania), 1.
131. Mittelstaedt, 5.
132. Pennsylvania Department of Commerce, *Pennsylvania Economic Revitalization,* 1.
133. National Council for Urban Economic Development, *The Ben Franklin Partnership: Linking Higher Education, Government and Business for Economic Growth* (Washington, D.C., November 1985), 18.
134. Pennsylvania Department of Commerce, *Pennsylvania Economic Revitalization,* 8. The undefined use of the word "ordinarily" presumably was intentional on the part of the legislature to permit the VCF managers broad discretion within general guidelines.
135. National Council for Urban Economic Development, *Ben Franklin Partnership,* 18.
136. Interview with Thomas Penn, manager, Genesis Seed Fund, Ltd., January 8, 1986.
137. Interview with Mazziotti.
138. The most striking example of this is the Seed Capital Venture Fund, which, while receiving $750,000 from the state through the Advanced Technology Centers, treats the ATC as any other limited partner.
139. Interview with Bill Cook, staff member, BFP, Harrisburg, Pennsylvania, January 14, 1986.
140. Interview with Professor Irving Hand, Pennsylvania State University, University Park, Pennsylvania, January 16, 1986.
141. Pennsylvania has had to contend with the traditional labor-management antagonism, inter-university rivalries that have hampered cooperation, and university-business suspicion. All of these have caused problems in the establishment of the programs and should be considered by any state.
142. Of special interest is a technical program designed to assist with the improvement of bridges throughout the state.

9

Science and technology policy has been discussed widely in Texas as a way of diversifying the state's economy. The need for diversification has become more urgent with the market downturn of the state's mineral and agricultural commodities and the increase in levels of unemployment and poverty. This urgency was expressed during the 1985 legislature, when research and economic development issues were debated intensely. Though a number of bills were enacted, funding for research and development was increased only moderately.

Interest in technology-intensive growth stems from the perception that the technology sector in Texas has two competitive advantages. First, the state has over the last two decades begun to build a strong university system and therefore posses a growing capability to assist technology industries. Second, the fastest-growing manufacturing industries in Texas during the 1970s were based on new technologies and may engender additional growth.

However, the impact of science and technology programs on specific statewide objectives for economic development—for example, employing displaced workers—has not been analyzed in detail. Moreover, Texas policymakers have not reached a consensus about what these statewide economic development objectives should be. They are defined alternatively as accelerating the job creation rate, reducing the job loss rate, mitigating structural poverty and unemployment, improving overall state income, providing business opportunity, and establishing new sources of state government revenues. Without a higher level of consensus, these general goals provide a weak foundation for significant state action.

Science and technology policy in Texas is in its infancy. Interest is strong, but actual state-funded programs are few and weakly supported. Given budget constraints and a conservative fiscal posture, the state government is uncertain about its role.

This chapter describes demographic and economic trends in Texas that define the environment for economic development, reviews the history of science and technology policy in the state, and outlines issues which will influence the evolution and impact of science and technology policies in Texas.

— *This chapter was written by Brian Muller. Michael Dowling wrote the section "Funding for Research in Science and Technology".*

Demographic and Economic Profile

POPULATION CHARACTERISTICS

The characteristics of the Texas population are changing rapidly. Some of the shifts, such as the composition of the labor force, will have a strong influence on economic growth in the state. Science and technology policy will need to accommodate the shifting roles and needs of different populations.

The Texas population has been increasing at substantially higher rates than in the United States as a whole; between 1970 and 1980 the Texas growth rate was over two-and-a-half times the national rate (Table 9-1). Much of the growth has been from immigration, both from Mexico and from other sections of the United States. The state's ample labor supply has provided a competitive advantage to businesses—including technology-intensive businesses—which have located in Texas.

The Texas population, like that of the United States as a whole, is aging. The size of the 65-and-over cohort increased slightly between 1970 and 1984, while the size of the under-19 cohort decreased substantially (Table 9-2). Overall, however, the Texas population is aging at a slower rate than the United States, producing a somewhat younger labor force.

An increasing percentage of the younger workers will be Hispanic. Immigration patterns and other demographic influences have significantly changed the state's racial distribution over the last fifteen years. From 1970 to 1980, the percentage of the white population decreased substantially while that of the Hispanic and other populations increased; the black population remained fairly constant (Table 9-3).

TABLE 9-1
Population of Texas and Percentage Change
Compared to the United States, 1970, 1980, and 1984
(in 1,000s and %)

	Texas	Texas Change	U.S. Change
1970	11,200	—	—
1980	14,200	27.1	11.4
1984	15,900	8.4	4.1

Source: U.S. Department of Commerce, Bureau of the Census, *State Population Estimates, by Age and Components of Change: 1980 and 1984, Population Estimates and Projections,* p. 7; idem, *1980 Census of Population, Characteristics of the Population,* part 1, p. 1.; idem, *1970 Census of Population,* vol. 1, *Characteristics of the Population,* part 11, p. 8.

TABLE 9-2
Age Distribution in Texas
Compared to the United States, 1970 and 1980
(%)

	1970 Texas	1970 United States	1980 Texas	1980 United States
0-19	39.5	37.8	34.3	32.0
20-44	32.5	31.7	38.3	37.2
45-64	19.1	20.6	17.8	19.7
65+	8.9	9.8	9.6	11.3

Source: U.S. Department of Commerce, Bureau of the Census, *1980 Census of Population,* ch. B, part 11, p. 37.; idem, *1980 Census of Population,* vol. 1, ch. B, part 1, p. 42.; idem, *1970 Census of Population,* vol. 1, part 11, p. 69.

TABLE 9-3
Racial Distribution in Texas
Compared to the United States, 1970 and 1980
(%)

	1970 Texas	1970 United States	1980 Texas	1980 United States
White	68.0	87.5	61.8	83.1
Black	12.5	11.1	12.0	11.7
Other	0.7	1.4	5.2	5.1

Source: U.S. Department of Commerce, Bureau of the Census, *1980 Census of Population,* ch. B, part 11, p. 17; idem, *1980 Census of Population,* ch. B, part 1, p. 42; idem, *1970 Census of Population,* vol. 1, part 11, p. 60.

234

Income, Poverty, and Unemployment

Per capita income in Texas increased substantially between 1970 and 1980 (Table 9-4). However, the increase started from a relatively low base and has not yet reached the national average.

The level of poverty in Texas decreased over the decade 1970-1980 (Table 9-5). In 1970 almost 19 percent of all Texans lived in poverty. By 1980, the figure had dropped to about 15 percent, which is still higher than in the United States as a whole.

During the 1970s and early 1980s, Texas performed better than the nation as a whole in generating jobs for its work force. Unemployment rates were 5.3 percent in 1981 and 6.1 percent in 1982, more than a point below U.S. rates in both periods. Since 1982, unemployment rates have increased significantly and reached 8.9 percent in 1986.

Changes in demographic and work force characteristics raise several questions for science and technology policy. The most important change is the increasing rate of unemployment. The state needs programs which will generate jobs quickly; that is, over the next five to ten years. Commercialization of a basic research project requires seven to twenty years. How can science and technology policy address short-term employment needs?

The expansion of the Hispanic population will also influence economic growth in Texas. Hispanics represent both an increasing percentage of the labor force and the highest percentage of poor and unemployed in the state. Moreover, Hispanic legislators have become a key political force in Texas; they played an important role in the 1985 biennium. But Hispanics and other disadvantaged Texans will not automatically share in the benefits of science and technology policy. They may require targeted programs for employment, training, and small business assistance. How can science and technology policies be designed to ensure participation of, and benefit to, minorities and other disadvantaged populations?

The relative youth of Texas workers has additional implications for economic development policy. Texas workers will be relatively less experienced than those in other states, and thus at a comparative disadvantage. A poorly educated labor force may represent a critical obstacle to economic growth. How can science and technology policy have a significant positive influence on the system of secondary and vocational education?

In sum, Texas will have significant needs over the next decade to upgrade the skills of its labor force and to bring economic development assistance to specific regions, population groups, and the unemployed. Will science and technology policy be able to link these economic needs with university-based research and commercialization efforts?

TABLE 9-4

Per Capita Income and Percentage Change in Texas
Compared to the United States, 1970, 1980, and 1984
(dollars and change in %)

	Texas	Change	United States	Change
1970	2,810	—	3,945	—
1980	7,205	156	9,494	141
1984	12,636	75	12,789	35

Source: U.S. Department of Commerce, Bureau of Economic Analysis, *Survey of Current Business*, August 1985, p. 18; idem, *Statistical Abstract of the United States, 1984*, p. 457.

TABLE 9-5

Individuals below the Poverty Level in Texas
Compared to the Unites States, 1970 and 1980
(%)

	Texas	United States
1970	18.8	13.0
1980	14.7	12.1

Sources: U.S. Dept. of Commerce, *Statistical Abstract of the United States, 1985*, p. 457; idem, *1980 Census of Population*, vol. 1, p. 397.

ECONOMIC CHARACTERISTICS

The Texas economy of the 1980s is characterized by shifts in both sectoral and regional shares of employment and output; traditional industries are declining and new ones are emerging. Some of these shifts—like the emergence of research-intensive industries—are used as a rationale for more active state support of science and technology.

Traditional Resource Industries

The economy of Texas has traditionally been based on agriculture and on the extraction and processing of natural resources. The current decline of the oil, gas, and production agriculture industries is forcing the state to consider diversifying its economic base. The decline has also inspired debate about making traditional resource industries more productive and efficient and expanding value-added processing activities.

The oil and gas industry has been a major employer, responsible for virtually all jobs in the mining sector and a substantial number in nondurable goods and other sectors. During the oil boom of the 1970s, employment in mining doubled. By 1982, the height of the boom, jobs in mining represented about 5 percent of the total state employment (Table 9-6).

TABLE 9-6

Non-Agricultural Employment and Share in Texas by Sector,
1972, 1977, 1982 and Percentage Change between 1972 and 1982
(employees in 1,000s, share in %, change in %)

	1972		1977		1982	
	Emp.	Share	Emp.	Share	Emp.	Share
Mining	103.5	2.6	159.3	3.2	311.6	5.0
Construction	259.3	6.6	345.8	7.0	423.6	6.8
Manufacturing	738.7	19.0	893.5	18.2	1,060.2	16.9
Transportation	264.5	6.8	308.8	6.3	386.1	6.2
Wholesale & retail	945.1	24.3	1,210.5	24.7	1,547.9	24.7
Finance & insurance	214.1	5.5	276.5	5.6	364.3	5.8
Government	714.8	18.4	875.5	17.8	1,023.0	16.3
Services	644.4	16.6	836.9	17.0	1,571.1	18.4
Total	3,884.4	100.0	4,906.8	100.0	6,687.8	100.0

Source: U.S. Dept. of Labor, Bureau of Labor Statistics, *Employment, Hours, and Earnings, States and Areas, 1939-1982*, vol. 2, pp. 709-723.

Since 1982, however, employment has become depressed. Jobs for oilfield workers dropped 17 percent between early 1982 and late 1984. Employment in oilfield machinery manufacturing dropped by over 50 percent during this period. Secondary employment was also affected: between 1982 and 1984 over 100,000 jobs were lost in Houston, the center of the industry.[1]

Future oil production in Texas is limited by dwindling state reserves. A recent study by the Bureau of Business Research predicts that employment in this sector will continue to decline through the end of the century.[2] This sectoral decline is a major impetus to the development of a state technology policy. As William L. Fisher, director of the Bureau of Economic Geology at the University of Texas at Austin, has said, "We are not arguing about whether we are running out of oil. The question is: do we have a little more time to diversify our economy?"

Agriculture has also suffered declines in employment over the past two decades. In 1960, over 300,000 workers were employed in the agriculture, forestry, and fisheries sector; by 1980, only about 63,000 people worked in this sector. This decline in agricultural employment includes decreases in the numbers of both farm laborers and farm operators.

The problems in the farm sector emerging since 1980—including international competition and the decline in commodity prices—have accelerated the rate of attrition among farm operators. According to one estimate, over 100 farmers in Texas are going out of business each week.[3]

Even as agricultural employment has declined, agricultural output has increased; rising levels of investment and new technologies have resulted in increased productivity. According to one forecast, agricultural output will grow at annual rates of over 4 percent to the year 2007—a growth rate second only to durable manufacturing among all sectors of the Texas economy.[4]

Emerging Manufacturing Industries

Most of the growth in manufacturing over the last two decades has occurred in durable goods. Employment in this sector more than doubled between 1960 and 1980; the fastest-growing industries during this period were nonelectrical machinery, electrical equipment, and instruments. Employment in the nondurable industries, however, increased by less than 50 percent between 1960 and 1980; their share of manufacturing employment dropped rapidly between 1977 and 1982 (Table 9-7). The sectors with the greatest relative decline were food and kindred products, apparel, and petroleum refining.

Much of the growth in durable manufacturing has occurred in the so-called high-technology industries (Table 9-8). Between 1977 and 1982, five of eight industries defined by the Congressional Budget Office as high technology experienced substantially higher growth rates in Texas than in the United States as a whole; one, electronic components, showed only a slightly lower growth rate. (Comparative data for the two industries are not available.) The pharmaceutical industry in Texas grew four times faster than in the nation, and the rate for office/computing machines was almost 30 percent greater than the national rate. In just ten years, high-technology's share of total manufacturing in Texas grew from almost 5 percent to almost 20 percent.

A Bureau of Business Research survey categorizes a different mix of Texas industries as high-technology.[5] To several of the sectors included in Table 9-8, this group adds ordnance and accessories, electrical distribution equipment, electrical industrial apparatus, and several other industries (Table 9-9). Most of the additional sectors did not perform well relative to the first group. The highest growth rates were in electrical distribution equipment and miscellaneous electrical equipment.

TABLE 9-7

Manufacturing Employment and Share in Texas by Industry,
1972, 1977, 1982 and Percentage Change between 1972 and 1982
(employees in 1,000s, share in %, and change in %)

	1972		1977		1982	
	Emp.	Share	Emp.	Share	Emp.	Share
Nondurable						
Food/kindred	77.5	2.0	84.8	10.2	89.9	9.0
Tobacco	—	—	—	—	—	—
Textile	6.4	1.0	7.1	.8	—	—
Apparel	67.0	10.4	73.4	8.8	66.7	6.7
Paper products	17.6	2.7	19.8	2.4	20.9	2.1
Printing/ publishing	40.6	6.3	47.4	5.8	65.7	6.6
Chemicals	—	—	67.7	8.2	74.3	7.4
Petroleum refining	32.7	5.2	35.3	4.3	39.4	4.0
Rubber & plastic	16.0	2.5	25.5	3.1	29.9	3.0
Leather	—	—	6.6	.8	9.0	1.0
Total nondurable	257.8	40.1	367.6	44.4	395.8	39.8
Durable						
Lumber & wood	30.9	4.8	33.1	4.0	33.4	3.4
Furniture & fixtures	16.1	2.5	17.4	2.1	15.8	1.6
Stone, clay, glass	30.0	4.6	35.6	4.3	39.7	4.0
Primary metal	33.1	5.1	38.6	4.6	39.2	3.9
Fabricated metal	67.3	10.4	78.3	9.4	99.3	9.7
Nonelectric machinery	70.8	10.9	115.4	13.9	169.7	17.0
Electrical equipment	54.6	8.4	67.8	8.2	99.3	9.7
Transportation equip.	67.4	10.4	61.1	7.4	73.0	7.3
Instruments	8.6	1.3	14.1	1.7	18.2	1.8
Miscellaneous	10.0	1.5	FF	FF	13.5	1.4
Total durable	388.8	59.9	461.4	55.6	601.1	60.4
Total mfg.	646.6	100.0	829.0	100.0	996.9	100.0

Source: U.S. Dept. of Commerce, Bureau of the Census, *1972 Census of Manufactures*, vol 3, part 2, p. 40-1; idem, *1977 Census of Manufactures*, vol. 3, part 2, p. 39-1; idem, *1982 Census of Manufactures, Geographic Area Series, Texas.*

TABLE 9-8

High-Tech Employment in Texas

and Percentage Change, 1972, 1977, and 1982

(employees in 1,000s, change in %)

	1972	Change	1977	Change	1982
Drugs	1.4	85.7	2.6	26.9	3.3
Industrial organic chemicals	26.0	23.8	32.2	2.2	32.9
Office/computing machines	—	—	16.3	73.6	28.3
Communication equipment	—	—	—	—	45.6
Electronic components	—	—	24.1	37.8	33.2
Aircraft & parts	—	—	32.7	32.1	43.2
Missiles/ space vehicles	—	—	—	—	—
Instruments	8.6	63.9	14.1	29.1	18.2
Total high-tech employment	36.0	238.9	122.0	67.8	204.7
All manufacturing	735.6	20.5	886.4	19.4	1,058.4
Percentage of high-tech	4.9	—	13.8	—	19.3

Note: Statistics for some industry groups are withheld to avoid disclosing figures for individual companies.
Source: U.S. Department of Commerce, Bureau of the Census, *1982 Census of Manufactures, General Summary, Texas,* table 5; *1977 Census of Manufactures, General Summary, Texas,* p. 10-7.

TABLE 9-9

Employment in Additional High-Technology Sectors

in Texas, 1972, 1977, and 1982

(in 1,000s)

	1972	1977	1982
Ordnance/accessories	9.7	4.5	5.0
Electric distribution equipment	1.5	2.2	2.7
Electric industrial apparatus	—	2.2	2.4
Electric lighting/wiring	3.1	2.3	3.5
Radio/TV receiving equipment	—	2.6	2.4
Miscellaneous electrical equipment	3.8	3.8	5.7
Miscellaneous transportation equipment	3.6	2.5	2.1
Total additional high-technology	21.7	20.1	23.8

Note: Statistics for some industry groups are withheld to avoid disclosing figures for individual companies.
Source: U.S. Department of Commerce, Bureau of the Census, *1982 Census of Manufactures, General Summary, Texas,* table 5; idem, *1977 Census of Manufactures, General Summary, Texas,* p. 10-7.

Finance, Insurance, Real Estate, and Services

The finance, insurance, and real estate (FIRE) and the services sectors have also experienced rapidly increasing employment in Texas. Both are discussed as targets for technology policy. FIRE has more than doubled its work force over the last decade. This rate of growth is greater than that of the United States as a whole, but because Texas started in the 1970s with a relatively smaller FIRE percentage (5.6 percent), in 1980 it had not yet caught up with the overall U.S. rate (5.9 percent).

The service sector has also seen dramatic growth, almost doubling its total number of employees between 1970 and 1980 (Table 9-10). The share of total state employment in services increased by about 10 percent from 1972 to 1982.

Between 1960 and 1980, the major areas of growth within the service sector were business services and professional services. Business services experienced the most rapid levels of growth, increasing about 125 percent each decade between 1960 and 1980. The Bureau of Business Research projects that business services will continue to expand at moderate rates of growth through the end of the century.[6]

Professional services experienced an enormous increase in numbers—almost 800,000—between 1960 and 1980. The rate of growth for this sector is also impressive: it almost doubled between 1960 and 1970 and increased by another 50 percent by 1980. Professional services are also projected by the Bureau of Business Research to experience moderate growth through the end of the century.

The other major employment sectors—construction, transportation, wholesale trade, retail trade, and government—all expanded at substantial rates during the last decade.

Three questions for science and technology policy in Texas emerge from the analysis of the Texas economy. First, can science and technology be directed to assist traditional Texas industries? These industries have experienced significant international competition but might be made more viable through application of new technologies.

TABLE 9-10
Service Employment in Texas by Sector,
1970 and 1980

Sector	1970	1980
Business	71,063	177,720
Repair	67,796	116,518
Personal	256,679	210,739
Entertainment	32,918	49,117
Professional	712,288	1,172,129

Source: Bureau of the Census.

Second, what incentives can be employed in science and technology policy to stimulate the growth of new industries? These range from sectors such as microelectronics—which have established an important presence in Texas over the last decade—to sectors that are small but rapidly growing, such as instruments.

The third question concerns the service sectors of the economy. While not producing substantial exports like the manufacturing sectors do, they represent a rapidly growing source of employment in Texas. How does science and technology policy relate to these secondary service, finance, insurance, real estate, construction, and related sectors?

Science and Technology Policy

HISTORY PRIOR TO 1980

The setting for the development of technology policy in Texas is shaped by the unusual political history of the state, in which a strong probusiness tradition is combined with anticorporate populism. A laissez-faire attitude coexists with active state intervention in certain economic sectors.

One dimension of Texas populism, the attitude that state institutional power should be dispersed, is manifest in the sharply constrained powers of the governor and in other aspects of Texas government, such as the election of commissioners to head six state agencies. This approach tends to weaken state government and make it difficult to coordinate policies for economic intervention.

On the other hand, Texas state government has taken an active role in some areas of economic policy. Texas has strictly regulated industries such as oil and gas to achieve specific development goals. In addition, the state has provided funding at a high level for research in agriculture and medicine.

The Texas Railroad Commission is an example of a regulatory agency which has played a key role in Texas' economic development. The pattern of decisions at the agency has represented the effort to balance technology with economic development policy. A guiding principle in decision making has been that technical concerns about oilfield conservation should be balanced with a state economic interest in capturing profits from the industry.

Another traditional focus of state technology policy has been agriculture. The state for many years has provided substantial funding to a system of land grant universities, experiment stations, and extension offices. Texas A&M University is the heart of the research and extension system and has played an important role nationwide in the evolution of agricultural technologies. Innovations in biotechnologies and the use of growth hormones in cattle feeding were pioneered at A&M. Scientists at A&M developed high-yielding hybrid strains of grain which have revolutionized agriculture worldwide. These innovations were transferred to Texas farmers through the agricultural experiment stations, the agricultural extension service, and by private companies.

The Texas Energy and Natural Resources Advisory Council (TENRAC) is a third historical example of technology policy in Texas. A product of the energy crisis of the mid- to late seventies, TENRAC was created in 1979 through merger and expansion of earlier programs. Its purpose was to plan, coordinate policy, and administer research grants related to energy and natural resources in Texas.[7] During its existence, approximately $8,500,000 was expended by TENRAC. Each dollar leveraged another $1.06 of external funding. Research was performed in a range of energy technologies from lignite gasification to alcohol fuel production.[8] However, TENRAC had a short life. After 1980, the energy crisis was perceived to be less urgent; the agency was terminated by the legislature in 1983.

THE ENVIRONMENT FOR RECENT INITIATIVES

In about 1980, emphasis in science and technology policy debate began to shift. New goals emerged: to stimulate growth in emerging industries and to improve the Texas' position in international competition. A new set of political actors and rationales were introduced. This shift, still ongoing, was also influenced by two critical changes. First, the decline of the oil and gas industry made economic diversification an imperative. Attention was drawn to the high-technology export industries like Texas Instruments that had expanded dramatically in the late 1970s and early 1980s.

Second, the funding base for the Texas university system expanded substantially during the 1970s. Major universities were better able to attract faculty with national reputations. Almost 800 endowed chairs were added to the University of Texas during the 1970s and early 1980s. Texas A&M also created significant new programs. Texas colleges and universities became aggressive supporters of legislation encouraging development of new technologies.

The first major public forum for technology policy was the Texas 2000 Commission. The commission's original research agenda had emphasized natural resources, but science and technology emerged in the course of the research,[9] and the commission issued recommendations in its final report related to science and technology policy. These included providing universities with "sufficient financial, physical, and human resources" to support research; establishing a science and technology council; developing technical assistance programs for small businesses and individual entrepreneurs; improving legal, regulatory, and financial incentives to private-sector research; and creating a communications program to expand awareness about the potential benefits of technology.[10]

Also during the early 1980s, the Microelectronics and Computer Technology Corporation (MCC), after surveying communities around the country for suitability as a location for computer research, chose Austin. The selection produced great excitement within Texas and publicity nationwide about the opportunities for technology businesses in the state.

Technology policy played only a minor role in the 1982 gubernatorial campaign, but emerged again in 1983 after the new governor, Mark White, began defining priorities. A staff slot in the Office of Economic Development was dedicated to policy coordination in this area.

Other new actors emerged. Individual universities, particularly the University of Texas at Austin and Texas A&M at College Station, became powerful advocates for technology programs at their institutions. Other governmental and quasi-public organizations began to assume roles, including the City of San Antonio, the Metroplex High Technology Task Force in Dallas-Forth Worth, and the Houston Economic Development Council. Private industry also became involved in policy discussion. This sector has been represented by the Texas Computer Industry Council, the American Electronics Association, the Texas Venture Capital Association, and the Texas Industrial Development Council, which represents organizations such as chambers of commerce.

This new wave of interest in technology policy differed from previous state involvement in several respects. First, it addressed a new set of industries—the high-technology firms—rather than traditional resource sectors. Second, it had a broader conceptual scope: high-technology intended as a vehicle for statewide economic and job generation rather than as a narrow incentive for an individual industry. Third, it tended to focus on entrepreneurship and the front end of the product cycle—that is, the creation of new products—rather than on increasing productivity and efficiency in established businesses. Fourth, it was given urgency by the evidence of increasing international competition and the decline of resource industries.

NEW INITIATIVES IN SCIENCE AND TECHNOLOGY POLICY

The structure of the new science and technology policies and programs in Texas has evolved from the 1983 and particularly the 1985 legislatures. So far, the steps taken are largely piecemeal and not incorporated into an overall state plan. Areas of emphasis include funding levels for university research funding and structure of secondary education, patent problems and other issues related to university-industry cooperation, and funding and design of programs for investment and assistance in new-product commercialization.

Two concrete actions were taken by the 1983 legislature. First, the legislature appropriated $1 million for INVENT, the Institute for Ventures in New Technology, located at the Texas Engineering Experiment Station at Texas

244

A&M. In addition, authority was provided by the legislature for the creation of
the Senate Interim Committee on Business, Education, and Technology. The
committee's most important charge was to produce a report that outlined
technology-related issues in Texas and proposed legislation to address these
issues, including encouragement of closer collaboration between universities
and industry, increased organized research funding, flexible policies dealing with
intellectual property, and improved methods of project solicitation funding.
This report had an important influence on the 1985 legislative session.[11]

In 1984, Governor White appointed the Science and Technology Council,
which was staffed from the governor's office. Comprised of representatives of
universities, high-technology corporations, the business service industry, and
others, the council's mandate was to develop policy recommendations and advise
the governor on a broad scope of issues ranging from university-based research
and development to capital availability.[12]

During the summer of 1985, a special legislative session was held to
consider reforms to the Texas educational system. Technology development
was never an explicit goal of this legislation, but debate during the session was
informed by a general perception that Texas needs a technically trained labor
force, strong in math and science, to advance its international competitiveness.

The 1985 legislative session was active in the area of technology policy. A
variety of persons and groups initiated proposals, among them the Science and
Technology Council, the major universities, and the lieutenant governor. The
Senate Business, Education, and Technology Committee and the House Science
and Technology Committee (created by speaker Gib Lewis during the 1985
session) introduced over thirty bills. The Senate Education Committee and the
House Higher Education Committee also played important roles in considering
technology legislation under their jurisdiction. In all, fourteen technology-
related bills were passed by the legislature, although most did not include
appropriations.

Two pieces of legislation may have immediate effects on science and
technology policy in Texas. One was the creation of the Texas Advanced
Technology Research Program, a $35 million fund awarded through a
competitive grant process. The other was the formation of the Select
Committee on Higher Education, which is mandated to hold hearings
throughout the state on the future of public education and to prepare proposals
for future legislation. Technology policy is an explicit area of concentration for
the Committee.

Science and Technology Programs

Participation by Texas state government in science and technology programs has taken a variety of forms. The four programs discussed below—the Houston Area Research Center, the research and development centers at public universities in Texas, the Institute for Ventures in New Technologies, and the Texas Advanced Technology Research Program—are representative of the different state roles.

THE HOUSTON AREA RESEARCH CENTER

The Houston Area Research Center (HARC) was created in 1982 as a research consortium of business executives and representatives from four Texas universities: Rice University, Texas A&M, University of Houston-University Park, and the University of Texas at Austin.[13] The consortium's goal is to transform scientific and technological advances into practical and commercial applications.[14] HARC receives no state funding; most money comes from federal and industry contracts.

HARC acts as a vehicle for joint research among member universities. The center undertakes projects that are too large for a single university, or whose chances of success are increased by a joint effort. In this way, HARC helps overcome institutional competitiveness and offers a cooperative working environment.

Areas of focus have expanded beyond local issues to those of state, national, and international interest. Research is conducted at HARC in eight areas, represented by independent research centers, including the Texas Accelerator Center, Geotechnology Research Center, Laser Applications Research Center, The Woodlands Center for Growth Studies, Materials Science Research Center, Innovation Center, Computer Systems Applications Research Center and the Space Technology and Research Center.

UNIVERSITY R&D CENTERS IN TEXAS

A number of research centers attached to public universities receive state appropriations. The University of Texas system supports twenty-six centers, nine of which were on the drawing board in 1985. Texas A&M University, the University of Houston, North Texas State University, and Texas Tech University sponsor the bulk of non-UT centers.

Only about twenty of the state's eighty centers emphasize high-technology research topics. Even fewer are involved in joint efforts with industry or receive private industry funds. For example, of the thirty-two research centers listed at the University of Houston, only nine can be classified under high technology; and only three of those perform cooperative research and development with industry.

Despite the diverse nature of the centers, some common factors emerge. All of the centers were created for research on a specific topic. Some of the topics are directly linked to the state's economic needs, such as oil and gas extraction methods. Resource-related centers include the Energy Systems Research Center (UT-Arlington), Center for Enhanced Oil and Gas Recovery Research (UT-Austin), Allied Geophysical Laboratories (UH), and the Enhanced Petroleum Recovery Institute (UH). Other centers related to the manufacturing and construction industries include the Textile Research Center (Texas Tech), the Construction Research Center (UT-Arlington), and the Computation Fluid Dynamics Research Center (UT-Austin) (which receives funding from aerospace companies). Biomedical research is conducted at the Howard Hughes Medical Institute (UT Health Science Center at Dallas), the Biomedical Engineering Research Laboratories (UH collaborating with Baylor and Rice), the Institute for Molecular Biotechnology (UH), and the Center for Biological Nuclear Magnetic Resonance (A&M).

Most of the twenty high-technology research centers in Texas were created in 1984 and 1985. Several are not yet operational, such as the Institute for Advanced Manufacturing (UT-El Paso) and the Center for Energy, Technology, and Diversification (UT-Permian Basin).

Funding for the centers overall is relatively small: few centers receive more than $1 million per year in state appropriations. About $17.5 million was allocated by the state in 1985 for *all* eighty research centers, including the high-technology ones. Among the more richly funded high-technology research centers are the Cyclotron Institute (A&M), which was awarded $800,886 (FY 1985); the Energy Resources Program (A&M) with $1.5 million; and Institute of Geophysics (UT-Austin), receiving funding of $1.7 million (FY 1985). Eighteen centers and institutes received approximately $500,000 or less; twelve were granted *no* state funds in 1985.

INVENT

The Institute for Ventures in New Technologies (INVENT) is a division of the Texas Engineering Station at Texas A&M. It assists entrepreneurs and inventors in developing their ideas into commercial products. Particularly, INVENT provides engineering and business management services to its clients so that they can attract venture capital.

INVENT was founded in 1983. In 1985 it operated on an appropriated budget of $1.165 million. The goal of the program is to make a transition to self-sufficiency, so that by 1992 its budget comes exclusively from investment return.

INVENT'S program features a selection process to determine who should receive full aid. Only 3 percent of all applications are assisted by INVENT personnel to set up operational business. Technology-oriented businesses are given preference, so that the program takes full advantage of A&M's engineering expertise.

THE TEXAS ADVANCED TECHNOLOGIES RESEARCH PROGRAM

The 1985 legislature appropriated $35 million for a new initiative, the Texas Advanced Technologies Research Program (TATRP). This program was designed to support individual research projects in the fields of microelectronics, energy, telecommunications, aerospace, biotechnology, materials, and other areas of science and technology that hold "substantial promise of great benefit to the people of Texas."[15] Rather than disburse funds based on a formula, the legislature chose to award the funds on a competitive basis. Researchers at private universities such as Baylor, Rice, and Southern Methodist University were excluded from participation.

The Coordinating Board of the Texas College and University Systems was given responsibility for evaluating proposals. The board consulted with Frank Press, president of the National Academy of Sciences, who suggested possible consultants to review proposals. The board then established guidelines and publicized criteria for ranking proposals:
• potential for industrialization in the field;
• potential for unusual opportunities in the field;
• prospects for rapid advances in a key area of science or technology;
• prospects for significant effect on other fields;
• demand for students and post-doctorals in the field; and
• relative significance of the scientific and economic contribution of the proposal when compared to other proposals.

Additional guidelines were introduced after consultation: projects under $250,000 were not encouraged, and agricultural research, chemistry, and physics were added as eligible fields. The format for proposals—length and content required—was developed and dates for submission were established. At the same time, an advisory panel of distinguished scientists from outside the state was created.

By the September 1985 deadline, 511 proposals requesting $300 million were received. The Coordinating Board staff asked that the larger schools prioritize proposals, and eventually a set of about 200 proposals was sent to each member of the advisory panel. The preliminary ranking of proposals showed that the University of Texas and Texas A&M systems would receive $32 million of the $35 million available. Since, according to the legislation, UT and A&M could receive only $23.33 million, or two-thirds of the fund, the panel adjusted budgets and priorities to select finally 87 proposals. In October 1985, the Coordinating Board accepted the recommendations without changes.

Funding for Research in Science and Technology

The enthusiasm about new initiatives in Texas science and technology so far has found only moderate expression in financial support. State research appropriations overall are dwarfed by both federal and public funding and are also small in comparison to state monies provided to traditional research efforts in agriculture and medicine.

Most present state support for science and technology goes to research and graduate education, as opposed to commercialization and manpower development. Exceptions include the appropriation for INVENT and for the agricultural extension service.

RESEARCH AND DEVELOPMENT FUNDING IN TEXAS

According to the National Science Foundation (NSF), in 1983 Texas ranked sixth among the fifty states in terms of federal obligations for research and development, but only about twenty-fourth on a per capita basis.[16] Table 9-11 shows that in 1983, federal agencies performed relatively less R&D in Texas than the national average, partly because there is no national laboratory in Texas. On the other hand, industry performed relatively more federal R&D than the national average.

TABLE 9-11

Federal Obligations for R&D by Performer
in Texas and Share Compared to the United States, 1983
($ million and %)

Performer	Funds	Share	U.S. Share
Federal facilities	229.1	16.2	27.1
Industry	903.4	64.0	49.1
Universities	235.1	16.6	18.8
State & local government	36.8	2.6	4.5
Other	8.3	0.6	0.5
Total	1,412.7	100.0	100.0

Source: National Science Foundation, *Federal Funds for Research and Development*, vol. 33, p. 142.

TABLE 9-12
Share of Federal Obligations for R&D in Texas
by Agency Source Compared to the United States, 1983
(%)

Agency	Texas Share	U.S. Share
Agriculture	3.1	2.2
Commerce	0.4	0.9
Defense	60.2	61.0
Energy	1.8	12.0
Health & Human Services	10.7	11.5
Interior	0.4	1.0
Transportation	1.7	0.9
EPA	0.8	0.6
NASA	19.2	7.0
NSF	1.8	2.8

Source: National Science Foundation, *Federal Funds for Research and Development*, vol. 33, p. 150.

Table 9-12 shows that in 1983 Texas received on average more federal funds from the Departments of Transportation and Agriculture and from NASA. The state receives substantially less from the Department of Energy and secures relatively few funds from the NSF.

Data on industrial R&D spending is incomplete and difficult to obtain. The most recent survey of industrial R&D spending did not release data for Texas because the operations of a single company would have been disclosed. In 1979, the NSF estimated that Texas industries spent $1.2 billion in the state on R&D, compared to the federal government's $1.0 billion.[17]

At present, the only area of state government funding for R&D are the state institutions of higher education, including universities, medical schools, health science centers, research institutes, and extension services. Public higher education is funded in two ways: by direct appropriations from the legislature and by the Permanent University Fund, a pool of state revenue earmarked for members of the University of Texas and Texas A&M systems. The interest income from the invested Permanent University Fund makes up the Available University Fund, which is distributed to the eligible universities for plant and equipment purchases and in support of certain programs.

250

STATE FUNDING OF UNIVERSITY RESEARCH

State funding of research at colleges and universities in Texas (excluding TATRP) takes two forms: organized research and special line item research. Organized research funds are nonspecific and are distributed among all the state's senior colleges, universities, and health science centers according to a Coordinating Board formula with special weight given to the number of masters and doctoral students in science and engineering programs. The funds are then allocated by the administration of each institution to individual programs or to the deans of particular schools and colleges within the university.

In addition to the organized research funds, the legislature also appropriates, on a line item basis, special funds for particular research institutions and programs, like the University of Texas McDonald Observatory or the Texas A&M Cyclotron Institute.

Table 9-13 shows that funds for organized research have remained relatively constant over the last fifteen years, but have declined in real terms. However, funding of special item research in the same period has increased dramatically, over 400 percent. This growth is primarily due to an increase in the number of special items. A review of the appropriations bills shows that in the 1986-1987 biennium, fifty-four programs or institutes were funded by special line item appropriation, as compared to twenty-five in 1972-1973.

TABLE 9-13
Research Funding at Texas Senior Colleges
and Universities, 1972-1987, and Total Change
(in $ thousand, and %)

Biennium	Organized Research	Special Items	Total	Change
1986-1987	13,590	35,780	49,370	- 6
1984-1985	18,218	34,474	52,692	13
1982-1983	17,339	29,384	46,723	31
1980-1981	14,327	21,458	35,785	-10
1978-1979	14,573	25,280	39,854	2
1976-1977	18,696	20,190	38,886	38
1974-1975	16,342	11,905	28,248	22
1972-1873	14,588	8,643	23,230	—

Source: Internal document, Coordinating Board, Texas College and University Systems.

TABLE 9-14
State-Funded Health Related Research,
1972-1987 and Percentage Change
(in $ thousands, and %)

Biennium	Organized Research	Special Items	Total	Change
1986-1987	$34,621	15,581	50,203	8
1984-1985	28,930	17,689	46,620	12
1982-1983	24,432	17,117	41,549	46
1980-1981	19,244	9,134	28,377	47
1978-1979	15,627	3,638	19,265	46
1976-1977	11,037	2,177	13,213	7
1974-1975	8,107	4,241	12,348	13
1972-1973	6,819	4,106	10,925	—

Source: Internal document, Coordinating Board, Texas College and University Systems.

STATE FUNDING FOR HEALTH EDUCATION AND RESEARCH

In addition to the funding of research at senior colleges and universities, the Texas legislature has strongly supported education and research at state medical schools and health science centers. Nearly $1.3 billion was appropriated for health education during the 1984-1985 biennium and $1.2 billion during the 1986-1987 biennium. The universities received twice as much funding, but had over thirty times as many students.[18]

Table 9-14 shows that both organized and special research funding for health have grown rapidly over the last fifteen years. Total funding for health research was half of total university research funding in 1972-1973; in the 1986-1987 appropriation, it has surpassed university research funding. Clearly, high priority is placed on health related research in Texas.

STATE FUNDING FOR OTHER RESEARCH

A significant amount of additional research is performed at various state institutes and extension services. The most important of these is the Texas Agriculture Experiment Station at Texas A&M University, which received over half of all the funds in the 1986-1987 appropriation. They also include the Texas Engineering Experiment Station, the Texas Transportation Institute, the Texas Forest Service Research Program, and others. Table 9-15 shows that this funding category has increased over 400 percent in this period, and is now greater than the combined funds for university and health-related research.

TABLE 9-15
Other Research Funds at Experiment Stations and
Various Research Institutes, and Percentage Change, 1972-1987
($ thousands and %)

Biennium	Research Funds	Change
1986-1987	136,773*	17
1984-1985	117,303	10
1982-1983	106,636	45
1980-1981	73,427	13
1978-1979	64,731	12
1976-1977	57,660	40
1974-1975	41,097	22
1972-1973	33,625	—

*Includes the $35 million for the Texas Advanced
Technologies Research Program.
Source: Internal document, Coordinating Board, Texas
College and University Systems.

OTHER SOURCES OF FUNDING FOR UNIVERSITY RESEARCH

The state is not the major source of funds for university research. An annual survey of research funding conducted by the Coordinating Board's Educational Data Center is summarized in Table 9-16. The majority of research funds in higher education come from federal agencies like the National Science Foundation or federal departments like the Defense Department. Private sources such as industry and foundations also support a significant amount of research.

At individual universities, the proportion of federal government support can be much greater than the state average. For example, the University of Texas at Austin has reported that for the 1984-1985 academic year its researchers secured $106 million for sponsored research projects, with $82 million, or 77 percent, coming from federal agencies. This is almost ten times the approximately $11 million the university receives per year for research from the organized research formula and for special line items.[19]

Implications for Science and Technology Policy in Texas

Existing state initiatives in science and technology do not represent a coherent body of state government policy. No firm consensus about policy goals and organization emerged from the 1983 or 1985 legislatures. Appropriations for post-1980 programs are relatively low compared to other states in our survey. Comparatively few innovative programs have been adopted by the Texas government. Those programs that have been undertaken—in state agencies, universities, local public organizations, and the private sector—are only loosely coordinated.

The relatively low profile of Texas—as a funder, initiator, and innovator of science and technology programs—corresponds in principle to the roles of state

TABLE 9-16
Source of Research Funds at Public Senior Institutions and
Agencies of Higher Education, Fiscal Year 1984
(in $ million and %)

Source of Funds	Amount	Percentage of Total
Public		
State appropriated	102.5	25.1
Institutionally controlled	17.9	4.4
Federal government	209.3	51.4
Private		
Profit	19.7	4.8
Non-profit	42.8	10.5
Other	15.3	3.8
Total	407.5	100.0

Source: Coordinating Board, Texas College and University System, *Public Senior Institutions and Agencies of Higher Education in Texas: Research Funds Report for the Fiscal Year Ended August 31, 1984,* December 1984, p. 2.

government in California and Minnesota. The private sector and universities have taken the policy lead in those states, with state agencies and the legislature acting as junior partners.

The constitutional structure of state government in Texas may prevent the governor, legislature, or state agencies from aggressively directing science and technology policy—the role Governor Hunt performed in North Carolina. However, an effective science and technology policy will require concerted legislative actions and arrangements for a high level of coordination among publicly-funded programs and between those programs and the private sector.

Government and the private sector have been cooperating actively on the local level in Texas, where much of the momentum for science and technology policy has developed. The city of San Antonio, for example, is helping to organize a biotechnology research program and industrial park based at the University of Texas and Southwest Research Foundation. Other local public-private programs include the North Texas Commission and the Houston Economic Development Council.

On the state level, however, the private sector has taken a lower profile in policy development than in the other surveyed states. For example, the Milrite Council in Pennsylvania, and comparable private-sector organizations in Massachusetts and Minnesota, play a highly visible role in defining and supporting public-private programs.

There is no firm evidence to support a comparison between states of private-sector contributions to joint public-private research and commercialization programs. However, several states such as Pennsylvania have established large matching funds programs in which state appropriations are used to leverage private research dollars. Texas has not used this policy tool as extensively.

Overall, private contributions to joint public-private programs—excluding agricultural research—are probably at a lower level in Texas than in states such as Pennsylvania.

The ability of policymakers in Texas to define a framework for both public and private coordination and concerted action—which works effectively within the unusual institutional structure of state government and education in Texas—is a major challenge to science and technology policy in the state.

Although there is no established science and technology policy in Texas, recent legislation reflects a number of principles that may provide a direction for policy development.

- Improved research activities foster new industries and new jobs (expressed in TATRP legislation).
- Research is a legitimate university activity (expressed in Senate Concurrent Resolution No. 118).
- Universities require aggressive intellectual-property policies (expressed in 1985 legislation).
- A well-educated work force is necessary for sustained economic growth (expressed in 1984 education reforms).
- More emphasis should be directed to home-grown industries (expressed in INVENT legislation).
- State government should fill some strategic gaps in the marketplace such as technology information-sharing and assistance in R&D for prototype development (expressed in INVENT legislation).
- State-sponsored research can help solve development problems of resource sustainability and infrastructure provision, including declining water supplies, inadequate transportation facilities, and soil erosion (expressed in the Texas 2000 Commission Report).

Even if these principles are used, the state legislature will still face a number of allocative decisions. Allocative issues in Texas relate to the following four areas: sectors, regions, populations, and institutions.

One allocative problem is that of distributing state monies for research, development, and commercialization among industrial sectors. In Texas, this problem concerns the balance among the three major industrial groups: the emerging, largely technology-based, industries; the traditional, largely resource-based, sectors; and the secondary sectors, particularly FIRE and services.

There is evidence in the surveyed states of growing competition between traditional and emerging industries for R&D resources. Mature industries in some states are complaining that their research needs are being neglected in favor of the high-technology industries. For example, Governor Martin of North Carolina has recently appointed an assistant secretary for traditional industries in the Department of Commerce to assist such industries with innovation and other development needs.

Most of the discussion about science and technology policy in Texas has focused on the so-called high-technology industries like microelectronics, robotics, and biotechnology. Research efforts are not completely absent in the state's traditional industries: the Geotechnology Research Center, a part of HARC, directs research efforts toward oil and gas, and agriculture is a longtime focus of research policy in Texas. But these and other traditional industries like textile and apparel manufacturing could benefit more fully from new science and technology initiatives. Production innovations, improved resource extraction processes, and new-product development could all help make these industries more competitive. In particular, the market and resource problems facing agriculture are massive. International markets for bulk commodities, such as grain and cotton, are becoming more competitive, reducing prices. At the same time, falling water tables, soil erosion, and other factors are increasing production costs.

In addition, the tertiary sectors like FIRE and services are critical to the Texas economy because they represent the largest source of absolute job growth. The experience of MCC in Austin suggests that most employment growth resulting from research-intensive industry location occurs in the service sector. Many secondary industries provide technology-based producer and consumer services. A disparate group of businesses, from software companies to hospitals to construction companies, can benefit from innovation.

Regional issues are also critical, because Texas encompasses a number of economic regions with different interests. Legislative representatives of these regions can be sharply divided over technology policy. Particularly, representatives of districts outside central Texas and the major cities are suspicious that their districts will not receive benefits from science and technology policy.

The University of Texas has begun to address regional inequities within its system by funding regional industrial development centers. Apart from this effort, little state funding goes to R&D outside the major universities. For example, Pan American University, the largest university in the South Texas region, receives only a few thousand dollars a year in organized research funding.

There are several problems inherent in the effort to distribute R&D resources broadly in Texas. Regional economies in the state are not equally equipped to host research-intensive industries, and regional institutions are not equally qualified to support such activity. Moreover, the basic research process tends to benefit from agglomerations around major institutions. In any case, economic benefits from research in one region of Texas can overflow into, and be oriented to, other regions.

In short, policymakers in Texas are faced with a quandary. On one hand, the research process may be more successful if concentrated among major institutions; on the other hand, demands for regional equity argue for a broader distribution of resources.

Allocative issues related to population groups are important because of the demographic data presented earlier in this chapter. These suggest that Hispanic populations in Texas will grow more rapidly than other groups and that the state may experience increasing rates of poverty and unemployment. The role of science and technology in addressing these social problems is not clearly reflected in the surveyed states. Nationwide, the growth of high-technology industries has probably done relatively little to reduce poverty and structural unemployment. Employment in some states, such as Massachusetts, however, has increased rapidly due to the growth of technology-based industries, and structural unemployment has been reduced.

It can be argued that research-intensive development policy is not the appropriate instrument with which to address poverty and unemployment. Incentives may be too long-term and results too indirect to be effective for this purpose. On the other hand, the potential for using science and technology policy to address specific problems of community and regional economic development has not been explored fully by the states in this study.

The issue of targeting resources to population groups—both income and ethnic—did not emerge in most of the state debates surveyed in this project. Failure to target could develop into a deeper controversy in Texas because of the state's large Hispanic populations and rising unemployment rates.

Finally, several institutional questions about science and technology policy have emerged in Texas that are also raised in other states. The most important of these are: Should private universities receive resources for technology policy? And what is the relationship between newer technology-related programs and older research programs created to aid economic development?

States with major private research universities—California, Massachusetts, and New York in particular—have experienced relatively little conflict about funding research in private universities. In Texas, however, private colleges have not yet achieved the status of those in California and the Northeast. The policy issues in Texas concern whether the state should devote resources to strengthening institutions such as Rice and Baylor.

The agricultural land grant university system in Texas, based at Texas A&M, illustrates some difficulties encountered between traditional and new science and technology programs. This system has undoubtedly been effective in the commercialization and dissemination of certain new technologies leading to increased productivity. But it can also be argued that the system has been sensitive only to a narrow range of research needs in agriculture. According to this view, priorities for agricultural research do not correspond to statewide economic objectives, such as resource sustainability and employment generation. Traditional agricultural research might benefit by incorporation into a comprehensive science and technology policy directed toward broad state economic objectives.

NOTES

1. "The Great Oil Boom Ends in Texas," *New York Times*, September 16, 1984, sec. 3.
2. Thomas R. Plaut, Susan M. Tully, and Patrick J. Henoff, *Texas Economic Outlook: Long-Term Forecasts*, Bureau of Business Research, The University of Texas at Austin, 1984, 5.
3. American Bankers Association, "Mid-Year Survey," Washington, D.C.
4. Ibid., 7.
5. Susan Goodman and Victor Arnold, "High Technology in Texas," *Texas Business Review*, November-December, 1983.
6. Ibid., 8-9.
7. TENRAC, *Annual Report*, December 1980.
8. TENRAC, *Texas Energy Development Fund*, September 1983.
9. Interview with Meg Wilson, former staff member, Texas 2000 Commission, Austin, Texas, October 5, 1985.
10. State of Texas, Office of the Governor, *Texas 2000 Commission Report and Recommendations*, March 1982.
11. Texas State Senate, Advisory Committee to the Committee on Business, Technology, and Education, *Report on Fostering Emerging Technologies in Texas*.
12. Texas Science and Technology Council, *Annual Report, June 1984 - June 1985*.
13. Houston Area Research Center, *HARC*. Brochure.
14. Ibid.
15. General Appropriation Bill for 1986-87 Fiscal Year, 111-122.
16. National Science Foundation, *Federal Funds for Research and Development*, vol. 33, 1984, 142.
17. National Science Foundation, *Research and Development in Industry, 1981*, 1983, 51.
18. Legislative Budget Board, *Fiscal Size Up, Texas State Services, 1984-85 Biennium*, 61, *and General Appropriation Bill for the 1986-87 Fiscal Years*.
19. Interview with Dr. Kenneth Tolo, associate Vice-President for Academic Affairs and Research, University of Texas at Austin.

10

SCIENCE AND TECHNOLOGY POLICY: PRESENT DEVELOPMENTS AND FUTURE TRENDS

The eight states considered in this study are very much concerned with science and technology policy. The specific form of involvement and reasons for concern vary among the states. In this chapter we compare the eight states and present generalizations derived from the comparisons on (a) goals and the policy development context, (b) policy clusters, and (c) program clusters. The chapter concludes with conclusions about the future of these state efforts.

Goals and Policy Development Context

In these eight states, four historical factors have led to, or greatly influenced, the general development of science and technology policies and shaped the particular characteristics of these policies in each state.

ECONOMIC DECLINE AND DIVERSIFICATION

A first important factor in the development of science and technology policies and programs is the perceived need to replace or invigorate declining industries and to diversify existing economies. Pennsylvania, New York, and Massachusetts all experienced slowed economic growth at the end of the 1970s and early 1980s. In some cases, manufacturing employment experienced an absolute decline. States that seem primarily interested in diversifying their traditional economic bases include Florida, Minnesota, North Carolina, and Texas. State involvement in science and technology policy has been largely motivated by economic conditions and designed to create jobs. Strategies have often been tailored to particular economic and scientific strengths and weaknesses in each state.

Given this concern with job creation, some states view science and technology policy as a component of economic development policy. These states have consciously tried to make this relationship direct and explicit, while other states have not. In some states, the broad goal of job creation through science and technology policy has been targeted for specific population groups or regions within the state. Underemployed population groups and recently displaced workers have been identified as preferred recipients of new jobs. Targeting of underdeveloped regions or regions suffering severe economic pressures has been attempted in some states in order to obtain a broad consensus for science and technology policies.

— This chapter was written by Michael Dowling.

ACTIVE LEADERS

A second salient feature of science and technology policies is the prominent leadership role played by individual state government officials, and in some cases, leaders from industry. This leadership almost always included the governor of the state.[1] Heavy reliance upon the leadership of a governor or other high state official does invite risks; support for their policies has often disappeared with administration changes. This was true both in California and North Carolina after Governors Brown and Hunt left office and in New York, when early science and technology programs put in place under Governor Rockefeller were disbanded. In fact, lack of continuous political support across administrations is one of the biggest problems facing states attempting to develop long-term strategies for high-technology development. These strategies cannot produce quick returns that are useful to a politician with a short term of office.

STRATEGY STUDIES

A third element frequently guiding science and technology policy development is strategy studies. These studies have taken several forms. For example, New York contracted with an independent consulting firm to evaluate the strengths and weaknesses of the state's economy in order to develop priorities for development of particular high-technology industries. This study led to the development of many of the state's new science and technology programs. In North Carolina, Governor Hunt appointed a Task Force on Science and Technology to develop strategies and programs and to garner support for their implementation. Similar studies were conducted in most of the other states. The studies seemed to be useful to policymakers in three ways:
• in developing strategies and priorities by objectively examining a state's relative economic, technological, and scientific strengths and weaknesses
• in increasing the visibility and public awareness of state efforts;
• in gaining political support for policies by involving various interest groups such as government, industry, academia, and labor.

EDUCATION

In several states, science and technology policies have been based on the strengths of existing education systems. The higher education components of these systems have provided an institutional base for industry-university research cooperation on high-technology programs. They also train scientists and engineers for high-technology companies. The best example of early emphasis on education is California, which developed in the 1920s and again in the early 1960s a plan for its higher public education system that laid the groundwork for the tremendous growth of high-technology industry in the state.

Several states, including Massachusetts, North Carolina, and more recently New York, have specifically linked science and technology development efforts to existing public and private research universities; for example, North Carolina's Research Triangle Park, with its Research Triangle Institute, is tied to the state's three major research universities. Other states are trying to improve poor systems by placing an emphasis on higher education; for example, Florida has made improving higher education, especially in engineering, its highest science and technology development priority.

Science and Technology Policy Clusters

Though a wide range of policies have been adopted in the eight states, a number of common themes can be identified. These commonalities are reflected in four policy clusters.

The most often encountered type of policy in the eight states focused on research and development for new products and production processes. There is a strong belief that breakthroughs can be best achieved when university research capabilities are focused on industry problems. The focus is almost always on applied rather than pure research, and the specific topics are often defined in collaboration with industry. This policy frequently, but not always, takes the form of government assistance in the forming of partnerships to facilitate technology transfers between universities and industry. This policy cluster can be seen as deriving principally from the product cycle model, in which new products and improved production technology are the source of regeneration and economic growth. If firms cannot conduct research through their own resources, then other capabilities should be called upon.[2] While research capabilities of public universities are an obvious focus of attention of state policymakers, many states also include private universities in these efforts.

A second type of policy, implicitly concerned with firms and firm life cycles, focuses on promoting entrepreneurship and incubation of new firms as well as assisting existing firms in adopting innovative production technology. The policies for entrepreneurship and incubation are usually focused on advanced-technology industries and firms. The policies on production technology are often designed for traditional, non-high-technology firms. In either case the intention is to strengthen firms.

A third policy cluster is focused on encouraging the location of branch plants of multilocational high-technology firms in a state. The focus can take the form of either promoting the advantages of the state or actually attempting to lower the costs of production in the state for industrial prospects. States with lower levels of high-technology resources tend to adopt the latter focus. Industrial recruitment is still common, but it no longer receives the emphasis it has in the past. Also, rather than developing programs that offer specific incentives to out-of-state firms, a concern has shifted to developing resources that make the state more attractive to high-technology firms, especially through the development of human resources.

The last cluster of policies is concerned with the development of human resources required by a high-technology economy. These policies are most frequently concerned with the training of engineers and scientists, but also include training programs and primary and secondary education. Strong educational systems are commonly viewed not only as a source of employees for advanced-technology firms, but also as the means to prepare people for the changes in all economic spheres and improve the quality of life within the state. This cluster does not focus on any single phase of the product cycle or the firm life cycle models. There is, in fact, evidence that a highly skilled labor force does play a role in attracting high-technology firms. Indeed, it was frequently reported that interest of businesses in university partnerships originated in having access to graduates rather than access to the actual results of research.

These four policy clusters were identified in the eight states studied and, given our method of selecting these states, the same clusters are likely to be found in the larger universe of states. Not every state pursues policies in each cluster, but virtually all eight attempt to use their universities and educational resources in some fashion. Some states, such as Massachusetts, Minnesota, and Pennsylvania, have placed emphasis on developing new firms and industries. Others, such as Florida, have actively recruited firms. North Carolina and New York have done both.

The range of policy clusters we encountered is relatively narrow in terms of traditional state activities. With the exception of education, science and technology policy is essentially divorced from the traditional functions of state government. Yet it is likely that technological innovation can usefully serve established state functions, like the delivery of infrastructure, and in problem solving, like water resource management and pollution control. This utilization of science and technology is not part of the current policy agenda.

Science and Technology Program Clusters

Each of the four policy clusters identified above can be implemented in several ways, and some programs actually serve several policies. From the programs in the states studied, six program clusters emerge (Table 10-1):
  • policy development and coordinating bodies;
  • university-industry R&D partnerships and technology transfer programs;
  • education programs in science and engineering;
  • financial assistance and business incentive programs;
  • job training programs; and
  • university research funding programs.

TABLE 10-1

Links between Policy Clusters and Program Clusters

POLICY CLUSTERS

PROGRAM CLUSTERS	Research & Development	Entrepreneurship & New Firm Development	Attracting Out-of-State Firms	Education & Development of Human Resources
Policy development bodies	•:•	•:•	•:•	•:•
University-industry technology transfers	•:•	•:•		
Science & engineering education				•:•
Financial incentives for businesses	•:•	•:•	•:•	•:•
Job training		•:•	•:•	•:•
Direct funding of university research	•:•			

All eight states have in place some kind of policy development body to promote science and technology development. These include various councils, committees, and boards, usually composed of a mixture of representatives from government, industry, academia, and in some cases, labor groups. Usually such bodies are appointed by the governor, but in Massachusetts, an influential council was formed by the private sector. In California, the most influential policymaking bodies have been committees of the state legislature.

Some of the bodies are purely advisory, as is the case with North Carolina's Board of Science and Technology. In other cases, they actually oversee the management of programs, such as New York's board of directors for the State's Science and Technology Foundation. Policy bodies that also oversee program implementation and are somewhat removed from political influence appear to be the most effective in increasing the coordination and efficiency of science and

264

technology programs. Purely advisory bodies often suffer from a lack of power to influence policy implementation, and are often too closely identified with a particular governor, which leads to discontinuance when administrations change.

In addition to policy coordinating bodies, many states have adopted programs to promote the transfer of knowledge and technology between universities and industries. Five states—California, Massachusetts, Minnesota, New York, and Pennsylvania—have established joint university-industry R&D centers to conduct basic and applied research targeted toward specific areas.[3]

In each case, they have established centers affiliated with one or more research universities, both public and private, and have provided initial funding for facilities, equipment, and in some cases professorships and graduate student scholarships. Targeted research areas have been chosen on the basis of each state's resources, needs, and perceived competitive advantage. Some overlap exists that may present difficulties. For example, Pennsylvania, Massachusetts, and New York have all established biotechnology centers; it is unlikely they will all be successful.

The extent of state involvement in maintaining these centers is at issue. Pennsylvania hopes that its centers will become self-supporting in the near future. New York and Massachusetts are less optimistic, expecting that continued state support will be necessary for the foreseeable future. At present, concrete data measuring the success of these centers in contributing to the creation of new jobs, new products, or new firms are scarce. The centers have been, however, reasonably successful in securing matching funds from industry and have improved the spirit of cooperation between university and industry researchers.

Another issue regarding the centers is location. Some states have also tried to promote regional economic development by geographically distributing them across the state. There are problems associated with this strategy. First, in some cases the centers were chosen for political reasons, not for the research strengths of particular institutions. Second, many argue that a "critical mass" of research capability and industrial infrastructure is required for the successful development of new industries, and states should therefore not spread their resources too thinly.

A third program cluster is in education. Some of the states have recognized the need to improve educational programs in science and engineering to increase the number of scientists and engineers available to high-technology firms. Such programs include Florida's investment in facilities and equipment for university-based science and engineering education programs and North Carolina's efforts to create a specialized high school for science and mathematics.

The emphasis on science and math education is important for the development of innovation and technology-based industry. However, these efforts may be made at the expense of general education goals. For example, in

North Carolina the governor's support of the new high school for science and mathematics has been deeply resented by educators in the traditional school system.

The fourth cluster identified concerns financial assistance. Most of the states studied are actually providing financial incentives to encourage the growth of new firms and the location of outside firms. Tax incentives and tax credits, traditional mechanisms for promoting economic development, are also part of the new effort to support high-technology development. Going beyond these traditional forms, some states have begun to supply seed funds or venture capital for startup companies, especially high-technology ones. These states believe that there exists a "funding gap" in which the private-sector venture capital markets are not willing to provide enough early-stage funding (less than $200,000) to small, risky enterprises. The states are beginning to act as brokers and suppliers of such funds. Both Massachusetts and New York have set up quasi-public corporations to fund such projects, and North Carolina has created a state authority to invest in new businesses and incubator facilities. Pennsylvania also includes a venture capital fund as part of its overall high-technology development strategy. These programs are a new step for state governments in an area that has been traditionally left to the private sector. However, opponents argue that a funding gap does not really exist and that state intervention is unnecessary.

Job training is another area of program cluster. In the states studied, job training programs are usually seen as important both in terms of vocational training for new workers in high-technology industries and of retraining for older workers displaced by declining industries, especially in heavy-industry states. One of the most successful programs of this type is the Massachusetts Bay State Skills Corporation, because it serves a very diverse group of clients and has been able to secure the active involvement of the private sector, including joint funding of training programs. However, information on numbers of jobs actually created or retained as a result of these programs is scarce and critics have argued that the programs waste state funds since industry would conduct the training in the absence of government effort.

Finally, direct funding of research, both basic and applied, at universities is used as a mechanism by some states to promote economic growth. Strong research programs are believed to attract superior faculty members and graduate students and generate spillover effects when innovations developed at universities are commercialized in new local companies. This latter relationship is seen as one important factor influencing the growth of new high-technology firms around Stanford University in California and the Massachusetts Institute of Technology. New York, with its Research and Development Grants Program administered by the state's Science and Technology Foundation, and Texas, with its recent Texas Advanced Technologies Research Program, are also focusing on university research as a means of replicating the success of such leading states as California and Massachusetts.

It is difficult to judge how effective these new university research support efforts will be because relatively long time periods are required to realize returns from such research investments. The successful high-technology complexes of Massachusetts and California, with their strong university research components, have been built over the last three decades. States trying to emulate them cannot expect quick success.

In summary, the goals of improving the business climate and creating jobs have been addressed by the states in this study through a variety of mechanisms. Some of these have been used traditionally to promote general economic development; others are more innovative, moving state governments into new roles. In the next section, the future of these efforts of state government is considered.

The Future of State Efforts

The two main factors leading to state involvement in science and technology policy were structural change in the national economy and the federal government's decreased level of activity in regional economic development. Structural change in the national economy has not yet run its course, and, given federal budget deficits, it is unlikely that the federal government will become more active in regional economic development. The incentives, therefore, for active state participation are not likely to lessen for some time.

Even though evidence of success, in terms of new job creation, is not yet available and hard to measure accurately in any event, these efforts have produced a number of indirect effects that also suggest a continuation of state efforts. The most notable has been increased cooperation among government, universities, industries, and labor in integrating key policy components like R&D, business incentives, entrepreneurship, education, training, and financial assistance. Different states are in different stages of implementation; those that are farthest along, like Massachusetts and New York, have recognized that by working together, different interest groups can further their particular objectives while pursuing the common goal of economic development and job creation.

Private-sector involvement has consisted of the active leadership of industry representatives in some states. For example, William Norris, the former chief executive of the Control Data Corporation, is active in Minnesota, as is the private-sector High-Technology Council in Massachusetts. Industry has also been supportive of particular programs by supplying matching funds for joint industry-university research centers and job training programs in several states. It appears that strong private-sector participation is essential to the development of successful high-technology development strategies.

Many states have been very innovative in their search for new mechanisms to promote science and technology development. Such innovations include new public interventions in the state and local economy, for example, through the provision of venture capital or incubator facilities for startup businesses. The states are also more innovative in the development of institutions to implement science and technology programs, including the use of quasi-public corporations and the establishment of joint university-industry research centers supported in part by state funding. These innovations are quite different from the traditional reliance on the tax code to achieve particular economic development objectives. Although firm conclusions cannot yet be drawn, these innovations and direct public investment may lead to more effective ways to target limited public funds for the support of particular areas of research, industry sectors, economic activities, and geographic areas. In addition, in some of the state studied, these public investments have been very successful in leveraging private investment in the same areas of interest.

Another important development is that the states are placing increasing emphasis on using research and educational institutions to further long-term economic development. These institutions are viewed as having great potential for promoting economic growth through new-product and technology development and spin-off companies. Some states, such as California and Massachusetts, have already begun to reap the benefits of outstanding educational and research institutions. Other states, like Florida, are behind in this area and are making impressive attempts to catch up. The utilitarian view of education is not held by all and some are fearful that the traditional functions of education in transmitting cultural and social values and the cause of pure research may be adversely affected by this attention and orientation.

While political support of state science and technology policy remains strong, there are several factors that complicate its future. Few of the programs examined have undergone objective evaluation, which make their value difficult to estimate.[4] As with most economic development programs, it is difficult to distinguish between effects induced by government policies and those attributable to other market forces. Most programs are in fact too young to evaluate meaningfully. Furthermore, many have developed no clear performance measures to gauge their success. Better performance measures should be built into the design of programs so that they can be evaluated as they mature. The best example of this kind of design is the PennTAP program in Pennsylvania, which reports cost savings to firms resulting from the advice and information provided through its technology transfer service as a performance measure. The program has monitored these savings throughout its twenty-year history. Other performance measures, such as number of jobs created and private funding leveraged by state funding, must be further developed and incorporated into new and existing programs.

The continuity of many of the policies and programs examined is endangered by the lack of consensus on overarching goals and strategies among the different actors in state government. Programs do need to change or evolve as more is learned about their effectiveness, but in several cases, programs have been dramatically changed, and even abolished, when administrations have changed. If such new initiatives are to be ultimately successful, they will have to be built on broad-based, long-term political support.

Fragmented political support in some states has led to a lack of coordination among the various programs and policymaking bodies involved in science and technology issues. The result is duplication of efforts, overlapping programs, and no clear overall strategy. In addition, in some state these new policies seem to have little linkage to more traditional economic development policies and programs.

A related issue revolves around targeting in many state policies. These policies may explicitly or implicitly favor certain industrial sectors, subregions in a state, or subpopulation groups. For example, "mature industries" and the service sectors may perceive that high-technology programs offer them little benefit. Also, there is often a basic conflict between attempts to distribute geographically the benefits of high-technology development and the need to form a critical mass around research universities and existing companies. This conflict is especially evident in states where high-technology industry is concentrated in a few urban areas. Governmental efforts to broaden participation have often been met with opposition from business and university leaders who feel that decisions concerning geographic distribution of high-technology development often reflect political concerns rather than research strengths and market potential. Even though some states are constructively facing the problems inherent in targeting, this will remain an issue in the future.

Perhaps the most troubling feature of current discussions is that science and technology policy has been, and continues to be, defined too narrowly. While the initial focus on the promotion of new technologies and products has been broadened to include innovation in production processes, thereby making traditional industry a potential object of support, discussions have not included the use of science and technology for other pressing problems. None of the states studied has considered the ability of science and technology to contribute to such long-term necessities as meeting infrastructure needs. The case for public intervention in ensuring the long-term availability and management of water resources may be stronger than that for promoting short-term economic development. Nor do most state programs consider the real needs of state and local agencies for scientific information or their capability of using advanced technology.

Whether the various efforts to develop and implement state science and technology policies will improve and diversify state economies and create new jobs remains to be seen. In the interim, they have been successful in increasing cooperation among key groups and achieving greater integration of programs to foster economic growth through the development of technology-based industries. In addition, a shift from an exclusive focus on competing for out-of-state firms to developing resources within states has occurred. The zero-sum game has, for the most part, been replaced by a more positive and comprehensive vision of economic regeneration. A new emphasis on education, research, and technology utilization is clearly visible, and state governments seem eager to innovate and play the role of catalyst.

NOTES

1. State leaders have included Jerry Brown (California); Bob Graham (Florida); Nelson Rockefeller, in the 1960s, and Hugh Carey, in the 1980s (New York); Richard Thornburgh (Pennsylvania); James Hunt and Quentin Lindsay, the governor's assistant (North Carolina); Rudy Perpich and William Norris, Control Data Corporation (Minnesota).
2. A private-sector response to this type of market failure can be found in research consortia, the most well-known example being MCC in Austin.
3. Area focus for the five states are: California—microelectronics; Massachusetts—biotechnology, marine science, materials science, microelectronics, photovoltaics, polymer science; Minnesota—microelectronics; New York—biotechnology, computer hardware and software, medical instruments, optical instruments, telecommunications; Pennsylvania—biotechnology, robotics, computer-aided design and manufacturing.
4. Michael I. Luger, "Does North Carolina's High-Tech Development Program Work?" *American Planning Association Journal*, Summer 1984, 280-289.

276

labor-business cooperation, Penn., 213-215
labor-management, Penn., 214-215
laboratories,
—in Mass., 77
—in Minn., 108, 113, 111, 112
—in N.Y., 136, 140, 150
Laser Applications Research Center, Tex., 245
Lehigh University, 216, 218
Lewis, Gib, Speaker of the Texas House of Representatives , 244
Lindeman, Wallace, MEIS, dir., 111
Lindsey, Quentin,
—as Science Advisor to the Governor of N.C.,176-178, 181
—and N.C. Board of Science and Technology, dir., 176-178, 181
linkages,
—private educational research, Penn., 204
—public-private, N.Y., 141
Long and Feller, 4
Long Term Program Support, N.C., 174
Low, George, Rensselaer Polytechnic Institute President, 143
manufacturing employment,
—in Fla., 40
—in Penn., 194-195, 197
—overview, 6
—sectoral shifts, Penn., 199-200
Marine Science Center, Mass., 89-90
Martin Marietta, and Honeywell, Inc., 45
Martin, James, Governor of N.C., 163, 177
Massachusetts Business Development Corporation, (MBDC), 78
Massachusetts Business Roundtable, 75
Massachusetts Capital Resources Company (MCRC), 80, 87-89, 92-94
Massachusetts Centers of Excellence Corporation (MCEC),75, 79, 89-92

Massachusetts Community Development Finance Corporation (MCDFC), 78
Massachusetts Governor's Office of Economic Development, 75
Massachusetts High-Tech Council, 75
Massachusetts Industrial Finance Authority, 76, 78, 85
Massachusetts Institute of Technology (MIT), 8, 69, 73, 74, 77, 89, 91
—and entrepreneurs, 77
—and federal R&D funds, 73
—and research grants, 89
Massachusetts Manpower Development Department, 75
Massachusetts Product Development Corporation (MPDC), 79
Massachusetts Taxation Commission report 79
Massachusetts Technology Development Corporation (MTDC), 75
—and capital formation, 78, 80, 85-87, 92-94
Massachusetts Technology Park Corp. (MTPC), 79, 89
Massachusetts, 260, 262, 263-268
Materials Research Center, 89-90
Materials Science Research Center, Tex., 245
Mauro, Frank, New York State Assembly Secretary, 145, 146
MBDC, 78
MBP, 108, 109
MCC, Tex., 243, 255
MCDFC, 78
McDonald Observatory, the University of Texas, 250
MCEC, 79, 90, 92, 93
MCRC, 80, 87-89, 92-94
MECC, 110, 115 119, 123, 124
MEIS, 110-114, 124
Mentor Program, N.C., 181, 182
MHTC, 112, 114, 117
micro-electronics, Tex., 241
Microelectronics and Computer Technology Corporation (MCC), 243, 255

278

North Carolina Technological
Development Authority, 176,
183-188
North Carolina, 260, 262, 264, 265
North Carolina, Department of
Community Colleges, 174, 185
North Texas Commission, 253
North Texas State University, 245
NSF, 89, 90
Office of International Trade and
Investment, (OITI), Mass., 77
Office of Training and Employment
Policy (OTEP), Mass., 78
Palo Alto,Calif., 3
partnerships,
—and job creation, Mass., 81, 88
—between academia, industry and
government, Mass., 73, 75, 79,
80
—for economic growth, Mass., 93
—for high-risk capital, Mass., 78
—in Fla., 50, 56
PCLF, 205
PennPride, 217
Pennsylvania Economic
Revitalization Fund, 204
Pennsylvania General Assembly,
213, 215
Pennsylvania Industrial
Development Authority (PIDA),
201
Pennsylvania Research Inventory
Project (PRIP), 205
Pennsylvania School for the
Sciences, 207
Pennsylvania State Planning Board,
202
Pennsylvania State Planning Board,
215
Pennsylvania State University and
NET/ATC, 216, 218-219
Pennsylvania State University, 209,
212
Pennsylvania Technical Assistance
Program (PennTAP), 196, 202,
207-212
Pennsylvania, 260, 264-262, 268
Pennsylvania, 262
PennTAP, 196, 202, 206-212, 267
pensions, Penn., 207, 213

Perpich, Rudy, Governor of
Minn.,100, 107
—and GOST, 122, 123
—and Minnesota Wellspring, 109,
119
Photovoltaics Center, 89-90
PIDA, 201, 207
Piedmont area, 167, 187
Plank, Raymond,
—Apache Corp. CEO,119, 121
—co-chair of Minnesota Wellspring,
119, 121
policies
—development and coordinating
bodies, 262
—development bodies, Mass.,
(EOEA), 74
—development bodies, Fla., FHTIC,
40
—in Minn., 106-109, 114, 117-
118, 124
—R&D, assumptions, 4
—technology transfer, N.C., 167
Policy Clusters, 263, 264
policymaking, 46, 47
policymaking bodies,
—in Minn., 108-109, 119-124, 122
—in N.C., North Carolina
Agricultural Extension Service,
Governor's Task Force on Science
and Technology, N.C., 172
—in Penn., MILRITE Council, 202
—North Carolina Board of Science
and Technology, 171
President Ronald Reagan, 203
Press, Frank, National Academy of
Science president, 247
Prime Computer, 69
PRIP, 205
Private Industry Councils, Mass., 78
private universities, 263
Productivity Development Program
(PDP), N.Y., 159
Program Clusters, 264
Program Development Group (PDG),
N.C., 139
program evaluation, 267
Promotion of High-Technology
Industry, Penn., 202
Proposition 2 1/2, 74